We Will Be Free

Overlanding in Africa and
Around South America

By

Graeme Robert Bell

WE WILL BE FREE

ISBN: 978-0-620-65299-5 (print)
ISBN: 978-0-620-65300-8 (eBook)
ISBN: 978-0-620-65301-5 (kindle)
ISBN: 978-0-620-65302-2 (epub)

Written by Graeme Robert Bell

Edited by Luisa Bell
Cover Photo & Design by Graeme Robert Bell
Photos by Luisa and Graeme Robert Bell

Disclaimer: The material in this book contains content/language of a mature nature.

MORE TITLES BY GRAEME BELL
Travel The Planet Overland
Overlanding the Americas "La Lucha"
Europe Overland - Seeking the Unique

www.a2aexpedition.com

For Luisa, Keelan and Jessica AKA Ginger Ninger, Schmidt and the Jellybean. I love you

Acknowledgement

I can count my good friends on my fingers and my enemies by my toes, that fact is not an indictment of those who don't enjoy my simple company but rather a reflection of my paranoia. I want to thank those dear friends who trudged through the early, horrible rough drafts of this book and steered me towards a clear vision. Thank you to John, Astrid, Rob, Stevie, Marinda and Jeandré.

A special thanks to my uncle, Alan Bell, a talented artist and the man who has continuously inspired me to be creative ever since I was a young man.

And a special offer of gratitude to Luisa, my love, my best friend, and the only person on this planet who knows me better than I know myself.

Glossary

Afrikaans and Other South Africanisms

Bakkie: "pick-up", a Blue Bulls player who likes to head-butt

Banky: A measure of dagga, one plastic Standard Bank bag full

Bloody: to make the word more appealing, angry, or exaggerated, 'Bloody hell Frikkie!'

Braai: BBQ, to grill meat on a fire, usually accompanied by a cold beverage or three

Dagga: Marijuana

DHA: Department of Home Affairs in South Africa, full to the brim with poephols

Eita: A casual greeting

Frikken: A classy South African way of saying the F word

Frikkie: an unfortunately common Afrikaans name

Ja Nee: "Yes No", sarcastic 'Sure'!

Jislaaik: "Yis-like" – To express astonishment

Knobkerries: A club with a large knob one end and used to hunt or clubbing an enemy's head

Koeksisters: A plaited deep-fried doughnut, Luisa makes lekker koeksisters

Lekker: Nice, cool, the Afrikaans word for a 'sweet'

Melk Tertjies: Milk tarts or a shooter made with one bottle of vodka, one can condensed milk, mix, shake, chill, serve, party!

Poephol: "asshole"

Rondavel: A westernised version of the round African style hut

Rooineck: "red-neck", English speaking South African. The name literally comes from the sunburnt necks of the British Army soldiers who wore pith helmets during the Boer Wars in South Africa and should not be confused with the American Redneck

Skrik: "Fright"

Sokkie: "sock", Social ballroom style dance with a partner

WE WILL BE FREE

Soutpiel/soutie: "Salt-penis", British oriented person in South Africa, whose feet are grounded in both England and South Africa with his penis hanging into the salty ocean below. A great compliment.
Uitendelik: "eventually"

South Americanisms
Arepa: A corn pancake, tastes like cardboard and eaten with Chicharron
Asado: Like a Braai but meat and booze are consumed simultaneously, in vast quantities
Blanco: White
Caipirinha: A Brazilian drink of crushed ice, sugar, lime and Cachaça sugar cane
Cerveza: Beer
Chicharron: Pork crackling
Churrascaria: An Asado restaurant
Churros: Deep-fried dough pastry, chocolate centred, nut covered epicness
Clube: Portuguese meaning Club
Jeito Brasiliero: The Brazilian way
La Nyapa: A bonus of meat or fresh produce
Marioca: Brazilian from Rio de Janeiro, easy to identify by the speedo or the G-string
Me Importa Un Chorizo: I don't care a sausage, also a restaurant in Chia, near Bogota
Mirador: Viewing point
Parilla: A Braai area, grill
Vino: Wine

To view categorised images of our journey, please go to
www.a2aexpedition.com

Introduction

My matric English teacher was a voluptuous, recent teachers' college graduate, whose ample bosom and pretty face fuelled many teenage fantasies, not least mine. Mrs Night was not yet a great teacher; she favoured the cool kids which I was not, but by instructing our class to write an essay with the banal subject, "The Street Where I Live", inadvertently led me to write the best essay I had ever written. Back home that afternoon, uninspired by the assignment, I sat down at our cork coffee table, lit a Chesterfield cigarette and wrote an honest essay I never intended to submit. I then lit a joint, put a Doors album on the turntable, and did the rest of my homework. If I remember correctly, the essay went something like this, *'The street where I live is dour and fantastic. The pavements straight, and filthy, cracked and trod by the feet of the working class. I love the street where I live. The rumble of the train every half hour and only a hundred meters from my bed. The Greeks in the corner store, the greasy guy who rings up the groceries and his large, equally greasy, scantily dressed girlfriend who shoves them in a packet, while eyeing you disapprovingly. The guys who sell sweets, cold drinks, weed, and something stronger at the railway entrance and the homeless guys who are their best clients. I love the atmosphere, the culture, that feeling that no-one has to try harder or be better because life is life and we are who we are, and nothing could change that. I admire and avoid the tough guys with the quick, cunning smiles and large old ladies permanently dressed for bed, the sexy teenage girls with thin, full ripe bodies, pushing baby prams overflowing with young screaming bodies. I love the junkies and the alkies, the dealers and the whores and the normal, hard-working people just trying to survive through it all'.*

The next morning, I hesitantly submitted the essay, as I had forgotten to write another, teacher-friendly essay and a few days later was surprised to be honoured by Mrs Night in front of the class and awarded with a mark of 98%. Her comments on the paper stated, "There was no need for foul language; you should become a (satirical) writer". That comment, justified or not, fuelled an existing ambitious dream which, without the opportunity for further education, would remain unfulfilled. In 1994 I applied for a junior journalist position at a small daily newspaper based on the East Rand of Johannesburg but lost out to an applicant with a journalism degree though the editor assured me that, based on my written submissions, I was a close second for the position. I was then introduced to a small film school by a wavy-haired curvy young woman who devoted two years to break my heart. I spent a few weeks as a volunteer carrying gear and running naked through a forest and was invited to enrol. The monthly tuition fee was equivalent to a third of my Mom's monthly salary, and I proposed that I would work nights as a barman and pay a third if my Mom and Dad would each pay a third. Mom said yes, but only if your Dad agrees to pay his share. Dad's second wife said, 'well, we are not even sure that you are his biological son, so, well, tough shit, I'm afraid'. Unfortunate and untrue. I joined the minimum wage masses and embraced alcohol.

21 years later, I sat down to write in a rented house on a horrible dusty Caribbean Venezuelan Margarita Island. The neighbour and his friends were pro windsurfers, low-slung baggies and exposed pubic hair. I arranged a little chair and table on the small balcony with a view of the dust, stopped smoking cigarettes and started eating chocolate. I loathed that island, the faked optimism of its expat residents, all of whom were living off the fat of a ruined economy. I particularly detested the landlady who could not perceive our travel-weary humanity, instead of trying to squeeze dollars out of us. That skinny Canadian yoga panted tit. There were giant frogs mating in the water supply, the house had almost no furniture, the wind blew constantly, and my mouth tasted of chalk. Venezuelan beer is bad, the food worse and the ruling regime is pure

shit. It was the perfect environment; I wrote all day and sipped Diplomatico rum at night, secretly inhaling the bitter smoke of cheap, fat cigars. I two-finger tapped 90 000 words, the skeleton of this book and perhaps another. I was born on 29 December 1974; no doubt pushed out by a large Christmas lunch. Luisa was born in November 75, hell-bent for revenge, but revenge for what and against whom we are still trying to figure out. Our lives ran parallel to each other; both were suburban and nomadic, our parents could never settle on just one house to live in. Luisa went to thirteen different schools before being kicked out into the world, and I went to at least seven schools before my Mom moved out. We were both the children of broken homes, but unlike my Dad's cowardly skilful and silently devastating abdication from the middle-class family throne, Luisa's dad left to sad applause. We were both raised speaking English in communities which were overwhelmingly Afrikaans and working class with all the associated negatives as there are few perks of being a minority within a minority, even though we both have more than a few litres of Afrikaans blood.

Growing up in secluded, isolated Apartheid South Africa and a household with almost no expendable income, travel was limited to piggyback weekends away and camping trips. Once I graduated high school, I was ready to see the world, to connect the music from countries far away with the lyrics they sang, the cities they described, and the people who sang them. Music, movies and books were my windows to the world that existed so far away from the tip of Africa that it may well have lived on another planet. I dreamt of being an African Bob Dylan, falling in and out of love as I roamed the countryside, a backpack on my back, a guitar in my hand.

The reality was that hitchhiking around the country to visit relatives in other cities was equally liberating and frustrating, those relatives weary of the longhaired kid standing on their doorstep. They had their problems and knew that I was problematic. The freedom and risk of standing on the side of the road, thumb in the air liberated. I had camping gear and cans of food, a book or two, a hunting knife, a small first aid kit, some warm clothing, too little money and a pair of Doc Marten boots, I could camp in the mountains and forests along the road, waiting for something or someone to show me the way. The solitude nurtured me and soothed my mind, sitting on a rock, the sun on my back, watching the breeze blow through the grass, a bird floating in the blue sky beneath the vapour trail of a high-altitude jet, sharing my simple breakfast with the creatures that exist beneath us. Quiet conversations with myself and a cigarette while I stood next to the road wondering which of the vehicles on the horizon would be brave or dangerous, how far I would get that day and who or what might be waiting when I arrived. But, it was the arriving which I dreaded most, questions which I would always answer incorrectly, an obligation, an attempt at happiness, the sarcastic smirk three hours after the welcome hug. 'What are you doing? Are you mad? Why do you dress that way? You can stay until Tuesday'. The exception was my Aunty Lyn. She always was a sweetheart.

My childhood friend, Brian, returned from travelling the Middle East and Scandinavia a better man the boy who had left. Over a few late-night drinks, he convinced me to 'get my shit together' and see the world. After some bar work back in hometown Krugersdorp, I had enough money to buy a return ticket to Israel, a popular destination for South African kids who needed to work to travel and even kids who did not. I spent a year in that massive, little country, returning unsatisfied, with more questions than when I had left, but that is a story for another time. Luisa had also travelled to Israel, three years earlier than I had and in a far more organised and disciplined manner.

Our worlds left their respective orbits and collided in January 1997. We have been inseparable, at Luisa's insistence mostly, since then. We were just two of those lost souls in a fishbowl. In 99 King Keelan

Michael Bell's wonderful, little blonde cone-shaped head was forcepted into the world, and five years later the stork delivered a Princess, Her Royal Highness is to be referred to as Jessica Luisa. Those kids saved my life. I believe that once a man becomes a father he has only one duty and that is to raise his children with love and respect, to protect them from a world which seeks to manipulate and exploit them, to find a way to turn the tables on that world and then teach his children how to do the same. My father had taught me how to be a father not by example but with 'Boy Named Sue' fight or fail absence. For that lesson, I thank him.

After ten years, a few false starts and some tough life lessons we together built an immigration business, and with years of hard, smart work, we achieved bittersweet success. Our strategy was to keep our overheads low and profits high while specialising in the engineering and construction industry. Luisa had a head for law, and I had a head for business, skills we had learnt over a decade of corporate service and skills which complimented each other. I would work on sales and marketing, dealing with the bureaucrats, and doing all the shitty jobs Luisa did not want to do. Luisa has an extraordinary skill of being able to work on a computer for sixteen hours a day without a pee. She is also the reigning queen of multitasking and can easily do the work of four, normal human beings.

Having achieved the South African version of the American dream, we should have been happy, right? What more can you expect from life than health and wealth, the golden keys to the Kingdom of Happy? If anything, we were too successful and were burning the candles at both ends for a few years. Our relationship with each other and the kids were starting to deteriorate. The Business became the most important member of our family, and we catered to it like a spoilt child. Every conversation ended when the phone rang, laughter subdued so that we could tell someone again what we had told them before. We needed balance, but The Business didn't need balance, it required constant attention and nurturing. Holidays would be cut short or planned around The Business, every decision we made was made with The Business in mind. We were successful financially, but I don't believe that is the only measure of success.

Every night I would lie in bed and dream of some form of escape, a way to leave this life of schedules, habit, routine and chronic boredom behind. We dreamt of a life of adventure and danger, a purpose that wakes you in the morning with purpose. A poster of a palm-treed exotic beach hung beside our bed where the cross should have hung. Most mornings, I would look at myself in the mirror, grey before my time, a belly of comfort and overindulgence, bloodshot eyes from the booze I had been medicating myself with. I would stare into the eyes staring back at me in the mirror, trying to find the adventurous, wild young man who had seen the world through the same eyes. He was in there, somewhere, usually lying strapped in a padlocked chest, scratching for freedom, whispering reminders of my betrayal. I had to find a way to free him, and by releasing him, I would free myself. He mocked me daily while I stood in line at the trough of life, A Pig in a Cage, On Antibiotics.

He was the one buying old Land Rovers, knowing that the new me would be seduced by the freedom they offered and promised. He had two parked outside and would encourage me to spend my weekends playing with them, washing and fixing them. He knew that at night I would sit on a plastic stool in the garage, sipping on beer after beer, staring at the off-road vehicles which beckoned me to load up, drop out, and disappear. He convinced me that the vehicle of my liberation was packaged in aluminium and history. But we needed a push out the door, a kick in the pants, a new philosophy.

Luisa's dad, André, had moved to Melkbosstrand in Cape Town a few months after we had in 2003. He was to become one of the most influential people in our lives. Luisa and André had a rocky relationship since he had divorced her mom, Christine, but now that we were living in the same town, we spent a lot of time together. André was a highly intelligent man, and he had a battle with alcohol for many years. He was completely sober for the last ten years of his life, and he was wise. We would talk for hours about religion, life and business, and in the last few years of his life, he realised that more than anything he wanted to travel and see the world. He and his son Jeandré were planning a two-month trip to Australia and Asia and invited me to go along for the adventure. I couldn't leave Luisa to handle all the work on her own, so I, unfortunately, could not go to Asia, though every cell in my body screamed for the escape. They had a great time and travelled on a shoestring budget even though he could afford not to. He was an interesting man. He rented a little house, no bigger than they needed, drove a cheap little car and wore simple clothing. Back in Pretoria, he had invested in real estate and had invested enough that he did not need to worry about money but did regardless. He kept a little notebook in which he scribbled little not0065s, and he believed in thinking so far out of the box that sometimes I would tease him that he lost the box completely. André was always there when you needed guidance or just a chat. He became the father that I never had.

Luisa succumbed to the idea that we needed a break, having not had a proper, forget about the world, holiday in almost five years and I eagerly enticed her to escape into escapist ideas and an addiction to travel porn. Luisa suggested we visit a beautiful island for a few weeks, but the costs were exorbitant. Because we liked to go camping in the Landy, we started toying with the idea of doing an overland trip. We bought some maps and started doing some research and the more we thought about the idea, the more excited we became. André would join us for some planning sessions and would sip a 0% beer while we threw ideas around. He encouraged and advised us, and we decided to take eight months to travel up to Kenya and then fly to Asia to backpack and then fly back to Kenya to drive home. André said he would probably join us along the road, maybe in Malawi or Tanzania or even Asia.

We might have relegated the idea to the bin of dreams. But, one morning, I received a phone call from someone I did not know, a lady sounding upset. She asked for Luisa, and I told her that she could speak to me. She was a nurse, and she had seen André collapse as he walked to his car outside a shopping area near the beach. André had months earlier had a quadruple heart bypass, but now his heart had given up altogether. The last number dialled on Andre's phone was our home, and the nurse told me that André had died. Luisa collapsed in shock. She hyperventilated and became completely disoriented to the point that I had to take her to our GP, Dr Meintjies, to be treated. Luckily my mom, Sue, was visiting from England, and she took care of Luisa for the next few days while she dealt with the loss of her Dad. We were devastated that we did not get to see him one last time and tell him how much we loved and admired him, how much he inspired us and how empty our lives would be without him.

With Andre's passing in 2009, we decided that we must travel. That life is too short to live just for money that we did not want to live this life with regrets. His life and passing was the catalyst that pushed Luisa and me in the same direction, onto the road to freedom from the soft, opulent prison we had locked ourselves in.

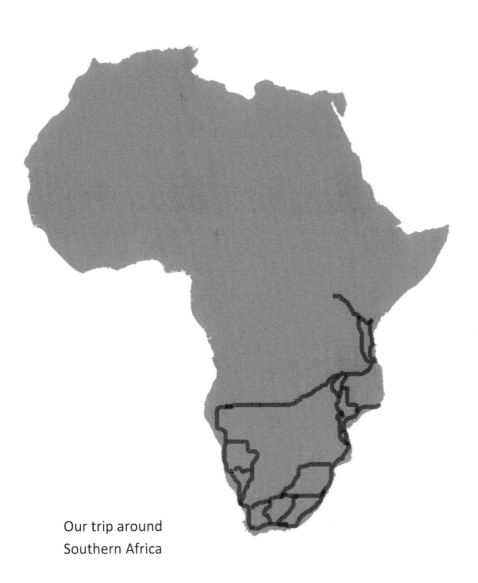

Our trip around
Southern Africa

1

A Vehicle for Our Dreams

The wheels were set in motion for a huge change. Our old 1982 Series 3 Landy, an ex-South African army R6, was great for camping trips but for a longer cross-border trip, we wanted something more reliable and lighter on fuel. Her 4.1 litre Chevrolet engine was gutsy and powerful, but she was as thirsty as I am on a Friday night. The 1980 Classic Range Rover two-door was great for making everything else look silly at the dunes or the off-road track but was just as thirsty as the R6, would need a complete rebuild and did not offer much space for a family of four and all the camping and outdoor crap. After looking at all the vehicles available, in the name of impartiality and thoroughness, we returned to our original and only real option, the Land Rover Defender 130. Style, toughness, off-road capability and load capacity, all of that in a sexy aluminium body.

We searched the internet and second-hand car magazines for a few months before Luisa found a 2003 Land Rover Defender 130 TD5 for sale in Bloemfontein. She was second-hand with 140 000 km's on the odometer and had belonged to a farmer who had used her to tow trailers, lug farm equipment and workers over long dirt roads. I did not want to buy an off-road ready, fully equipped Landy partially because they are expensive, partially because I wanted to do all the preparation work myself, but mostly because I did not want a vehicle which had been over-revved and forced to do things it did not want to do. This Landy was essentially a blank slate, a hard-working girl, unglamorous and unassuming but with a strong back and a strong heart. We negotiated with the dealer and requested a complete inspection by the Automobile

Association. The dealer said he would replace the gearbox at no extra cost because he was not happy with the fifth gear and the gear lever did not feel firm in the box. The decision made, I flew up to Bloemfontein to have a look at the Landy and stayed in the little cottage of an Architect who was far from impressed with my assessment of Afrikaner architecture. Not that the cottage, a converted garage, wasn't nice in a wannabe hotel sort of way, though it was freezing cold all night long. I was referring more to the face brick houses with bright blue or green gutters, pillars holding up corrugated metal roofs, burnt orange curtains and fluorescent lighting. Ja nee.

The white 130 stood in the rear display section of the showroom with the other trade-in vehicles. I fell in love with her the moment I slid into her grey, black and white interior. The only accessories were a raised air intake, a bullbar and a long-range fuel tank. Everything seemed as it should, and the chassis was in very good condition, too good almost for a vehicle which had spent the last few years working hard. Dry Bloemfontein is at a reasonably high elevation, and therefore there was not a spot of rust visible. I did notice that the bullbar had been badly welded, white overspray paint speckled the heater inside the engine compartment and the left front wheel arch was a different colour to the right front wheel arch. I asked the dealer if the Landy had been in an accident, but he shrugged, 'no, I don't think so'. If the Landy had been a double cab Toyota Land Cruiser, it would have been sold in a heartbeat, the Land Cruiser is the wagon of choice for Free State farmers and anyone else in a 300-km radius who owned a fishing rod and a rugby ball. The Land Rover is seen in these parts as a rooinek, soutpiel 4x4, envied for its off-road capability but distrusted because of its perceived unreliability. A farmer has enough machinery to worry about without wondering if his bakkie is going to get him back from the sokkie. Also, a Land Cruiser of similar year and mileage would fetch twice the price, so the dealer was happy for this soutie to take the dark horse off his hands and out of the showroom where it was intimidating the Toyotas. I took her and a junior salesman for a drive to a local off-road track where I put the low range box through its paces. The road tyres she was wearing were not up to the job, but she still climbed up and over and through everything I pointed her at, the salesman holding on tight to the grab handles. 'Jislaaik' he said as we drove the now muddy Landy back, 'this thing can go anywhere', a smile nudged at my ears. Luisa transferred R160,000 into the dealers account and the Landy was booked into the Land Rover dealer for the gearbox exchange, but the arrogant little snot who ordered the new box had ordered the wrong one and had to have another sent from Johannesburg which arrived the next day, a Friday. The mechanics worked until 11 pm, and I fed them KFC while watching them work. I had a lot to learn about the Defender having only owned Series vehicles and the old Range Rover in the past. The owner of the franchise showed up at the workshop with Brandy on his breath and handed me the keys to a new black Discovery 3. Go home he said, the bakkie will be ready tomorrow. Hookers waved at me as I drove down the city streets back to my cold cottage. The Disco was fantastic in every way and drove like I imagine a 4x4 Rolls Royce would. The morning was crisp and sunny as I collected the 130 from the dealer, completed the paperwork and headed for the N1 highway to Cape Town. The Landy had a one-month, 1000 km guarantee and home lay 1100 km's away. The engine lost power, and black smoke billowed from the exhaust, 300 km's from Bloemfontein. With a skrik I pulled over and checked the oils and fluids, everything seemed OK, and I made the difficult decision of continuing slowly to Cape Town and not returning to Bloemfontein where I would have to wait until Monday to have the Landy looked at. Oh hell, I have bought a bloody lemon! It was a very long and stressful drive, but she got me home after 16 hours where Luisa waited with a patting foot. On Monday the local indie had a look at the engine and scratched his head. He threw out phrases like 'blown turbo', or ' blown head gasket' but after twenty minutes he spotted something that made him look up at me with a smile. He took the Leatherman off his hip and fiddled around with a hose for a minute. Problem solved! The turbo hose had come loose from the intercooler which meant I had driven 800 kms without air going to the turbo. She pulled like a horse with the turbo operating at full power. A free fix is the very best kind. The mechanic also convinced me to have a Little Black Box (LBB, remember this acronym, you will be tested later) engine management system installed and for that, I owe him a crate of whisky, a case of wine and a warm, uncomfortable cuddle.

I had been planning the perfect expedition vehicle for months and decided that I would do all the modifications needed in my little garage at the end of the cul-de-sac. The first step was to search the internet for inspiration and ideas. European Land Rover campers tend to be 'live in' with the vehicle modified with either a pop-top or a slide on camper unit. Both systems offer secure internal sleeping and cooking facilities, while the pop=top arrangement generally offers less space while the vehicles off-road performance is not significantly compromised. The slide on camper units tend to be large, cumbersome, and too bloody tall, the height a major problem for intercontinental Overlanders as it will usually be taller than 2.5 metres and therefore unable to fit in a standard or high cube-shipping container. We could not afford either European setup and having had for a few years owned a rooftop tent which we enjoyed, decided to buy another large roof tent for this trip. Searching the internet, we found the tent we were looking for, the Howling Moon Tourer 2.4m. The seller was based in Durban and assured us that the dimensions were of the correct tent, and a relative agreed to have a look at the tent before we handed over the cash. The relative also assured us that the tent was the correct size and in good nick but when the tent arrived, we found that there was 600mm of tent missing. After a few grumpy phone calls the seller agreed to refund about R1, 000 and we installed the tent which was in almost new condition, though it did smell as if a mineworker had been living in it. Luisa also insisted on buying a second, huge, ground tent which was essentially a dome tent with mosquito screens as sides and was completely see-through.

I installed an aluminium canopy on the rear load tub, built a drawer system for two fridges and six wolf storage boxes, a kitchen area, fuel and water jerry cans, a sixty-litre gravity feed water tank and a booze decanter. I paid twice for the aluminium canopy because I had drawn the R9, 000 asking price in cash from the bank then went to the local Pick 'n Pay to buy some groceries. Melkbos had always been really safe, and I left the folder with some paperwork and the cash in the trolley while I walked the aisles. I turned my back for a minute to get a can of salsa, and when I returned to the trolley, the folder was gone. What an idiot. The security camera caught a local worker walking up to the trolley but glitched for a few seconds, long enough to not capture the theft or the thief. I confronted the worker, a Malawian and asked him "please, achimwene (brother in Chichewa), just return the money, and I will not call the cops". He gave me an innocent smile and insisted that he had done nothing. The police had already been alerted which, unfortunately, meant I could not practice CIA interrogation techniques on the guilty, Malawian. The cops told me that they could not do anything without a witness or proof and a search of his locker turned up no cash. Lesson learnt. I went back to the bank, withdrew more cash and returned home to face Luisa's wrath. The build continued in earnest once the canopy was installed and it took almost three months of planning, design, labour and many cases of beer but I was very happy with the end result.

2

On The Road

So once, you have made the decision to hit the road and live that romantic traveller's lifestyle, you have to divorce yourself from the nest builder you are supposed to be. The kids must be approved for homeschooling, and a bunch of paperwork needs to be sorted through before you can even get close to a map or a guidebook. We sold the little Fiat, ordered an AA Carnet, had to have visas issued for Tanzania and arranged with a client that we could use a mobile satellite thingy in exchange for some immigration services. The little square satellite receiver would enable us to send and receive emails out in the bush and by plugging in a standard landline type telephone; we would have a satellite telephone in case of emergencies. Time became scarcer than a bearded Chinese, as our planned departure date loomed.

We had a house sitter lined up to take care of our house and Boxer, Roxy, but at the very last moment, the night before we were due to leave, the dick dropped us with some lame excuse. We had only met him a few days earlier, and for some reason, I did not take to him and perhaps had grilled him a bit too thoroughly. We were all packed and ready to leave, sitting in our garage wondering what the hell we were going to do when our landlord came to say goodbye. He laughed and made a few phone calls. A friend of his came to meet us and agreed to take care of the house and the dog for as long as we were away. We left the next day with Jeandré and his beautiful Spanish girlfriend, Iera, along for the ride until we reached Durban. The Landy was heavily loaded partly because we had been told by the internet experts that we needed enough food and medical supplies to last us six months and partly because we had the extra load of two young people and their luggage.

We had not told most of our clients that we were going on a trip and had to make sure that we were always connected to ensure that no-one was left hanging. An assistant had been employed and trained to take care of the phones and running to DHA, and we prayed that he would be up to the job. Leaving home was extremely stressful, and both Luisa and I were on edge. What the hell were we doing? Dreaming about an adventure is a hell of a lot easier than leaving for an adventure.

Our first camp was near Mossel Bay, about 400 km's from Melkbos, at Hartenbos AKTV which did not have any space available until Jeandré spoke to them in perfect Afrikaans, a space miraculously appeared. We were greeted in the camp by an old Apartheid-Era South African flag blowing in the breeze and cold stares from the Afrikaner retirees. We were clearly not welcome, and I wished that I could have some black and gay friends with me to help complete the conservative Afrikaner hate list. A group of stony faces arranged their garden chairs to watch us set up camp. A friendly wave was ignored by the entire group except for one kindly old man who was quickly put in his place by his stony-faced wife. One night was enough in this particular paradise.

The Landy was handling the load very well, and that night we camped in Plettenberg Bay, 600 km's from Cape Town. The camp was slightly run-down but had direct access to a magnificent beach littered with giant rocks. We braaied (BBQ) that night and celebrated our second day on the road and met some interesting people, a couple of French Overlander surfers camped next to us in a van and a crazy South African called Mr Rose who drove a Series 2, wore a handkerchief on his head and spoke in an English schoolmaster's voice. I hung out with Mr Rose and discussed philosophy and Land Rovers for a while. A few days later, we drove on to the city of Port Elizabeth where a close friend, Johan, joined us for another braai and a few beers. The next stop was Coffee

Bay in the Transkei, and we left Port Elizabeth on a hot Saturday morning to drive up and over the Kei Cuttings mountain pass to access the Transkei. The road from the N2 highway to Coffee Bay was one of the worst we had ever driven, giant potholes and a winding road led us down through green hills to the bay and the crazy parties which were waiting for us. The camp at the bottom of a backpackers was protected only by a small fence and a few stray dogs and had direct access to the beach. The heat was unbearable until nightfall, and then the noise was unbearable. I had a joint with Jeandré, which I instantly regretted. Luisa and the imminent birth of Keelan had put an end to my stoner ways and I hardly ever smoked the wacky weed which had become far more potent and mind-blowing than the stuff I used to buy for R10 a Banky. There was just too much going on around me, and the setting was just too surreal, huge white eyes were peering at us through the bushes and voices saying "boss, boss!" The eyes were trying to sell us drugs or crayfish or prawns or firewood. I was paranoid and hallucinating slightly, a house on hill looked like a temple of some sort, and I began to suspect the nefarious intentions of a hippy cult. Luisa lost the Landy's keys which made me really uptight and had us all searching for half an hour before she found them in the tent. This was the kind of stunt Luisa pulled whenever I was stoned, just to make sure I had a terrible time. Jeandré eventually convinced the peddlers to go away. Our little posse settled in for a couple of days of surfing and chilling.

I had been trying to think of a good name for our Landy, and a group of Xhosa ladies sitting under a tree selling beads and bracelets gave us the perfect name. Looking at Keelan and me, wobbling back from the beach in our plump suburban bodies the ladies giggled and called us, 'eita mafuta, you look very strong'. 'What is mafuta, mama?' The ladies explained that mafuta means big and strong in the Xhosa language. Suitably impressed I decided to name the Landy Mafuta. Only later did I learn that the word mafuta refers to fat more than it does to strong, but you must understand, to a traditional Xhosa woman fat is a good thing. A fat man is a wealthy man who does not do manual labour, and when looking for a good husband, she looks for a fat husband.

We had been very low on fuel when we arrived, and our first task was to find fuel which we found at a very old pump station. Coffee Bay was the most "African" place we had found in South Africa. Jeandré had surfed, and we had swum in the sea, explored and found snakes and huge bugs, but it was good to leave the night-time camp madness behind and hit the road again. We crawled back up and out along the terrible road and rejoined the N2 and the terrible drivers on the road through Mtata, where some more Tstotsi's tried to sneak up on us in the traffic leading out of the city. Iera spotted them, and we took evasive action, rolling up our windows and quickly changing lanes. We had been camping for just over a week, and we were all a bit sun-dried and dehydrated so when Luisa's mom offered to let us use her accumulated time-share points for a week at the Wild Coast Hotel and Casino we, especially the girls, did not refuse. The Landy looked completely out of place outside the glitzy hotel reception, and we attracted some sidelong glances as we made our way to the rooms with our possessions packed in crates and cardboard boxes and loaded on the luggage trolley. Iera, who had assured us that she often camped in Europe, had a really hard time under the African sun, her hair frizzing and her skin erupting in rashes and pimples. Because both she and Jeandré loved to sleep every day until at least 11 am, I always made sure that they pitched their tent in a spot most likely to be cooked by the sun every morning. They did not catch on to my deviousness, and every morning they would crawl from the steaming tent, sweaty and red while Luisa and I would enjoy a good laugh and a cup of tea in the shade.

Iera greeted the white sheets and air-conditioned room with exasperated relief while I sat on the floor and played with the camera, sulkily accepting the civilised break in an otherwise adventurous journey.

GRAEME BELL

Jeandré and Iera had booked a flight from Durban airport for their return to Cape Town. They were having some domestic issues, and there was a tension in the air which I was happy to have cleared with their departure and happy to have some space and weight liberated from the Landy. While in Durban, staying with Luisa's mom we made arrangements to have a leak in the gearbox looked at by Land Rover Pinetown. The gearbox replacement by Land Rover Bloemfontein carried a one-year warranty, and while I had accepted the leak as a Land Rover inevitability, Luisa had not. How do you get oil out of a stone? Put a Land Rover badge on it.

The work was done over three days, and we rejoined the highway north of Durban and were almost back on the N2 highway to Mozambique when the Landy cut out. I stopped, turned her off and on again and drove ten kilometres before it happened again. I phoned my mechanic back in Cape Town and told him what work had been done on the Landy, and he advised me that there is a sensor on the left-hand side of the gearbox and if it had not been plugged in properly the engine would cut out! We had a look and fiddled with the plug then took the Landy to Land Rover Umhlanga as a precaution. The mechanics that helped us had no idea what was wrong with the Defender and their computer would not read the Defenders ECU. The Landy was getting a lot of attention from the staff and management though unfortunately, most of that attention was just photo taking. We left when it was obvious that they were unable to help and cautiously headed for Richards Bay further up the North Coast. That night's camp was in a beautiful and expensive campground surrounded by camper vans and caravans of holidaymakers who had satellite dishes and armchairs, microwave ovens and carpets. We abandoned the green lawned retirement village and aimed for Zululand where we had booked a rondavel and enjoyed a dinner of traditional Zulu food.

WE WILL BE FREE

The Zulus had always impressed me as a nation. Before Europeans arrived in Southern Africa, the Zulus were the dominant force in the region and gained international notoriety when they defeated the British Army at the Battle of Isandlwana in January 1879. Shaka was the Zulu king who united the Zulu nation in the early 19th century and was acclaimed as a military genius due to his innovations such as the introduction of the larger shield and the short "Iklwa" sword for close combat fighting which combined with the bulls' horns fighting formation, led the Zulu army to continuous victory. Luisa and I had both spent a few years living in Durban as kids, long enough for the most obvious aspects of Zulu culture to be something we appreciated nostalgically.

We were woken that fresh morning, by a Zulu softly strumming a guitar and singing a gentle song. He would strum and sing outside each door until he sensed the occupants were awake before moving onto the next hut. I wanted to follow him around all morning, a Zulu Pied Piper. We enjoyed a huge breakfast and threw some spears at an elephant skull with the Zulu men before buying two knobkerries and hitting the road for Kosi Bay at the Mozambican border. The knobkerries, wooden fighting clubs, were named Wacky and Slappy and Keelan loved both dearly. He would arrange them on either side of the ground tent entrance and mock attack anything which moved. Our next destination, St. Lucia, is a beautiful town which serves as a hub for the Greater St. Lucia Wetlands Park, we camped at a rundown camp where we were regularly raided by monkeys and hippos, and crocodiles lazed in the sun a few hundred metres away. The local pub promised free beer tomorrow. The drive north to Kosi Bay was interesting and a bit sad. South Africa is well developed and industrial with sophisticated agriculture and that one beautiful city, but this corner of South Africa was the poorest and least developed part of South Africa we had ever seen. Drums resting on sticks indicated the entrances to remote homes and litter hung in the few dry trees. We were nervous about entering Mozambique after all the stories we had heard and our last night camping in South Africa was an opportunity to eat some meat, drink some beer and catch up on last-minute work while we still had mobile phone connection. The square satellite receiver was extremely expensive and difficult to use. Luisa would connect the dish to her computer, and I would move the receiver around like old bunny ear aerials. The receiver would beep if contact was established and often would only hold a connection if I stood on a chair, arms fully extended with the receiver art a 45-degree angle. Luisa would have me stand in this position for ages while she pretended to work, sipping on a beer while I sweated, reminded of the military training we had received in high school and the sadistic seniors who loved to punish us for breathing out of sequence.

Many family and friends told us that we were being irresponsible travelling into "Africa" with our kids, some even suggested that we might die. For many South Africans, South Africa is not 'Africa', and a drive north of our borders is considered a trip back in time, to a dangerous, dark and foreboding Africa. Namibia and Botswana are 'safe', Mozambique is OK for a December holiday, but the rest is thought to be wild and dangerous and definitely not the place for plump suburbanites from semi-European Cape Town. There may or may not be some truth to that.

3

Mozambique

Crossing the border was relatively easy considering that we had never driven across a border. We were stamped out and in within thirty minutes and tentatively drove onto Mozambican soil. Immediately the road changed from good tar to dirt then deep sand, the tracks crisscrossed and there was no way of knowing if we were on the correct track but engaged low range and just kept going forward with the sea to our right somewhere. My God, is this how the Mozambican roads are going to be? We kept going, careful not to bash into vehicles coming the other way and quickly climbing up, off the track if we saw another vehicle coming around the corner. Our shock absorbers were not handling the terrain, and we were bouncing along the deep sand tracks, I had been very careful when selecting them and had even phoned the technical manager of the distributor who assured me that they had nine settings and were up to the challenge. In the morning, we tried adjusting the shocks and driving over bumpy terrain, but every setting was as equally shit as the last. The Defender was handling the deepest sand sections without any major problems -but often we would have to stop and wait after Daddy's Nissan full of South African kids or overloaded local vehicles got bogged down then had to be pushed or towed out of the way. Before we had left I had bought a set of 32 11.5 R15 BF Goodrich KM2 Mud Terrain tyres and they, along with the low range gearbox, were keeping us moving along despite the weight and the terrible shock absorbers. I was later to learn that the load rating of those tyres was not ideal for the heavy Landy, but that was only one of the very many things I still had to learn.

That night over a few beers, we had a look at the road to Maputo, the Portuguese-speaking nation's capital. The only logical route we could find was along back roads, through a National Park which eventually would emerge across the bay from Maputo.

Mozambique had been ravaged by a civil war that began in 1977, two years after the end of the war of independence. It was similar to the Angolan Civil War as both wars were directly influenced by the Cold War. The ruling party, Front for Liberation of Mozambique (FRELIMO) and the national armed forces FAM (Armed Forces of Mozambique) were violently opposed from 1977 by the Mozambique Resistance Movement (RENAMO) which received funding from then Rhodesia and South Africa. Around a million died from the fighting and starvation and the war eventually ended in 1992 with the imminent end of Apartheid in South Africa. It had been very important for the white South African government, that both Angola and Mozambique were destabilised and that no regimes sympathetic to the ANC and South African communist movements would be allowed to exist in the region.

Almost twenty years later, the effects of the war could still be seen. Roads had not been maintained, and the infrastructure had crumbled. The towns we drove through on the route up to Maputo were almost exactly as they had been when the Portuguese fled except for the dilapidation, overgrown flora and tin shacks built in the grounds of once beautiful homes. A long-forgotten gazebo stood in the middle of an overgrown park where once families of Portuguese settlers had picnicked in the cool evening, perhaps listening to a band playing from that small stage. These towns are ghosts of what they used to be, with names like Bella Vista, inhabited now by people without the means to appreciate the purpose of the layout or to maintain the infrastructure which would serve them well.

WE WILL BE FREE

We drove along rough tracks of Route 201 through the Maputo Elephant Park, past signs warning of elephant and rhino, though neither species had survived the war. The animal population of Mozambique had essentially been wiped out during the civil war as starving citizens killed and ate everything edible. A road continued parallel to the coast once Route 201 ended, potholed tar tracks gave way to mud, and sand and dirt until eventually our Landy emerged in an unnamed town across the Baia De Maputo from where we would cross by ferry into the city, visible across the water. We unknowingly drove to the front of the queue and bought ferry tickets from a young man in white socks, who ran across the red clay road, pool cue in hand, to direct us to the office. He tried to sell us the tickets at three times the official cost but eventually settled on the correct price and some small change. A large, relatively modern, ferry had just docked, and a mix of cars, 4x4's, and people loaded with goods were scrambling for a path off the pier. We were the second vehicle to drive onto the ferry and were directed to reverse into a corner from where we sat and watched the impossible manoeuvres of the other embarking vehicles. It was a chaotic but strangely efficient system which eventually filled the ferry. The weather changed suddenly as the ferry began its departure, the sky turned charcoal and damp, large drops began to plop onto our filthy Land Rover. Within seconds, sheets of water were showering us, and the wind began to howl the bay into waves. The drawbridge was raised, and the Captain attempted to steer away from the dock then piloted the ferry back towards the dock, and a few wet women jumped into the load area over the high steel walls. The ferry slowly moved in circles away from and back to the jetty a few times before finally setting off across the bay. By now we were nervous of a slow Indian Ocean death and were relieved to eventually reach the city and drive off the ferry once the storm had settled. The bay was still heaving, and we watched from the Landy as three heavily armed soldiers struggled with arrogant ineptitude to dock a rubber duck, the many, wet spectators laughing and jeering as the soldiers struggled.

Maputo has a reputation for danger, and we wearily drove the filthy, wet streets looking for a hostel. Fatima's hostel, where we had planned to stay, was full and very expensive so we spent a few hours driving around the city looking for a safe place to stay before the sunset, and the night-time assholes came out from wherever they lurk during the day. Eventually, we booked into the VIP Hotel close to the harbour and across the road from a relatively up-market mall and office complex where Price Waterhouse Coopers and Delloites boasted of their residence. The rooms smelt dank, but we were grateful for the beds and clean bathrooms. Escorpiao restaurant, where we had an early dinner, is old school in every way, from the bow-tied waiter to the lace tablecloths. We had delicious, fat LM peri-peri prawns and chicken with salads and French fries, each occupying their own plate on the crowded table, under which mosquitoes feasted on us. The food was so good that a year later, we drove back into the city, far out of our way and sat in traffic for four hours just to have that meal again only to find that they were closed on Monday and our luck, it was a Monday.

Leaving Maputo, the next day through terrible traffic, the Landy bounced through potholed streets and found more traffic. The tropical heat, exhaust fumes and noise were terrible but, after three hours, we escaped onto the EN1 Route heading north. City and slums gave way to dusty villages and palm trees. The road was decent tar for many kilometres, and as we arrived at a camp in Xai-Xai thick, black storm crowds loomed over the sea. The owner, a tough South African who had lived in Mozambique before and throughout the war, offered us a huge, spooky cottage at the top of a steep dune. We accepted as the cost was low and had a braai on the balcony, in the stormy wind, overlooking the sea and chatting about how much fun we were having in the exotic country and with the sense of adventure. That night we slept uneasily as the storm raged and the ghosts prowled our cottage and awoke to a fresh, cloudy blue sky and headed back onto the EN1. Turning right at the intersection which had led to the beach, over a hill, the sight of the road ahead caused us to recoil. Mud as far as the eye could see. The soil banks surrounding the road had crumbled and collapsed with the storm, and the entire section of the EN1 national road was a mud pit. The rain began to fall again, and the vehicles in front and behind us turned around and headed back to wherever they came from, except for one Isuzu 4x4 flatbed truck which pushed on. We engaged low range and followed in his wake past vehicles stuck up to their chassis' in the thick clay. The truck ploughed on, and we followed, at one-point dipping into a huge hole, and mud sloshed up over the windscreen. Luisa urged me on with a shout, and I accelerated up out of the ditch and up a long gradual rise. After eighty kilometres of this watery, muddy mess, we finally hit tar again and sped up our progress to Inhambane. Along the way, we saw awesome islands lying off the coast with forests of palm trees, crystal clear water and no sign of access. It was only after the mud road had made way for tar that we discovered that we had left the knobkerries, Wacky and Slappy, back at the haunted cottage. Keelan was devastated and begged us to go back, which I might have considered had the road not had been so terrible. We promised that we would get them back somehow and carried on down the road with a very sad little boy whimpering quietly in the back seat.

Just before the Jangamo turnoff to Inhambane lunch beckoned at a roadside restaurant in the shade of a huge Khaya tree. We had read in our guidebook that the author loved to eat local food and he advised strongly that we should do the same. The restaurant seemed popular enough, and many travellers stopped for a cheese sandwich and a coke before hitting the road again. I had heard so many great stories about Mozambican peri-peri prawns and chicken (and had great food in Maputo), so we sat down and ordered a peri-peri chicken and two Prego rolls. The meat which eventually arrived could barely be recognised as either chicken or beef, but we picked at the food until we could bear it no more. The "chef" then stepped out of the "kitchen" unfortunately leaving the door open behind him. Now, one interesting anomaly which we had observed so far in Mozambique was that every little town had a resident, dreadlocked madman. Usually dressed in filthy, ripped brown clothing and usually with one or both hands stuck in the air, these madmen would strut or limp or stagger along the EN1 screaming abuse or mumbling or staring into space. It was unnerving, but every village had one as if they were issued by the state. Well, our "chef" was an identical madman, dreadlocked and filthy with a weird grin. We plump, pale suburbanites had been fed whatever by whomever and just the thought of how he prepared it still upsets my stomach. To hell with the guidebook. From now on, we trust no-one, when it comes to food anyway.

We arrived in Inhambane with Luisa still screeching in my ear to look for a place to camp. It had been a very long day and after driving around searching for a few hours gave up on the idea of camping and were directed to a lodge run by WhenWe's (a name South African's have for white Rhodesians who had left Zimbabwe for whatever reason and often lamented the days, 'When We...'). The lodge was well run, and the cottages were large and spacious. We agreed on a price of R1, 000 a day, unpacked and washed the filthy Landy before settling in for a few Laurentina beers. That night I went for a swim next to the almost perfect bar and smashed my shin on the way out of the pool. It hurt like hell, but the only damage seemed superficial though the wound would stay open for five months. The next morning, we booked a tour with the lodge to the Bazaruto islands where we snorkelled in the warm water and rode the currents along the reef. After a day in the water and sun, we packed up and climbed into the little speedboat for the ride back to the mainland but after ten minutes in the boat, on the sea, in the howling, cool wind, one of the boats' engines failed. A few calls were made to the shore, and one of the WhenWe's instructed our "captain" to keep going. A ride which should have taken twenty minutes took an hour and a half of windy unpleasantness. Cold and grumpy we arrived back at the lodge, had a beer with the WhenWe's and went to bed. At about 2 am I awoke feeling ill and threw up. Half an hour later, my stomach joined the party. Head and arse were competing for the attention of the porcelain. Then a hammer started slamming into my left ear. This continued for a week at the lodge, a week in which I lost over 15 kg's and survived on Ultra Mel custard and painkillers. A daily routine of vomiting and diarrhoea reduced my days to misery. Trying to sleep, being too tired and too wired to sleep and my world the crumpled blankets, the mosquito netting, the bucket, the odd terrible cigarette, the slamming hammer.

I was having constant nightmares, and my thoughts ran in slow desperate circles as my body fought the mysterious infection. Aching, sweating, cramping, weak and disoriented. Malaria was ruled out as the symptoms were not typical of Malaria and we had been taking our Malarone treatments religiously at 9 am every morning at Keelan's insistence. The Malarone was extremely expensive and set us back R20 000 for the four of us, but we were not prepared to take a risk, especially with the health of our kids. Many Africans simply cannot afford the preventative prescription or the relatively cheap treatment, and for many, the disease is a death sentence. My illness was a mystery that we simply could not diagnose. The WhenWe's told me not to bother with the local doctors, and the local pharmacy shelves were stocked with eye drops and plasters, not much else. If I was inclined to be paranoid, I might suspect that the WhenWe's had slipped something in my drink. They were a bunch of wankers and had the most to gain from me being stuck, sweating in their bed for a week. Luckily, I am only paranoid when Jeandré is around.

During that week, Luisa drove into town, and I received a phone call from her. The right rear shock absorber had broken off at the joint. A young, blonde WhenWe offered to take us into town to search for a shock absorber, and we climbed in the back of his bakkie for the ride. He took us to a few parts places, but they only had Toyota parts. A Nigerian told us he could order a shock which would take a week to arrive. WhenWe then drove to the market and left us in the back of the bakkie, far from the shade, for an hour while I fought nausea and an unsettled stomach.

On the Friday, a shock absorber arrived at the Nigerian parts dealer in town. I dragged myself out of bed and drove the Landy into town, found the Nigerian and set about replacing the rear shock with an obviously sub-standard replacement. The nuts supplied did not fit the bolt of the shock. The Nigerian went off to find one who did. Using the bottle jack and whatever strength was left in my arms while lying in the dirt outside the little shack shop, I replaced the shock, bolted it in and drove back onto the road. I looked left, I looked right. My idea was to drive down the road to test the shock then turn around and head back to the lodge. I pulled into the road with the sun setting in my eyes and noticed a commotion in my left-hand wing mirror. A huge Mercedes truck had veered off the road to avoid hitting my Land Rover. Pedestrians scattered amidst the dust, plastic bags of groceries flying through the air. I drove on for a kilometre trying to decide what to do and realised that I had nowhere to go except back the way I came and stopped the Landy on the side of the road.

A black car slowed down and screamed Portuguese obscenities at me. I apologised and stooped. The Mercedes truck pulled up behind me, and six angry Mozambicans jumped out and rushed towards me. In a daze, I walked up to the largest, most aggressive man, shook hands and apologised. Man by man I shook hands and stooped, I am sick, I am tired, I am sorry, is everyone OK? They were obviously not accustomed

35

to humble white men and told me off, "who is going to pay for their groceries"? Don't worry, I will fix it. They forgave me and drove off, pretending to be angry. I turned around and headed back to witness the carnage I had caused which was actually minimal. Mozambicans are accustomed to terrible drivers and build their stalls a good distance from the road. I saw a broken bag of flour and some unhappy faces but kept on driving, only an idiot would have stopped. I headed back to the lodge and collapsed into my sickbed. Ear pounding, stomach-churning, exhausted.

Luisa was impatient with my illness, we needed to keep moving. Where many women would have headed back to South Africa, which wasn't far away, Luisa wanted to keep heading north and so did I. She packed us in the Land Rover and headed for Tete and the border with Malawi, a long and horrible road. I had recovered enough to be able to drive, but the road to Beira had disintegrated into a horrible potholed mess. One long stretch of road was absolutely terrible; it was easier and far more comfortable to drive on the mud verge than it was to drive on the acneed tar, banging the tyres into the rims of sneaky sharp-edged holes. The road would even out until we reached a comfortable speed then BANG! Another hole.

After many exhausting kilometres, the road levelled into comfortable, flat, Chinese tar and we wound through the little villages and the palm trees and green tropical forests. On the verge, around a bend, a gold Mercedes sat stricken. The driver was British, his loopy co-pilot American and in the back seat sat two stoned, reading, unconcerned Swedish girls. What's wrong? Head gasket. Need a tow? If you don't mind. We hooked the fat golden girl up to the Land Rover and towed them 200 km's to the next town which had a mechanic and a service station, and a new Ford F150 parked around the back. Good luck. Here have some Cuban cigars. Thanks, Happy Pants and on we went until the turnoff to Tete where the sun was setting to find accommodation run by WhenWe's dressed in camouflage clothing, crocodiles in a pit. We stayed in a filthy little rondavel, ate a basic dinner and woke up early for the drive to Tete.

4

Sweet Malawi

Leaving Mozambique was welcome. We had a horrible time and hoped that Malawi would be better. The border crossing was easy enough. Follow a tout down a path, past a bar and brothel to buy insurance, then figure out where to stamp out and where to stamp in, find customs and into English speaking Malawi.

I was still horribly sick and weak as we reached Blantyre and started searching for a hostel and a hospital. Luckily there was a private hospital close to the first hostel we had a look at; unfortunately, the staff was not as efficient as the modern building suggested they might be. A small black doctor had a look at me after a large nurse squished a cockroach which was bothering me. The doctor was not friendly; he had a quick look in my ear, told me I had wax build-up and gave me children's antibiotics. Kids antibiotics for a 130kg man. We booked into the Blantyre Holiday Inn with the entire Indian population of Malawi. Screaming spoilt kids, fat smoking men and nervous women.

While waiting for Luisa, my body and mind went into shutdown. I could not sit down for fear that I would not be able to stand again. I could not stay standing for fear that I would faint. Pains were shooting through my chest, and the hammering in my head grew absolutely unbearable. The receptionist was moving slowly, Luisa was asking questions, an Indian man interrupted their conversation. It was the sickest I had ever been. I am convinced to this day that if I had a weaker heart or spirit I would have had a heart attack that day, standing on the stairs, fighting to stay on my feet. After two days of a new hell, we left for Cape Maclear and Lake Malawi. I first tried to fix a connection on one of the fridges but was unable to concentrate in the heat and fog of my mind. Luisa was by now very impatient with my illness, I had been lying around for almost two weeks, and she had to pick up the slack and do all the driving. Real Men don't get sick you see, they fight through the illness and carry on regardless, Real Men don't expect sympathy or medicine or bed rest, Real Men kick disease and illness in the arse then make their wives an amazingly romantic dinner while raking in large piles of cash with large, glistening, muscular arms.

The road to Cape Maclear from Blantyre is mostly straight and mostly flat, the green countryside reminded me of Natal. The many police roadblocks were mostly problem-free with the exception of one tall Charles (all Malawian men are called Charles it seems) who wanted South African magazines. We had been told by internet friends to stay at a budget lodge called Fat Monkeys and turned off the decent tar onto the washboard dirt road which led up over a large hill and down into the bay. After creaking along over some large ditches in the road (and me throwing up a few times), we arrived at the large red gates at the entrance to the lodge. A worker opened, and we drove into heaven. There was space to camp a few metres from the lake under a large tree. The first night I had a beer and went to sleep in the tent, the second night I had two beers, the third night three and eight or more on the fourth night. Maybe it was the serenity of the camp, maybe it was the fresh air, or maybe the children's antibiotics were doing their job, but after a week, I was back on my feet and ready to explore.

In the mornings, we would wake to the gentle voices of the villagers passing our camp, feet wet in the fresh lake. Fish Eagles circled overhead while little Kingfishers would use the trees around us as launch pads for their hunting. Islands lay to our left and to our right with others visible further out in the lake. Each morning a waiter passing on his way to the kitchen would ask if I wanted tea, which he would serve to our camp on a tray. Breakfast of banana pancakes for the kids, eggs, toast, tomato and sausage for us in the little restaurant. A swim in the lake, maybe some snorkelling at the island with its array of tropical freshwater fish and Fish Eagles fed fish from a boat, then lunch, an afternoon beer and, depending who was in the bar, an evening party. The kids spent their days in the lake on our inflatable mattress, playing pirate, the boys teaming up against the girls.

We stayed for two weeks and made friends with a group of students from Norway, friends who are still friends and who we look forward to meeting again when we eventually overland Europe. I befriended the camp guard, Fanta, a peaceful, intelligent guy in whose presence I always felt completely at ease. Fanta and I would chat, or he would just watch me reading a book while I lay in a hammock, his gaze never feeling intrusive or uncomfortable. We would share a cigarette and talk about Malawi, South Africa, the lake, the people and the future. Fanta had plans to move to South Africa to make some money as many Malawians do. I looked at his life, running a few fishing boats, guarding the camp, living a tranquil life, and I did my best to discourage him. In South Africa, he would find poverty, aggression, racism, xenophobia, crime and despondency. No car or television or leather shoes were worth the sacrifice of the peace he had.

When we left, we were all pretty sad and grumpy. That lake had been what we had been searching for when we left home, and no other camp in Africa which we found could match the atmosphere, comfort or peace we had found on those calm shores.

Something strange happens when you find a nice camp while travelling long-term. You settle in, stuff gets spread around the camp, and you begin to feel uncomfortable with the thought of leaving. You just don't know when you will feel this safe and comfortable again. Inevitably and eventually you do leave, and the first half-hour back on the road is not a great deal of fun. Then you see new things, meet new people, and begin to enjoy the road. I have an English Overlander friend who calls it the Overlanders disease. There have been people who roll into a camp one day and never leave. Yes, they are usually retirees, but it is not uncommon to hear of people camping in one place for three years. After a month or two, you are no longer an Overlander, you are a resident.

The next camp was also on the beach, next to a hotel. The wind had whipped the fresh lake into almost surf-able waves. We chose our spot under a tree and waited for the Indian families to leave before moving out onto the beach to camp and braai and enjoy a few beers under the stars. A group of middle-aged Englishman in a Defender had been eyeing our spot under the trees with lustful eyes and moved into the spot as soon as we left. Unfortunately, a crowd of drinkers arrived in trucks and pumped very loud music while having mock fistfights mere steps from the English camp. It was a long night for them and a peaceful night for us.

Our next stop was close to the Tanzanian border but first we had to climb up from the Lake to an industrial town called Mzuzu before heading down an extremely tight mountain pass back to the lake and a camp run by a Dutch couple who would not have been more out of place if they had just arrived from Neptune. He was a tired, ponytailed hard rocker type and she a very tall Goth with a large black Great Dane pet to match her long flowing black dress in the African heat. The camp was nice enough, grassy and cool. A British couple arrived in a Land Rover Defender and searching for a place to camp we suggested that they camp on our piece of lawn. We swapped stories, they had driven down from the UK, and a green snake with a frog in its mouth slithered between us and climbed a tree. We had a beer, I destroyed our ground tent, and the most dreaded of all African travellers arrived. The big, yellow, or orange overland truck. Packed with ex-students, party animals, fat popular people and thin thirsty people, the serene camp exploded in a blossoming of canvas tents. Each passenger was eager to set up and get on with the drinking and fancy-dress parties they would hold every other night. Our British friends were invaded with tents being erected within pissing distance of their own. I marked my territory, and we were happy that no canvas was erected near us.

When these 'adventure travellers' pull into camp clean toilets become an explosion of tampons, toilet paper and loitering vomiters. Quiet pubs morph into testosterone puddles and a quiet night under an African sky transform into a London club frequented by slutty, heart-broken American Australian Swedes. We do not know why though we try to understand, perhaps it is the group mentality of people who think they are on an adventure, who love how the folks back home applaud their courage, safe in the group but anxious of their place in it, the alpha males, the lonely girls, the safety of the truck, the dishes, the long daytime recovery naps en-route to the next valley, river, viewpoint, sand dune, animal, party. We did make friends with the overland truck drivers though, they respected us, and we respected that.

We left our new friends and the hung-over the next morning. First, though, Keelan and I traded most of our milk powder, rice and sugar for a carved earth, walking sticks and a strange wooden man with enormous nostrils and hands stretching his buttocks, either a good luck charm or an evil token depending on who you asked. Those internet gurus had been wrong about the countries outside of South Africa, perhaps because most avoided human contact and drove directly to national parks and wildlife reserves. The weight of all the extra gear was making life hard for our Landy, and we were glad to free up some space.

5

Tanzania

The Tanzanian border lay up in tropical forested hills and was a simple affair partly because we had taken the time to organise the Carnet from the AA with which we could leave and enter most Southern and East African countries without having to complete a temporary import permit. Luisa was not doing well, her stomach cramping and twisting from some unknown bacteria which had affected only her. She begged me to find a toilet, and I struggled to drive fast enough to get anywhere which might have facilities and slow enough to stop on the winding road should we spot an uninhabited stretch of dirt road. For over an hour, we drove while Luisa squirmed in desperation. Eventually, at the top of a hill, we found a fuel station which looked vaguely modern. Luisa jumped out and waddled feverishly across the forecourt. The fuel attendant, recognising the face of digestive agony, ran to retrieve the keys and open the door to heavenly relief which turned out to be a slippery Muslim keyhole. She returned to the Landy with a look of mixed disgust and pure relief.

A road leads up a hill from the Dar es Salaam road to the town of Iringa where, later that same day, we needed to top up on fuel, cold coke and directions. A gang of cheeky kids surrounded the Landy and joked with me while I wandered around the Landy checking tyres and getting a clean shirt out of the clothing crates in the back of the Landy. With the tank full, we waved goodbye to our new little friends and drove up another hill to sit and wait for a robot to turn green. A large group waited for a bus, vendors wandered between the vehicles and a man approached my window, no thank you and I waved him away. He persisted, 'no, thank you'! And another wave. Another man joined him, and they continued to rap to me in Swahili then switched to English, 'the back is open'. Oh shit. I pulled over to find the top back flap of the canopy wide open, the clothing crates, computer bag and portable satellite sitting there staring at me, calling me an idiot. Luisa called me far worse. I had forgotten to close the flap at the fuel station and could only thank the road gods for the kindness and honesty of every one of the fifty people who was standing at that intersection.

The road into Tanzania and up to Dar es Salaam is at times tree-lined and mountainous and dips down into a national park where you are equally harassed by massive speed bumps and amazed by elephants and giraffe grazing by the roadside. We drove into the night and were horrified by the culture of driving in Tanzania. A Muslim country, most drivers are rushing to meet Allah, and basic road rules are disobeyed. Drivers will not use their headlights at night but will leave an indicator on until they turn, when they turn the indicator off. Truck drivers and bus drivers will hang dead goats and fish from the windscreen while overtaking on blind passes around blind corners on roads without a verge. After a long, dangerous tree-lined stretch of madness, we gratefully reached the Kisolonza lodge which offered camping and chalets. Keelan had been running a fever every night for the last week, and we decided to book a tartan-curtained chalet. I made sausage pasta on the tailgate of the Landy while Luisa tried to cool Keelan. In the morning, he was fine again, and we took the time to relax, clean, repack the Landy and have a look around our surroundings. The lodge is run by a Scottish and English couple who had built an amazing lodge from the ruins of an old clay village. The restaurant is a thatched roof erected over a ruin and filled with ambience, art, chairs and tables and lit by candles. As we approached for dinner, a man on a bicycle raced towards us and told us to stop, wait. After two minutes he called to us, Kuja! He was the drummer who sat by the door and invited guests, and he would not be happy if we did not enter to the sound of his gentle drumming and the sight of his friendly grin.

The showers are revitalising hot water heated by a wood-burning "donkey", and the loos are scentless long drop, both built with care and flair. Luisa scared the kids with a flashlight demonstration of what lay in the three-metre hole beneath the toilet seat and walked in on an old man using the toilet without locking the door. She had grabbed the door handle and absentmindedly stepped in to find a hairy pair of legs and a white bottom attached to a khaki shirt and a grizzled face. He sat and stared at her, she stopped dead in her tracks and stared back at him, the two caught in an embarrassed introduction. She apologised while he just looked at her with a wooden expression, then returned to share her embarrassment.

Dar es Salaam is a city with many charms within the central district and has a relatively fascinating colonial history beginning with its construction in the 1860s by the Sultan of Zanzibar. The Germans ran the country for a while then lost it to the British who ran the country after World War 1 until 1961 when independence was won. Roughly half the country is Muslim, and the call of the mullah and the Muslim dress lent the city an exotic air and made us feel very far from home. We fought our way through the city traffic, down Nelson Mandela Avenue and, in the dark after a meal of Steers fast food found the Kigamboni ferry to the south of the city where we would search for a camp. A fat cop jumped out of the shadows when Luisa drove down a poorly marked, wide, one-way street in the diplomatic area and tried to fine us, but we smiled and waved him off before escaping to join the ferry queue.

Mikadi beach camp is hot, sweaty, and well run by a Chilean, Lucho and his Zimbabwean wife, Jo. They knew what we needed as soon as we arrived, and we booked into two small Banda's, a room on stilts, hooked the Landy up to the power and settled in for a beer in the large, communally arranged pub. We left early the next day to look for another camp because Luisa had spent the night shielding Keelan's ears from the loud romantic acrobatics of the couple in the next Banda. I was reluctant to leave, and after a search, we found no better camp so returned to Mikadi to plan an indulgent break on Zanzibar Island. Mikadi camp is almost as wonderful as Fat Monkeys. Based on the beach between villages we would wake every morning to the Mullah's call, ALLLLLLLLLLLAAAAHHHHUUU AKBAR!

I enjoyed the pub the most. Lucho has the greatest music collection in the short history of humanity, and we had lost our impeccably prepared iPod just before we left South Africa. For the last few months, we had been listening to one dreadful Burning Spear CD. The cold, cheap, tasty beer and Lucho's music filled my head with calm, tranquil thoughts and I enjoyed the conversation of the travellers we met especially an Indian kid trying to make his way as a pilot and a British girl with whom we all became close. Sundays, the restaurant would serve a huge, delicious lunch while we watched the local Indians having verbally violent confrontations about whose mother or wife had brought the most samosas. Jo's mom took the kids searching for shells while we dealt with the drama of running a business remotely. One corporate client, an Indian with her own samosa issues, had not followed our instructions and had made her own work permit application a bureaucratic nightmare. She was the new head of the Human Resources department and took particular pleasure in turning her mistakes into our nightmare.

I was not the only fan of the bar. Locals would wander in from the beach, friends of the owners would arrive throughout the day, and there was a nice group of local, old school travellers who had made Africa their home. Young American NGO volunteers, teachers, or health workers arrive on the weekends for a bit of R&R after short or extended stays with remote villagers inland. Some had become Africanised, wore the local dress and carried stuff on their heads which is a hilarious sight. A few of the girls were desperate for affection after months of necessary celibacy. One American girl, a chubby khanga wearing Kirstie Allie lookalike, was particularly randy and unflatteringly cozied up to men in the bar, trying her luck with the tall blonde Kiwi, the ugly little French man, the taxi driver, the barman, the Masai and even me, each one of us repelled by her advances and desperation, though I am sure someone took advantage of her desperation later in the evening. A Friday night with that story unfolding in front of us, Lucho's soundtrack and potent punch is pretty much the best fun to be had in Dar. Keelan proved to be a pool playing whiz kid and defeated everyone in the bar until a local pro showed up to take on the little prodigy. Keelan lost two games out of three before being sent to bed before the action became unsuitable for a ten-year-old.

Another reason that Mikadi Beach Camp was intriguing was the young Masai security guards. These tall thin men are not the fake Masai who wander the Tanzanian tourist's traps; these guys are tough, unfazed and disciplined. One night I was sitting on the steps of my Banda smoking when I felt a presence, I turned and found a Masai sitting a few metres away from me in the dark shadows. He did not move a muscle, but I could see the whites of his eyes and knew that he was wide awake. I decided not to move until he moved. I lasted maybe five minutes, and he was still sitting in exactly the same position the next morning. Drunken day visitors who refused to leave the bar at night were, as a last resort, motivated to leave by the smiling Masai. One chap who had arrived in a new Range Rover refused to leave until his drink was finished but would only take mock sips while being loud and abusive. A Masai "accidentally" knocked the drink out of the man's hand and his big smile and unsmiling eyes convinced the man that it was time to leave. Drunken weekend invaders from the nearby village would be whipped like cows back into their territory. You don't mess with the Masai.

WE WILL BE FREE

We planned our trip to Zanzibar in the quiet hours, and Lucho and Jo were kind enough to let us leave the Landy safely in their parking lot for the two weeks we would be on the island. We took a tuk-tuk out over the bumpy road to the Kigamboni then walked with a huge backpack full of dirty laundry to catch the Fast Ferries ferry to the island. The backpack was full of laundry simply because the water at Mikadi is brackish and soap does not sud, and although it was sweltering most days, the extreme humidity kept the clothes from drying. The ferry was relatively modern but not fast because one of the engines was broken. Arriving at the island, we found ourselves in famous Stone Town, set amongst clear water and many colourful fishing boats. These guys do not realise that they live in paradise. We lumbered off the ferry and pushed through an excited crowd of touts to find a Taxi to take us to the east of the island and the paradise which awaited us. The taxi ride was hot and sweaty through the impoverished tropical centre of Zanzibar and arrived at the lodge which had looked perfect on the internet but was horribly messy and mismanaged by a pair of young Italians who were completely inattentive and forever on their phones. A large wedding party of Johannesburg accented South Africans wearing very thick silver chains around their necks were hanging out in the pool, swigging brandy and coke while our kids tried to find a spot to wash off the sun and humidity. After one night, we left the litter-strewn disappointment and headed to a five-star hotel on the west coast which was very well run and comfortable with the most delicious breakfast and dinner buffets we had ever seen. Unfortunately, there were none of the Mikadi beach type characters there, only dour Germans, arrogant Italians and the ubiquitous loud Americans. We were dressed in our overused, stained and deteriorating overland clothing and did not really fit in with the Armani / Louis Vuitton crowd. I had to buy a few t-shirts at the gift shop to look somewhat presentable and had to ask the general managers permission to enter the dining area with shorts on because we simply did not have any trousers. We explained that we had driven up from South Africa and he allowed us to break the rule. The setting was beautiful, and the Italian girls in G-strings improved the view significantly but not enough to save me from boredom. The kids played in the pool for hours every day while we enjoyed the sun even though Luisa had to spend many hours in the business centre taking care of the business back home, Zanzibar is not far enough from home for us to be able to escape our responsibilities.

The departure from the hotel was not grand. The doorman called a taxi and promised a fee of $8.00 for the trip back to the harbour at Stone Town. The taxi was an old Toyota which had been on the island for so many years that the seats were slimy and green fungus grew between the cracks in the dashboard. The taxi overheated four-time en-route to the harbour and arrived too late for us to catch the midday ferry. The driver then demanded $80, but we laughed, took our bags out of the boot and paid him $10 before trudging off surrounded by loud touts to try and find the ticket office. The touts were unbearable in the clammy heat, shouting at us and each other they followed me noisily down the road to the ticketing area, trying to direct me to other offices, not the official ticket office. When I bent my head close to the thick glass to hear what the clerk was mumbling, they all started shouting again. I lost it and chased them away swearing in pure Afrikaans and some unsavoury English. They finally understood that there was no money to be made off me but still hung around and followed us at a distance. We booked the first-class air-conditioned ride back which we enjoyed to the sights, sounds and smells of a group of burping, farting, cheesy-footed Chinese men.

Arriving back in Dar we took a short walk, the ferry across the harbour, another overloaded bumpy tuk-tuk ride and arrived back at Mikadi. We should not have left but should have saved our money and hung out at Mikadi, which was far more entertaining and enjoyable than anything I had experienced on the island. Stone Town was incredible though with its crumbling history and tropical setting. I had also seen one of the sexiest women I had ever seen. She was dressed in a full Burka which outlined her magnificent naked physique perfectly with its sultry, seductive midnight black fabric, her eyes expressing what most eyes could never.

Before leaving Mikadi, I explained our musical dilemma and the loss of the iPod to Lucho who asked for our hard drive and transferred 80 GB of the greatest music known to man. Even now, four years later, we have a folder under music called Mikadi Music, and we listen to it often. We said our goodbyes, promised to visit again and return a book I had borrowed (which I did post back to them a year later) then headed back into the madness of Dar to buy new shock absorbers to replace the one old shock and the dodgy part sold to me in Mozambique by the equally dodgy Nigerian, which I fitted in the parking area of a mall at the top of Nelson Mandela Avenue while the family shopped for new clothing. Dar is the best place we have seen in East Africa to buy Land Rover parts as the police and military still use Land Rovers. I had serviced the Landy at the Land Rover dealership before we had left for Zanzibar and had gone looking for Landy parts. I found a road with over thirty stores selling Land Rover parts mostly for the older petrol and TDI diesel engines.

The new shocks took care of most of the bouncing over the many terrible speed bumps on the road to the Serengeti, a road which has no speed limits and many overturned trucks and busses. We never felt unsafe in Tanzania except when driving on the roads surrounded by completely incompetent and unpredictable drivers of mostly un-roadworthy vehicles. A lone, policeman stood on the road surrounded by banana plantations and motioned for us to stop. We greeted each other respectfully, and he leant inside to see if he could see anything worth appropriating and spotted a few notes in the cup holders. 'I am very thirsty Mzungu, I need some money to buy a cold drink', 'we don't have any money Bwana', his eyes widening and a small disbelieving smile, 'but we have a cold drink for you', and we handed him the remaining half of my Fanta Orange. He let us go with a wave, and we continued past the hilly banana groves and onto the flatlands where sisal plantations lined the road.

Arusha is a horribly bustling little town crammed into a corner of paradise. East of the town and visible on a cloudless day is Kilimanjaro, to the west lay the Ngorongoro Crater and the Serengeti. We drove into town with Luisa again suffering from severe stomach cramps, asked around and were directed to the surgery of a Dr Mohamed, parked the Landy and went to sit in the filthy little waiting room while Luisa writhed in pain and the kids and I played with children dressed in their scruffy Sunday best. Eventually, Luisa was summoned into the grumpy, nose-picking doctors room where he lay her down and jammed his fingers into her tortured stomach. 'Does that hurt'? 'What the fuck do you think?' He scribbled a script, and we headed to the pharmacy which worked inefficiently on a system of pushing, shoving, shouting and indifference. I muscled in, pushed our script through the mouse hole, pleaded with the fat, slow pharmacist, retrieved the little box of magic and led my unhappy posse back to the Landy. We camped at Meserani Snake Park run by Ma and BJ, South Africans who had left South Africa before the first democratic elections. Ma was sweet but firm, BJ a Land Rover expert. The camping was free, set on an unkempt lawn. The highlights of the camp were the snakes and critters which lazed in ramshackle displays and the bar which was plastered wall and ceiling with memorabilia from the many thousands of travellers who had passed through. A dried crocodile hung and eyeballed you from the ceiling, t-shirts, stickers and graffiti-covered the walls which unfortunately could not speak.

There are many expensive tours available into the Ngorongoro Crater, but we like to save money and have an independent experience. Being

Africans, we had grown up going to nature reserves, and national parks so did not need a guide to explain the difference between an Impala and a Kudu. We unpacked most of the load from the rear of the Landy and set off early in the morning to explore the Crater and the adjacent Serengeti. The best tar in the entire country lies on that short ribbon from Arusha Airport to the park, and we made good time, arriving before most of the tours and their cargo of khaki dressed cameras. The fee had to be paid at the office at the gate. 400 dollars for our family and vehicle for less than nine hours. Tanzanians paid ten dollars. We argued with the park manager that we were African, not frikken Europeans or Americans, surely there was a discount for Africans? Not a cent, but we did get a smile and a sticker for the Landy. Feeling financially violated, we drove up the muddy roads to the rim of what has to be the Garden of Eden. A huge green bowl lay before us, herds running or grazing and a rainbow across the northern curve of the bowl, a cool blue sky. Actually, entering the crater would have cost an extra 200 dollars which we refused to pay; instead, we had to be satisfied with the view from the rim. The roads inside the parks are corrugated neglect, and the poor Landy shuddered as we drove along the rim stopping often for photos and to be harassed by "Masai" children selling trinkets. I stopped to help an old Land Rover with a flat tyre, the Indian owner did not have any tools, not even a wheel spanner and it had been so long since the tyres had been changed that the nuts were stuck in place. I retrieved my socket wheel spanner and spent a few sweaty minutes forcing the nuts off. His humble, uncomfortable wife sat in the vehicle the entire time, imagining that she was somewhere else. Our new friend thanked us as we left.

We drove on towards the Serengeti enjoying the herds of Giraffe and Wildebeest and Impala, straining our eyes to spot a cat, explored the little side tracks and drove so far that we eventually reached a lodge near a wetland which was accessed by helicopter. We drove up to the reception, settled in the lounge area and ordered some beer and cold drinks for the kids. Germans in camouflage gear carrying well-hung camouflaged cameras stalked the lodge garden for anything with wings or a heartbeat. We felt smug, covered in thick dust. After the large and very expensive beer, we drove back down the track we had entered on and headed for the entrance to the vast grass plains of the Serengeti. It was tempting to wander off into the wild and find a place to camp but the fine for reaching the exit gates after 5 pm was equal to the entrance fee. We had to rush to get out in time. I regret not spending more time in the park but to fully appreciate the place you would need to spend at least a week following the migrations and searching for animals. We simply did not have that kind of budget and, except for the blissful scenery, had pretty much seen it all before. Growing up surrounded by African wildlife is a privilege you only truly appreciate when you travel far away to lands without such magnificent beasts.

Returning to the gate, Luisa took over the driving. It is only right that she gets to enjoy the experience of not being only a passenger but also a participatory, one of very few who could say that they had driven through this magnificent setting. Unfortunately, she also earned the dubious honour of being one of the very few to drive a Land Rover sideways in the Serengeti. Approaching a small bridge around a corner, Luisa was using a bit too much throttle. The rear of the Landy was bouncing on the corrugation, and as we turned the corner the rear swung out, and we were very close to rolling, Luisa screamed but stayed calm, she did not brake but instinctively geared down, accelerated and counter steered and in a cloud of dust and flying stones we emerged safely back on the road. Poor Luisa was shaking, but I encouraged her to keep on driving, stopping then would have been terrible for her confidence as a driver. We pushed on towards the gate and ran into our Indian friend again who had broken down with a loose alternator. I gave him a 22 spanner and told him to pull his head out of his arse and buy a toolbox before leaving him with the tool and heading off back to the gate and that perfect tar and a rainy drive back to the camp, me playing DJ and doing my best to make Luisa cry with sad, happy music. No easy task, but I succeeded.

6

South to Malawi not North to Kenya or East to Asia

Back in the camp, a debate raged. Originally the plan had been to store the Landy somewhere in Kenya and the family would then fly to Asia to backpack for a few months; however, we were having a problem staying in touch with our clients and ensuring that they were receiving the service they deserved. Our assistant was doing a good job but needed our input for legal advice and the resolution of problems. One client, the incompetent Human Resources lady, was being extremely difficult and demanding, waging a revenge campaign against Luisa who had made the lady look silly when we had no choice but to inform her employers that she was making a mess of a relatively simple procedure. HR lady even had an over-ambitious non-specialist lawyer phone us to argue a point in a field in which he had no experience. This phone call took place in the Mozambique bush, interrupting a family rendition of Barbara Anne from the beach boys and lasting for half an hour as Luisa battled to control her anger. HR lady had to be appeased, or we stood to lose one of our largest accounts. The Department of Home Affairs in South Africa is by far one of the most incompetent bureaucracies in Africa and many European clients simply could not believe that a government department could be as dismally pathetic as this administration. Asia was now out of the question. I wanted to continue into Kenya and, at least, reach the Equator but was overruled by a persuasive Luisa, the decision was made to head back, pretty much the way we had come, to Malawi and then back home.

WE WILL BE FREE

It took a week of backtracking to get back to Cape Maclear and Fat Monkeys, back to soaking up the sun and enjoying the peace and tranquillity. Returning to any place where you have made friends and have left, promising but never expected to return, cements the friendship and encourages deeper friendship. By now we had been overlanding continually for over four months and we had learnt a lot about ourselves. We had crossed borders and travelled to many places we did not know existed, we had taken ourselves very far from our comfort zone and we had returned to a place where we felt comfortable outside of the box. Another two weeks of Malawian bliss and time came again to leave, to hand over a large pile of dirty, weak currency, pack the Landy and head out into the relatively unknown. The Landy climbed to Lilongwe and headed for the Zambian border. Along the road, I had an epiphany. The African people outside South Africa's borders had surprised me with their charm, friendliness, work ethic, attitude and hospitality. Having been raised in Apartheid South Africa, I had been educated to believe that humanity was not possible. I turned to Luisa and said, well, you know these people are awesome; these people are great, these people just need this and that and they will be on their way. The words were hardly out of my mouth when we overtook a dark blue car carrying a group of men who had been throwing chicken bones out the window as they drove. As we passed them smiling one of their group threw a large empty glass beer bottle into the road immediately in front of us. The bottle smashed and peppered the underside of the Landy. The message was clear. This is still Africa, don't get too comfortable. They slowed, and I pulled over to check the tyres, then waited for them, furious, knobkerrie in hand foolishly believing in my anger that I could take on a car full of men. They approached and slowly drove past, a windscreen full of huge grins.

7

Zambia

The Landy was fine, luckily, she is a powerful beast and I had fitted those excellent tyres before leaving. Soon enough we reached the exit to Malawi and the very well run Zambian border which even boasted an ATM. We were soon in Zambia, again fascinated by the difference a line in the soil can make. Malawi has everything she needs to prosper into the future, but, as it always happens in Africa, she has bad management. Politicians should not be motivated by personal wealth in the perfect world but, for me, the definition of third world or Developing Nations as they are now called is a country run by their elite for the sole purpose of self-enrichment. And many African governments are like poverty-stricken but strong, talented athletes. They rise from nothing to something, mistake that for success and buy a Gold Bentley. A Gold Bentley is a measure of dismal failure, of wasted opportunity, of an empty, futile mind. But most people in these nations look at the Gold Bentley and see wealth and power. The future is not a Gold Bentley but those who can afford one but who want to farm, grow, travel, learn and create. Not consumers of status symbols or mass-produced Chinese plastic crappiness but those who realise that their freedom and progress comes with a simpler life of self-sufficiency, sustainability and limited consumption complimented by education and small, healthy families. Many African countries have the dubious advantage of not having infrastructures based on old technology. The mobile phone GSM networks are a good example. Where developed nations have millions of kilometres of expensive telephone lines which most of Africa cannot afford to install and maintain, the GSM cellular network operates on a system of towers which can serve a large area and bring telecommunications to impoverished areas and, as private corporations invest and build the networks, Africa has the fastest-growing market in the world. Solar power and other 'green' energy systems find a natural home in Sub Saharan Africa where the sun almost always shines and often the wind blows and rivers flow. Now, if we could just keep those pesky, environmentally ignorant and indifferent Chinese out of Africa, but I am afraid it is too late. The dwindling rhino population proves that.

Zambia is rolling green hills, Chinese billboards depicting co-operation of which there is little evidence. We camped at a beautiful camp called Mama Rula's. It was beautiful until one of those big yellow "overland" trucks arrived and set about their usual destruction. I confronted them over a bonfire. 'Hey guys, you guys are awesome. I really enjoy how you embrace your freedom, who needs clean, who needs to flush, just spread that shit around. Now that is freedom'.

Leaving camp, we headed along the main route to Lusaka, parked outside a lovely hotel and spent a restless night camped on manicured grounds; every one of us had nightmares that night. That morning, while packing to leave, little Jessica rolled out of the two-metre high tent and landed flat on her back on the hard concrete soil. She had been living in that tent for over four months; an angry African spirit must have shoved the poor girl. Her cries did not end for what felt like hours and we rushed to Lusaka to find a decent hospital where Luisa located the private hospital and an Irish doctor who, thankfully, found nothing wrong with Jessica who I carried on my back for another two weeks mostly, I suspect, because she loves a good piggyback ride. That fine Irish lady had been in Africa far too long and had become like many European expats who love Africa but not necessarily the African inhabitants.

Lusaka city is a surprisingly clean and relatively modern city. At least the parts we visited are. There is a mall and a restaurant called

Kilimanjaro which serves an English breakfast large enough for the largest Englishman. We scoffed mushrooms, bacon and buttered toast, eggs and orange juice, a treat. The supermarkets we had come across only sold tinned goods from South Africa and very expensive fruit. Grapes are worth more than whisky in Zambia. Unless you are a fly in fly out National Park traveller, you will find that most survive on maize, bread and local produce.

Our stay in Zambia was not to be extended and we took a drive down to a camp called Eagles Rest (vague Storm trooper association) where dangerous hippos lazed on the lawn and crocs patrolled the water. Our next base was Livingstone, where we visited the Victoria Falls and took a day trip to Botswana to visit the Chobe National Park. The decision was taken not to drive into Botswana in our Landy but instead took a tour with one of the many South African run tour agencies operating out of Livingstone and was relieved that we did not have to queue with the many trucks for the old ferry across the mighty Zambezi. Chobe itself was exactly what we had expected, wood and thatch lodges, European prices, boats and Land Cruisers stuffed with the ubiquitous khaki-clad, sunburnt tourists. The park has approximately 70 000 elephants crammed into 11,700 square kilometres. Since the elephants became the darlings of conservation in the '80s their numbers have recovered and swelled to the point that there are quite simply too many elephants and too few resources, especially in Chobe. Elephants are the bulldozers of the bush and, unless Chobe finds a creative means to lower those numbers, the park will soon become a treeless expanse. Poachers these days focus their pestilent attention on the few remaining Rhinos whose magnificent horns, when ground and taken orally, helps little Chinese men to achieve significantly less impressive horns of their own, even though the horn has absolutely no medicinal properties.

8

Namibia - An Afrikaner Paradise

Leaving Zambia, we drove along the 450 km long, straight Caprivi Strip and almost drove straight past the Zambian customs and Immigration office, a little house hidden behind a large tree. A little old lady helped us with our Carnet and I showed her how to complete the section to exit before we could exit. The Caprivi Strip was once considered extremely dangerous; as it was here that the SADF confronted the SWAPO threat. The landmines had been cleared and fishing lodges now dot the map along the road. Arriving in Namibia, near Rundu, was an eye-opener and an indication of why Namibia is such a successful country. Driving up to a complex of glass, steel and porcelain buildings, we entered an air-conditioned office and were served by professional staff. The toilets were even clean. Namibian roads are a pleasure to drive mostly and often you will be alone for many kilometres of rumbling tyres, snoozing kids, road trip music. The landscape is generally flat and arid with a few small mountains visible on the horizon to the left or the right but not usually where you are headed. We felt like we were back in South Africa and a stop at the Spar supermarket in Grootfontein confirmed this. Afrikaans speaking farmers filled the supermarket and the adjacent restaurants, high school girls identical in every way to the high school girls from the farming communities near Bloemfontein or Upington, waited at the Wimpy burger joint for their parents to fetch them after a weekend school camp, all legs and giggles. The supermarket itself was packed with fresh fruits, vegetables and the butchery must have been almost fifty metres long.

We wandered around staring at the bounty and were amazed later when we realised that we had bought only a few apples and some water. We had been so accustomed to going without good food that when we had the chance to buy some we did not but made up for silliness the next day when we stocked up on South African delicacies, droewors, biltong, All Gold ketchup, boerewors and rib-eye steak.

It is a strange feeling driving in a relatively civilised, safe, prosperous country after becoming accustomed to the opposite. And it is actually quite boring, the thrill of adventure does not course through your veins quite as much as when you have no idea if you will find a camp, a meal and a good road ahead. Namibia is a Sunday afternoon, Africa light. Slow and easy, beautiful and calm. It is possible though to find yourself out in the desert, out of water and very far from any form of civilisation. There are more deadly scorpions than people and plenty of those kinds of snake which will kill you with an untreated bite or rot a leg off. Our tour of Nam, as the locals call it, was to be cut short by the demands of the business back home and we did not get to visit the Himba or journey into Angola, a country I have long dreamed of visiting.

Swakopmund, a small city along the coast, surrounded by desert is a piece of Germany dropped into the sands of Africa, the centre of town proudly displays Germanic architecture and the one bookshop stocks 90% German-language books. We stayed in a hostel which suffered from a sewerage backwash at high tide. The smell of human waste would come shooting up the pipes and fill the room with every large Atlantic Ocean wave which broke against the shore. The owner of the hostel, a lovely blonde Afrikaner lady, had invited us to watch a rugby match at her house in a quiet suburb. Luisa and I both have Afrikaner blood, sharing a love for most things Afrikaans and had truly missed the weekend braai and Rugby matches over the almost six months away from home.

WE WILL BE FREE

Sossusvlei 'is a salt and clay pan surrounded by high red dunes, located in the southern part of the Namib Desert' according to Wikipedia and lies roughly 350 km's south, south-east of that little German hamlet. We had not booked camping and arrived at the entrance to the pan to be shown to the overflow camping which had no shade and no toilet facilities. By now the family had lost most of its suburban fat and were lean, tanned and scruffy-haired from those months living in and on top of the Land Rover. Keelan and I walked to the office to look for a toilet, and assembled tourist watched us as we walked by in our crumpled dusty clothing. Now, I don't like to be a show-off, but I did enjoy the attention, I must admit, feeling like Crocodile Dundee stepping out of the Land Rover though we all know he drives a bloody Toyota UTE. Back home I was nothing to look at in my blue jeans and black collar shirt, standing in the queue at Home Affairs making small talk, waiting for my turn to kiss ass, playing a game on my phone, checking I had all my papers in order, breathing the breath and odours of my fellow inmates. But, there, in the imagination of the tourist sipping cold drinks in the shade, we were a wild family, perhaps we worked with lions and roamed the desert, perhaps we worked with the Himba and the San people, perhaps we had just completed a long a difficult journey into 'dark' Africa. Perhaps we now deserved a second look.

At 4 am, we awoke and packed up our little camp. The buzz is that you simply have to visit the pan at sunrise or sunset to get the best photographs. The Landy joined a queue of tour vehicles in the blue dark of morning, a traffic jam in the middle of the desert. A park official wandered around in front of a boom which protected the pans and asserted his authority. Chatting on a walkie-talkie for a while, a paper needed to be read, control maintained. By the time the boom lifted an eager anticipation and impatience had grown, engines revved and red-eyed drivers eager to move jostled for position while struggling to obey the speed limit. I imagine this is a scene that has unfolded every morning for the last twenty years and will continue until a week before the apocalypse. At the end of the concrete road, we left behind the buses and poxy little 2x4's and ventured onto the sand dunes in the wake of Land Cruisers, full of sandy eyed cameras. I did not bother airing down the tyres as the big muds eat sand-like sandwiches and skirted past the adventurous girls in the bogged Mitsubishi. The landscape is truly magnificent, but, as always, I was irritated by the touristness of it all. We climbed a dune and ran rolled down the other side; we took photographs and had an argument with our picnic under a tree full of hungry birds and Germans.

A friend invited us to stay at her hunting lodge close to the South African border, but first, we had to stop and collect some beer for their lodge. Twelve cases of beer and a case of spirits waited for us at the bottle store. Where the hell was I supposed to put all of that? I made some space in the back by tying gear onto the roof of the Landy and set off for the long dirt road drive to the farm. We don't hunt unless we have to, and we never have had to, but do enjoy shooting and had a great time teaching Keelan how to shoot. My family proved to be capable of killing an orange at 100 metres with a Tikka 25.06 scoped. We visited a big cat rehabilitation farm championed by Brad Pitt and the one with the lips. A large male lion charged me while I was taking photos, Luisa choosing that exact moment to stand behind me to my permanent annoyance. Luckily there was a fence between the lion and me, or I would have been forced to hurt him with my bare hands or a Nikon camera. Who am I kidding; I have seen lions bite through car tyres as if they are made of liquorice.

We arrived back in South Africa after driving through the Richtersveld and headed back to Cape Town, spending a week in Langebaan while waiting for the house sitter to leave our house. Getting back home on a beautiful summer's day was bittersweet. Within days we would be back at work, permanently dedicated to the old life which since travelling had lost some shine. We became restless, bored, unfulfilled. The simple life of living in a Land Rover and seeing new places and having new experiences is addictive. On the road, I felt like the man I was born to be, I felt free and in control and challenged. Back at my desk or standing in queues waiting for bored inefficient public servants, I was dreaming of the road, of the simple pleasure of driving in silence, watching the world go by, meditating on the movement of the machine, the hum of the engine and wind on my face.

9

Home, Oh, God, No

Driving to the store in Melkbos one weekday morning I spotted a very large dorsal fin in the ocean, I stopped and walked onto the beach to find a Killer Whale was swimming along the shore and phoned Luisa to get down to the beach. The Orca swam slowly parallel to the beach as Luisa joined me and a small crowd gathered. The Orca stopped swimming and beached herself on a small sandbank close to Slabbert se Klippe. For a few minutes, our small crowd watched for movement before Glen, a friend and fellow bodyboarder and I waded out to try and help the large predator. A few other locals joined us, and we managed to get the oily skinned mammal upright and using wave action managed to get her off the sand. An oily black substance was bubbling out of her blowhole, she did not move, and she was not breathing. After standing with her for half an hour in the cold Atlantic, we decided that there was nothing we could do for her, that she was dead. I was moved. In the shadow of the nuclear power station I had held one of the oceans most beautiful creatures and I had felt her life slip away, I could not help her, we left her in the surf where I had spent so many hours to the prodding, poking and photo-taking of the crowds who came down to the beach to witness her end.

I had started surfing again in 2003 after many years; Jeandre was my surf buddy in those cold Atlantic waters. It was the perfect escape from the pressures on land. When you step off the "continent", you are free, un-contactable, tasting and feeling Mother Nature. Riding a wave is ecstasy, once you learn to do it properly and, like overlanding, it is addictive. Either weekends were spent in the ocean at our local break, or we would take a road trip to a wave called Gas Chambers. If the swell was small and the waves weak in Cape Town, Gassies could always be relied on to provide a huge backbreaking barrel reserved exclusively for Bodyboarders, who were able to make the steep drop off and bottom turn into the beast. If you miscalculated the take-off, the wave would slam you into the sand, rolling your wetsuit up over your elbows and knees before spitting you out onto the beach. Getting to Gassies is not easy and Jeandre and his mates would visit my house during my Friday night beer drinking sessions, to tell me how I was the greatest bodyboarder who ever lived and convincing me to drive them twenty kilometres out to the Nature reserve parking lot for the six-kilometre dirt road walk to the break. We started going out there when Jeandre and his friends were just fifteen or sixteen years old, which was a stress for me, I would be responsible if one of them was bitten by a shark or broke their backs on the huge waves. The shark problem was a real problem being the Cape, which has the world's largest population of Great Whites; though the West Coast of Cape Town is not as sharky as the East, (one of the kids we surfed with was attacked by a Great White near Gordon's Bay in 2013 and died from his injuries). We surfed mainly West Coast rights, but every other weekend we would surf spots up the East Coast, Betty's Bay and Hermanus mainly. I had nightmares about sharks, but that did not stop us from surfing for hours in wild, deep waters. Jeandre and I started surfing a wave we called Back Wave Corner. It was a deep wave, about 750 metres offshore on large days. We know of no-one else who had ever surfed that wave. Sitting watching the sea one day, we saw these huge waves peeling off in the direction of Koeberg Nuclear Power Plant. We decided to give it a go and paddled out from the left side of Slabbert's se Klippe (Slabberts Rocks). Getting out to the break could take up to 40 minutes and we would lay there waiting for a set to roll in, often asking ourselves if we were too deep.

Sitting there feeling like shark bait was unnerving and one day just after Jeandre had taken a wave in a Southern Right Whale popped up twenty metres from my board to ask me what exactly I was doing. I told him I was surfing, man. He told me I was mad and swam away.

The wave itself was intimidating; rearing up from a flat ocean, a wall of water would head straight at us. It was not a left or a right, just a large wall with a crumbling lip. It usually did not barrel, and the deep-water wipe-out was ten times easier than Gassies, but you did have to hold your breath a lot longer. The trick to catching the wave was to triangulate your position, a technique we learned from the inspiring Riding Giants and to have enough speed to catch the wave before it peaked. The ride is a high speed shot down a face, left, or right, then straightening out to catch the reforming white water face to the beach. It is not a Hawaii type big wave, but it was our big-ish wave, and we surfed it alone.

On one of the first attempts to surf Back Wave both Jeandre and I arrived back at the beach at the same time and were walking along excitedly talking about the ride when ambulances and National Sea Rescue Institute 4x4's came heading along the beach towards us. Someone from Orca restaurant had called them to report two surfer's way out in deep water. Was that us? Yes. Are you ok? Yes. Are you crazy? No, but we are going to go out again, ok? It was not ok with Luisa who had come running down the beach behind the rescue vehicles. Stop being an ass, you are not a kid anymore, and you have a child to think of. Ok. We went and surfed again.

We surfed together any chance we could until Jeandre's friends aged enough to drive themselves and I was secretly happy. Waking up at 5 am to go surf waves which could break bones, was getting to be too much. I had been keeping up with a teenager for five years, but it was time now for me to surf old man waves with the other old men.

A few months after arriving back in Melkbos, Luisa and I decided to have one of our Strategic Business Meetings, or SBM, we like to make our most important decisions when intoxicated. A few drinks and a hot fire convinced us that the time had come to make another move, to start again; surely a new environment in a beautiful setting would distinguish the fire of longing that we both felt for those six months of travelling adventure. Plettenberg Bay was where we had our honeymoon and Luisa had family in the nearby village of Knysna. We searched the internet for houses to rent, I was looking for a surf shack with a hammock, what Luisa found was completely the opposite. South Africa was going through a slump in the property market and Luisa found a house in a security estate, with a sea view, for R12, 000 per month. At that time R12, 000 was just over a $1400 US and since we worked from home we were actually saving money as opposed to renting both a house and a business premise. We took our Volvo for the drive up the coast to have a look at that and a few other houses. We met with the owner of the house, a charming, retired one-armed Afrikaner named Mr Theron. Mr Theron had lost his arm in a flying accident when he was a nineteen-year-old trainee pilot in the South African Air Force. He had been trapped under the wreckage and received 3rd-degree burns on most of his body before a local farmer, who had seen the crash, could pull him, sans arm, out of the flames. After almost a year in hospital, Mr Theron went on to study law, marry his childhood sweetheart and have three healthy sons. The house was simply fantastic. Surrounded by the palaces of the local and foreign rich, it was a boast of pillars and glass and luxury. Four bedrooms, each with a full bathroom, a Jacuzzi and swimming pool, a large deck and 200-degree sea views. We were sold and within two months we had made the move from Cape Town to our new home. I was speechless the first night we spent in that house. I simply could not believe that we had come so far in our lives. Surely this was what people think of when they talk of success. Two beautiful kids, a fantastic wife, a couple of great cars and a house fit for a movie star. The entire front of the house facing the ocean was walled in glass and it was not uncommon to stand in the shower and see dolphins and whales frolicking through the porthole in the shower wall. A beautiful, quiet beach lay five minutes' walk away and to the left, the Robberg Peninsula jutted out into the sea. We bought furniture and impressed locals with our address, I bought a few golf shirts and we had salmon for lunch and prawn for dinner. The weekends spent at the local farmers market, at the beach, entertaining family and friends.

Personally, I like to measure success by achievement from a starting point. The son of a millionaire is born a success, but until he has made his own way in life, I would not consider him to be a success. The son of a poor man who is raised poor and works his way into a mansion should be considered far more successful. But if you define success only by material wealth then I believe the definition to be faulty. We were not millionaires, but we had made some very good choices and we had worked very hard. As we sat at night and stared at the sea and the lights of the town, we congratulated each other, we were on the way to the top, our neighbours were the captains of industry and we were two poor kids, with kids, living a dream.

It did not take long for that little voice to start whispering challenges again. A beautiful view becomes a background, a comfortable life vaguely unpleasant, the neighbours a nuisance. A new routine replaces the old routine. Within six months we decided to take the Landy and drive up to Malawi through Mozambique. We arranged that the kids could have a week off either side of a two-week school holiday, arranged a house sitter and excitely hit the road early one Saturday morning. Expecting Mozambique to again be a hard slog of bad weather and terrible roads we were surprised to find new Chinese tar and a few great places we had missed the first time there.

10

On The Road Again - Yeah

While overlanding between Mozambique and Malawi we found that we weren't exactly lost, but our GPS and National Geographic African Adventure Atlas we're having a bit of an argument. The GPS insisted we should turn back, 'No ferry!' The atlas, stubbornly and rather predictably, insisted that this dirt track, devoid of any vehicular or pedestrian activity for the last 50 km, led to a ferry which traversed the croc and hippo populated Shire River. The sun was setting, and our fuel was running low.

With Luisa in the unenviable position of navigator and the kids as passengers and technical advisers/critics, we had made the decision to leave the tar roads and trucks and to follow the dirt tracks to a lesser-known border crossing at Marka, Malawi. We had decided, when planning our route, to leave the beaten track as often as possible and have faith in the good nature of the Mozambican hombres.

This faith was proven to be justified as we arrived at the Shire to find a ferry and a couple of friendly locals who were travelling from Inhassoro to the interior. They had arrived at the Shire half an hour before us as the sun was setting to find that the ferry closed at 17h00 on a Friday. They had sent someone to fetch the ferry master who agreed to take both our vehicles across at a slightly inflated rate. The ferry was operated via a human-powered pulley system. We engaged the diff lock and drove the Defender down into the mud and onto the two rusty metal beams provided as a ramp to the ferry and 20 minutes later repeated the procedure to disembark in the now complete darkness.

The one golden overlanding rule is that one should never drive at night, but with our new friends taking the lead we drove the 30 km of goat track to the next town hoping to find suitable accommodation and fuel. It was 25 June 2011, Mozambique Independence Day and celebrations were in full swing as we entered the town of Morrumbala after some interesting water crossings and mud negotiation, to find that there was no fuel station in town. Mozambican dance music was distortedly pumping through an army of unseen speakers, the roads were unmaintained dirt and the population seemed in very good spirits inspired, no doubt, by strong spirits. We thanked our new friends and headed for the border, which we had been advised was open until 20h30, deciding instead to take our chances entering Malawi.

The road to the Mozambican border is another goat track passable by vehicle but definitely not constructed for that purpose. The Landy's headlights decided that now was a good time to fail and would only illuminate the track if I held the light stalk in the 'brights' position. At 20h30 with the fuel light well and truly burning my retina, we approached the Mozambican border and were greeted by a guard armed with a rusty AK 47 and a large, yellow can of Laurentina Premier Beer. Closed! Independence Day! In our terrible Portuguese we explained we had no other options and eventually the guard was kind enough to disturb the immigration official, who in turn roused the customs official who promptly and slightly begrudgingly disappeared with our passports and AA Carnet to return 15 minutes later with all our documents stamped and in order. Now to negotiate no man's land and the Malawian border.

It was not to be that we would enter Malawi that night. Instead, we were greeted, thankfully in English, by the Malawian border guard, Charles, who informed us that it was impossible to enter, but yes, we could camp in no man's land. The wife was not happy. This was the first time that our planning had let us down so spectacularly, but the Land

Rover is fully equipped for bush camping, so we rustled up some pasta and had a cold beer while watching locals arrive in their vehicles, lift the boom and head off to Mozambique with no documentary complications.

Not long after the rooftop tent was opened, and the kids put to bed, a particularly inebriated and unpleasant soul decided that he would pay a visit and inspect our vehicle. I puffed out my chest and approached him before he could get too close to the family and vehicle. His name was Thomas (that night without the silent H), and he persistently stepped over my imaginary boundary and, after two hours of testing my patience, was about to receive an unpleasant physical intervention when Charles approached and introduced Thomas – the customs official! Great timing. For the next hour, we endured Thomas and his opinions, learnt that he was a good Muslim and fed him cigarettes. Eventually, he grew bored and returned to the Immigration building to sharpen a large knife. In the morning, I greeted him with 'Salaam alaikum.' He was astounded, 'How did you know I am Muslim?' Poor Thomas had an obvious hangover and no clue how to complete the Carnet. He proposed a customs fee of $150 – thanks but no thanks! After a bit of negotiation, I paid him $25 and entered Malawi to look for fuel.

I drove the Landy into the first gas station with a sigh of relief and cheerfully asked the attendant to fill her up. He just laughed. 'Don't you know that there is no fuel in Malawi'? Malawi's president, Bingu wa Mutharika, had expelled the British High Commissioner, Mr Cochrane Dyet after he was quoted in a leaked cable saying that the president does not accept criticism and has become less tolerant. In response to the expulsion, the British (and the World Bank) retracted their aid to Malawi which accounted for 40% of the countries budget. As a result, foreign currency became as scarce in Malawi as a tolerant president and essential exports and fuel supplies ran dry. Ordinary Malawians and a few South African travellers paid the price for the diplomatic spat. Leaving the border with almost empty fuel tanks we spluttered along the wide dirt road before we reached a town with a fuel station. Again, we were told that there was no fuel and I was asked not to smoke on the forecourt - why? There is no fuel! But they insisted, and I left the station on foot to look for black market fuel. Perhaps they had some reserve fuel saved in their tanks for when the price went through the roof. An Indian man behind the counter at the Macro store told me that I should ask a scruffy gentleman loitering outside for fuel. Mr Scruffy had fuel, at twice the pump price and poured 20 litres into the Landy through a funnel and a tea strainer, enough fuel for us to reach Blantyre and join a queue outside a Petroda gas station where we hung out with the locals and waited for a fuel tanker to arrive, frequently asking the manager how much longer and frequently being told - "one hour". After four "one hours" our new friends came running towards us, their hands full of plastic containers and jerry cans. "BP has fuel, let's go!" A few guys jumped on the Landy's side steps and we raced, as fast as a Landy can race, down a few blocks to the BP station. We were at the end of a long queue and the policeman directing traffic instructed us to park on the other side of the road so as not to obstruct traffic. And so, we waited in the heat. I took my jerry cans and went and sat in the field adjacent to the station with a group of almost 100 men who languished, each with plastic containers or jerry cans waiting for the tanker to finish filling the underground storage tanks. A policeman and the owner of the fuel station entered the field, walked directly to me, handed me an official document and explained that the document was a directive issued by the government and they wanted me to read it to the crowd. Perhaps they thought the crowd might react better to a Mzungu (white person) breaking whatever news they had brought. I was one of the crowd, sitting on my jerry cans, watching the fights and jostling for position. I spoke to the station owner, explaining that I had heard that there was rationing of fuel. He nodded; I asked him if it was possible to fill both my tanks. He agreed and called the crowd to come listen to the announcement. I stood on top of my jerry cans and read the document which stated, something like "the Honourable Minister of Energy had decreed that from this day on no persons will be permitted to purchase fuel if said fuel is to be decanted into portable containers, including but not restricted to jerry cans, bottles or plastic containers. Only the owners or drivers of vehicles with standard fuel tanks may purchase fuel". The crowd erupted in fury which, thankfully, was not directed at me. I stepped off the jerry cans and chatted with a few of the men who came over to read the document, shrugged my shoulders and carried my cans back to the Landy. The men in the field huddled together chatting and debating. The sunset and the policeman who was controlling the queuing left, leaving chaos in his wake. Vehicles began joining the back of the queues we were not allowed to join and the forty vehicles which had been instructed to wait on the other side of the road were no longer part of the queue. A few arguments broke out and I decided to take control of the situation. I spoke to a few taxi drivers and made friends with a few large guys, then took up residence in the middle of the road and controlled the merging of the vehicles as those at the front filled up their tanks and left. The men with the portable containers were still hanging around, but none were carrying their containers. Odd. I had a look around and discovered that, while I had read the document and accepted the law unquestionably, they had found a loophole and had arranged with the taxi drivers that, at a small fee, they would place and fill the containers inside the taxis thereby not falling foul of the police. While we were waiting impatiently police and military vehicles would approach from the other side of the station and fill 160-litre drums in the bin of Land Cruisers. I continued to direct the traffic and drivers who tried to jump the queue were evicted by my new, large friends. We were slowly making our way forward, tired, hungry and desperate for ablution and wheezing from the fumes of so many vehicles idling in the still evening. I asked a fat policeman to be equitable in his control of the pumps, but he laughed at me. "Which queue are you in?" "That one". No wonder you want this queue to move faster hahaha". Fat cops are the worst cops. By now we estimated that the station's tanks must be very close to empty. A hundred or more vehicles had been in front of us, including taxis with their" illegal" containers and the authorities had been draining large amounts. Only one yellow truck stood between the pumps and us. I had let the truck go in front of us to display fairness and gain the trust of the crowd and once the driver had assured me that he only had one 100-litre tank. He moved forward to the pump, filled the 100-litre tank then slid open the tailgate to reveal five 160-litre drums. I gathered my allies and had the driver kicked off the forecourt before eventually rolling up and filling my tanks with 125 litres of liquid gold. We left the fuel station hell after 12 hours of waiting and fighting and went looking for a place to sleep, found a little lodge run by a Frenchman, the room had a double king size bed and mirrors on the ceiling, we did not care, instead queued again, this time for the loo, then slept the sleep of the dead.

Soon after leaving Blantyre, we were back with our friends in Cape Maclear and all too soon we were back home dreaming of the road.

11

You Have Got To Be Kidding

A seed had been planted and we had one of our SBM's to discuss life. Fuck it, the wine said, let's just pack it all in and hit the road. We shook on it and started dreaming of a new adventure. Driving through Africa was fun, but we wanted to do something more challenging. How about driving across the Americas? OK, why not?

The decision to leave had to be one of these most difficult decisions we have ever made. Sitting in that amazing house, looking at the ocean and contemplating life, I reached a point where I had to seriously consider where I had come from and where I was going. My past failures had been as spectacular as my recent success but who wants to open the door to failure. Why, when you have reached a level of "success" envied by your friends and family, would you want to just throw it all away? We worked so hard to get where we were. Were we being impetuous, ungrateful, unrealistic and frivolous? All around us, we could see poverty and people struggling to make ends meet, friends and family who perpetually failed. Had we been merely tremendously lucky? I prefer to think that we made our own luck. Yes, we had made some huge mistakes in the past, but we had learned from those mistakes. By liberating ourselves from debt, we had freed ourselves from the cycle and we had earned enough to be able to save. We counted our pennies and though our lifestyle seemed expensive, we had found ways to ensure that we were not just handing over our hard-earned money to others. Experience is the best school.

As a kid, I learned many skills purely because we did not have money and in my teen years, my Mom was often not at home. I learned to sew and repair my clothing, I learned how to cook, I learned how to repair anything we could not afford to replace, and I learned how to work.

Being surrounded by the wealthy only served to remind me where I came from. Yes, you can dress like them and have Sunday lunch at the Polo Club, enjoy a good whiskey, but they would always have something I would never have, and I had experience of what that they fear the most. Poverty. It is as etched into my skin as are my tattoos. Not extreme poverty of course, but the poverty of circumstance, opportunity, education. But never did I submit to the mentality of poverty. The idea that they have, and we don't, and they will always have, and we never will. Education, self-education, is free with the desire to learn and curiosity. Self-education won't get you the diploma or the degree and usually won't get you the job but once you realise that you are free to educate yourself and free to choose how, to follow your interests and not be guided by a syllabus or the fodder that fills that syllabus, you won't want the job because you have liberated yourself. Poverty allowed me to be a free thinker purely because I had to work and made time for my own education and betterment with enlightenment the only goal. And I know what it means to have nothing, to have less than nothing. And once you realise that you have nothing to lose, you realise that you will never lose as long as you have what matters and what should matter, love, curiosity, self-belief.

I believe in myself and I believe in Luisa. I believe that we will always have what we need and will always overcome whatever life throws at us because we have been tested and we were able to overcome our own weaknesses. A world where worth is determined by material wealth is a world unbalanced. I choose rather to determine my wealth by my potential, by what I can achieve and by the industry of my mind and hands. We will never be poor even if we have only the change in our pockets, we will never be desperate because we will plan our lives and equip ourselves with the mental tools to build and rebuild. We have a work ethic.

And music. Music in our hearts and music in our ears. Good music never sings of wealth and cars and mansions and lust love. Good music speaks of the heart, of real love, pain, dreams, desire and life. The music I love is the music which had always inspired me, which spoke to me through melodies, lyrics, beat and bass. Music which is the tortured soul finding sweet release. The poetry of a life lived for experience, art. Music is art and art is what separates us from the beast, the art of the soul of consciousness, of rising above your memory psychology, past, pain and failure. Music which was my greatest comfort and friend when the world was only dark. Dazed and Confused. A Pig in a Cage, on Antibiotics.

As an Agnostic, I don't have the promise of an afterlife, either burning or glowing. I don't have the cultural belief system which drives most of us to work in the morning and to church on Sunday. The idea that I only have this one life, this one opportunity on this planet, this miracle of time and flesh, both liberates and imprisons me. Agnosticism and non-dogmatic spirituality requires courage. The courage to accept that you are mortal, not divine, that you will grow, die and decay and whatever you have had of this life, you will have no more. Only blackness and rebirth through the soil, in the air and water. And if you only have one life, what you do with it, how do you live it. This is the mindset of rebellion.

12

I Want To Break Free

It is astonishing how difficult it is to extricate yourself from LIFE. It took 18 months for us to wrap up and sell the business and sever the ties which bound us. I refused to try and run the business while we travelled. During those six months, while we were travelling in 2010, the priority had never been finding food or fuel or campsites. The priority had always been Wi-Fi and we would spend many precious hours every day driving around town looking for internet cafes or Wi-Fi hotspots. The kids and I would then wait in the Landy while Luisa put out the many fires. I would rather stay at home than do that all over again.

Those eighteen months before we left were filled with hard work, daily doubt and sleepless nights staring at the ceiling. About 1% of the entire planning for this journey was dedicated to maps and on the road logistics. 99% was dedicated to pure mental slog. Selling the Volvo, removing the kids from school and having them approved for home-schooling, organising, selling or donating all of the extra crap we had hoarded, cancelling debit orders, magazine subscriptions, packing and moving what was left into storage, arranging shipping of the Landy to South America, vaccinations, full medical check-ups and million-other small but significant tasks. Our greatest challenge was to be selling the business whilst operating daily. I had a very good idea which of our competitors would be best equipped to serve our client database and that was to be a significant consideration. We might have been able to sell the database to a lesser company for more money, but we truly believed that our clients deserved a company we believed would serve them as well as we had. The contract negotiation was an intense effort of concentration which had to serve and protect both parties, a goal we achieved. Our clients accepted the new service provider, which provided us with a guaranteed income for the first eighteen months on the road as that was the limit of the income agreed in the final contract.

While planning the South American journey we made contact with Overlander groups on the Internet. There are many sites and blogs dedicated solely to Overlanding which are an incredible source of information. Through one of the sites we made contact with a Norwegian couple who had just finished the Pan American (Pan Am) route and were shipping their Nissan Patrol to South Africa, so naturally, we invited them to stay with us for a while, while they prepared for the drive up through Africa. Espen and Malin's true passion lies in Antarctica and as they travel, they would park the Patrol and fly to the Antarctic camps to work through the summer "tourist" season. Their journey through the Americas had been very rapid by most standards and they completed the 60,000-km journey in less than four months, which, after travelling the length and breadth of South America, I can scarcely believe. Initially they planned to spend a few days with us but those few days turned into a few weeks while I filled their bellies with South African food and beer and they recovered from those months on the road in our comfortable home. At night, pouring beer over maps, they explained the PanAm route and shared their experiences with us. We went camping in the Baviaanskloof and they laughed at how much gear we had and how long it took for us to set up camp. In two minutes they were set up and filmed me inflating mattresses and taking out chairs and tables, zipping on extra tents and preparing a feast. A few weeks after they left a German couple, Andrea and Georg came to stay after completing the same trip as the Norwegians and we only had one night with them before we handed them the keys to the house and drove 1,000 kilometres to Johannesburg to the Landy Festival.

The festival was a great meeting of Land Rovers and on the last day we joined a convoy of just over 1,000 Landy's in an attempt to break a Guinness World Record. The festival actually started off when photographer Craig Dutton began a project called, 'My Land Rover Has A Soul', which he used social media to promote. The campaign was a massive success and soon had thousands of followers who started asking when the mother of all Land Rover get-togethers might actually happen. The first festival was held in 2012 and I only wish that we had been able to get the record because we clearly had the numbers but, in true Jo'burg fashion, we also had too much speed. The gaps between the vehicles were too large to qualify for the world record. This is actually the second Land Rover world record attempt we had been a part of, the first taking place in wet Cape Town where there were 380 Land Rovers. Maybe one day, when I am big.

The festivals were an expensive distraction. We were emulating what we had seen on the TV and internet. A Land Rover covered in stickers, on an expedition, waving a flag. Looking back, I would have done things very differently. A few months earlier, searching the Internet "after hours," we were inspired by the stories of great expeditions. All had a few things in common - adventure and charity. We had the adventure part covered and began searching for a specific cause to support. Water Aid and Clean Cook Stoves seemed worthy efforts as did education programs.

When we first travelled out of South Africa into the neighbouring countries we were prepared for almost any eventuality because we had been sobered by the warnings of friends, family and experts on the internet that the surrounding countries were unsafe, that food was scarce and that we should travel very, very cautiously especially as we had our children with us. We saw plenty of positive ambition throughout the countries we travelled to. African leaders seem, slowly but surely, to be turning their backs on the powerful dynasties of the "big men" which has plagued Africa since the sixties. Countries like Nigeria and Rwanda are growing as democracies. Namibia and Botswana are extremely successful and stable democracies. I was amazed by Malawi and Zambia. But, Africa has a massive mountain to climb. Poverty, Malaria, pollution, a lack of educational and medical resources.

When I was ill in Mozambique, our initial suspect was Malaria and when Jessica fell ill a year later in Malawi we again suspected Malaria. Luckily there was an Irish clinic located nearby on the banks of Lake Malawi and a midnight visit to the sister put our minds at rest, too much lake water and maybe too much sun. Had she had Malaria though she would have received immediate, potentially life-saving treatment. We both recovered fully, but these experiences had left us all with a stark realisation of what life must be like for the average citizen of these countries. Most cannot afford to be evacuated to South Africa for treatment in our world-class private medical facilities, we couldn't. And there are simply not enough clinics.

But. We had seen many white NGO Land Cruisers whizzing around Southern and East Africa. Somehow, they never seemed to get anywhere except for the next hotel and we could not see much evidence of their many years of labour in Africa. We would see well-dressed NGO types at hotel conference centres rushing to buffet lunches and trudging back to the boardrooms. We had read and seen enough to understand that AID in Africa is a business, a business which is worth billions of dollars annually and employs thousands of people. Toyota alone makes a fortune from the sale of white Land Cruisers. A mid-level NGO manager based in Africa will cost approximately US$500,000 a year according to some estimates. And often NGO's with competing interests will operate in one small town or area, the one trying to save the wetlands, the other trying to drain the wetlands to deprive mosquitoes of breeding areas. Neither group is getting much done, and both are spending a fortune which could be directly invested in the community, in education, which would save the wetlands and kill the mosquitoes. I am not an expert, but Richard Dowden is, and his book, Africa, Altered States, Ordinary Miracles answered most of the questions I had about Africa and puts the Aid industry into perspective.

We found a Malaria NGO on the internet, which seemed to be very different from your typical aid agency. They had a clear goal to end Malaria deaths. They had an established distribution network, high-powered backing and, most importantly, they could prove that they were distributing nets, that Malaria deaths were plummeting in the areas where they operated and that they had only one goal and that was the eradication of Malaria. This was not an aid for business NGO and that is what we were looking for. Their approach was fresh and set specific goals while promoting fundraising with an entrepreneurial approach.

Supporting a charity gives an adventurer an opportunity to raise funds for a worthy cause and often attracts sponsors to adventure who have interest in either the charity or the adventure or both. Sponsorship is a slippery slope, though. Financial sponsorship is extremely rare these days and it stands to reason that any corporation who will pay towards an adventure or expedition will want to have a measure of control over the route, the marketing and the team. We calculated that we had enough money saved to cover the majority of our expenses for a two-and-a-half-year period if all expenses totalled less than US$60 per day and therefore we did not need or necessarily want, financial sponsorship once we had done the maths. The entrepreneurial approach appealed to us though. We researched ethical entrepreneurial charity work and fundraising and found out that this was a new trend. If a fundraiser sets a financial goal and achieves that goal, then a percentage could be allocated to cover the fund-raising expenses. As we had enough funds to cover our expenses for 30 months our expenses incurred would not impact the fundraising but, we might be able to consider a further partnership which would allow us to travel further and raise funds and cover expenses. The idea being that all donations and fundraising would be directed to the NGO directly and we would not compromise our integrity by accepting cash donations. One hand washes the other, and both are clean. We contacted the NGO in New York and had a few Skype sessions to explain our fundraising ideas. They were excited about our ideas and mentioned that they might even be able to arrange for us to be interviewed on CNN. We were then enrolled by the organisation to complete their online training course to be Malaria spokespersons. The training was professionally coordinated through a dedicated online training company and Luisa and I set aside our free time for almost a month, studying the course material, learning about the history, biology and treatment of Malaria, we spent many hours preparing a PowerPoint presentation as a final assignment and successfully completed the training and were awarded official certificates and badges to wear on our lapels. Our goal was to raise $300,000 for the Malaria NGO specifically by doing hands-on fundraising once we reached the USA (the language barrier would make fundraising in South and Central America almost impossible) and by directing traffic to their donation page through a dedicated page on our website.

As part of the fundraising plan, we came up with an idea to raffle GoPro cameras at the Landy Festival, a rock festival and a beer festival. GoPro agreed to sell us three GoPro's at wholesale prices and we had banners printed to adorn the stall. The main goal was to raise awareness for our expedition, attract traffic to our website where people would find a link to the Malaria NGO website where they could donate. The raffle of the GoPro's would help raise funds for the shipping of the Land Rover which was one of largest initial expenses. At the festivals we learnt some very hard lessons. Firstly, not very many people cared about Malaria, perhaps because it is not a problem in South Africa and secondly, many people we spoke to were sceptical of both the NGO and our attempts. Thirdly, it was a complete financial failure. The cost to prepare for and to attend the three festivals was roughly R13, 000 and the raffle sales only amounted to about R3, 000 which barely covered the costs of the GoPro cameras. Having never done any kind of public fundraising, this was a steep and expensive learning curve.

Luisa and I had designed a sponsorship proposal and sent it out to a few companies whose products were aligned with our travel. The idea is that we could use and promote particularly South African products while we travelled and were lucky to receive some high-quality gear. Melvill and Moon provided us with a full set of indestructible and beautifully made seat covers. Howling Moon agreed to provide us with a huge 2.4m Tourer rooftop tent with the proviso that we return the tent once we have finished travelling and Frontrunner provided us with a bash plate and a gas can holder. We were unable to source a local adventure clothing supplier, so Luisa had me phone Craghoppers in the UK and they sent us a box of clothing which lasted us for almost two years of hard travel. That, my friends, is the complete extent of the sponsorship we received for the journey that followed. At that time, we would have loved to have a lump of cash handed to us, but not a cent was received, which in retrospect was perhaps a good thing. My advice to anyone seriously considering financial sponsorship for a long-term trip would be, think again. Unless you are Bear Grylls or Sir. Fiennes, chances are corporations will not take the time to look at your extensive and thoroughly researched proposal and remember you are one of many knocking on the door.

At the Johannesburg festival, we met Rob, who took a great liking to Keelan, who had decided to work at Rob's stall and he introduced us to a family from Port Elizabeth who had driven around the world in a Land Cruiser motorhome. Gary, Jo Anne and their two kids came to spend the weekend with us and share their experiences.

Inspired by our world traveller visitors, we refocused on getting on the road. Within a month we moved our furniture out of our beautiful Plettenberg Bay home, packed it all in a storage garage and headed down to Cape Town to spend a few weeks with Luisa's step-mom, Marinda, while we finalised all the other things which we had to. For almost a year we had worked sixteen-hour days to make this dream become a reality. Moving out of that house was the final nail in the coffin of our old lives and the portal to a new existence, a new life which was almost entirely unpredictable. I was ready, the kids were excited, and Luisa was nervous. After two months in Cape Town the day arrived to ship the Landy to Montevideo, Uruguay.

The shipping had to be one of the most difficult tasks in actually getting on the road in South America. We could have bought a vehicle in Uruguay or Argentina, but the Landy is one of the family and we had spent so much time travelling in her and so much effort preparing her to Overland that we could not bear the thought of using another vehicle. We contacted a few shipping companies and most came back with ridiculous quotations. I decided to try a more direct approach and approached the offices of one of the largest shipping companies in the world. We explained our journey and what we planned to achieve, and the logistics manager responded that they would love to help. They even suggested that we might be able to accompany the ship and the Land Rover over the pond. That would have been a great saving for us and an amazing way to start the journey. I was excited but nervous at the idea of sailing across the Atlantic; the deep ocean scares the crap out of me. We had been discussing the shipping with them, and I sent them a sponsorship proposal. All seemed to be organised until I received an email stating that the shipping company could no longer assist us but wished us a safe journey. I waited a few days then phoned the logistics manager. I accepted their decision but just wanted to know why they had a sudden change of heart. She explained to me that she had sent the sponsorship proposal to the bigwigs in Japan. The proposal stated our proposed route, possibly including Brazil and promised that we would put the company logo on our Land Rover in the hope that they would receive some positive publicity. The Japanese had baulked at that idea purely because Brazil is regarded by the Japanese as a very unsafe country. She explained to me that when the Japanese executives travel to Brazil for business, they fly in, take a helicopter from the airport to a hotel or conference centre. Thereafter all travel within Brazil is done by helicopter and they never, "touch the ground". The fear was that if we entered Brazil with the company logo on our vehicle, we WILL be abducted, and the company WILL be held ransom, a risk that they were simply unwilling to take. I processed this information and responded by email that we would not put the logo on our vehicle and would not list them as a sponsor on our website or in any other publication. This compromise suited them, and they agreed that they would provide a discounted shipping container but, unfortunately, we would be unable to sail with the ship.

We stayed with our Overlander friends, the Allie's, in Port Elizabeth for a night then drove the Landy to the port to be shipped. I had heard that the vehicle has to be spotless and had spent a week scrubbing every part of her to ensure that we had no problems. The shipping agent accompanied us, and we entered the port, waited a few minutes and then the moment of truth. Would the Landy fit into the Hi-Cube container? We squeezed her in and that was that. Once those doors closed on the container we were past the point of no return, everything, even moving out of our house, was a temporary move on the road to the road but once the Landy was in and committed, there was no going back. We rented a car and drove up to Luisa's mom's house in Durban to say our goodbyes. From there we drove up to Johannesburg and spent a few nights with family and friends in a Highveld Spring October before almost missing our plane to Buenos Aires. We love you, South Africa, wait for us to return!

Only once the wheels left the tarmac did the excitement and terror finally set in. We had some savings, some guaranteed income for the next eighteen months and a few shares. This was going to be the greatest risk and greatest adventure of our lives. That was October 2012, and I don't ever regret the decision to leave.

GRAEME BELL

Our trip around
South America

13

Argentina and Uruguay

Touchdown in Buenos Aires, our eyes wide, dragging our tired, wired selves out of the airport and setting foot on a new continent, a continent which we had researched extensively but still knew almost nothing about. A taxi sped us along the highway to the city. A Fiat tried to kill us, the neighbourhoods varied from German-style homes to grey rundown apartment blocks, to large green areas and industrial areas. We had booked at Hostel America del Sur in the San Telmo district. At first, we thought the taxi driver was taking us to the wrong address. The streets were dirty and unmaintained; the buildings reflected that squalor and were camouflaged far above street levels in graffiti, monsters and aeroplanes, cartoons and dinosaurs, politicians and political statements. The architecture colonial and astoundingly detailed but completely unloved or preserved, the atmosphere post-apocalyptic, the ruined streets of a city which belonged on another continent while lovers kissed passionately with skin-tight jeans and vinyl, beards, tattoos, old ladies pulling groceries, a grey sky and traffic. With two weeks to kill while waiting for the Landy to swim across the pond we decided to spend a week in Buenos Aires before heading off to Uruguay. I would wake up early and go for long walks around the city as the sun rose, photographing the architecture and soaking up every sight and sound. In the afternoons we would do the tourist thing, walking tours, visiting churches and palaces and museums admiring buildings which could only have been the consequence of great amounts of surplus wealth. Spanish was going to be a tough nut to crack, having expended all of our time, effort and energy on the logistics of departure, we had not taken the time to learn any Spanish, and we were paying dearly for it. Argentina has a duel exchange for American dollars. There is an official exchange rate and an unofficial, black market rate which was almost double in 2013. There are signs of decay and unrest throughout the city and the government is playing at African politics. We met a friend of the family in Buenos Aires, a retired American journalist. He had covered the wars in Angola, Mozambique and Vietnam, he had written for the New York Times and The Washington Post and he gave a tour and an insight into the country and city where he lived with his Argentine wife. The government reforms are all about control and entrenchment, restricting personal freedoms and ensuring the privilege of the ruling classes. Essentially doing what governments do globally but with more malice, less subtlety. The alternative lifestyle scene in Buenos Aires is alive and kicking. Metal bands with names like Kiss My Ass display posters on the walls of private residences, black is the colour, the hair long, tattoos and piercings and skateboards. The meat is excellent, and my favourite was the Choripan and Asado, served by a tough smiling man with a boxer's battered face, at a small place where the locals hung out drinking beers, where the tourists don't go.

The sky had not yet fallen on our heads and we enjoyed Quilmes beer at night to celebrate our bravery. Taking the ferry to Uruguay across the Rio de la Plata is expensive and we had to take a bus from the city of Colonia to Montevideo. Luisa and I had our first fall out of the trip at the Colonia Port when she disappeared while I was waiting in the queue. She was looking for something and holding us up, and because of my agitation, the immigration and drug guys decided to take a closer look at our luggage. Obviously, they found nothing because we get liquid kicks and we headed onto into the bus where I sat next to a stinking toilet and Luisa started chatting to an expat South African, Piet, who had been living in Uruguay for almost twenty years and had enjoyed Luisa and I swearing at each other in coarse Cape Afrikaans.

Montevideo is similar to Buenos Aires in its gritty beauty, both cities had been rainy and grey and cool. Our first night at the new hostel Impeccable, the owners invited us to try Grappa Miel, a delicious honey port which is communally shared. An unattended glass is free to anyone who enters the room to enjoy, similar to the custom of Yerba Mate tea which is an Uruguayan addiction. To paraphrase the Mate brochure; "Mate is an infusion made by steeping yerba mate – the ground, dried leaves of the Llex Paraguariensis plant – in hot water. Its origins date back to pre-Hispanic times and the Guarani indigenous culture. When the drinking of tea was taking hold in Europe in the 17th century, the drinking of Mate began to spread in South America and especially in Uruguay". You will see people drinking Mate everywhere and it is not restricted to age or class, but children do not partake. Groups of people will share Mate; it is taken to the beach, the office, the bedroom (I assume), pubs, clubs and church. There are street vendors who sell leather Mate and flask carriers and every supermarket has a range of Yerba to choose from.

The invention of the flask did what the cell phone did for telecommunication and made Mate mobile. These days the "Uruguayan pose" is a flask under the arm and a Mate in hand. I asked a corporate type if Mate was healthy and he replied, "of course, you are drinking water!". Well, Grappa Miel is not water. We had a few sips and a beer or two before being invited to the local pub where Uruguay was playing Argentina on the telly. The people were great but a little surprised to see our kids hanging out with us, so we took the kids back to the hostel and put them safely to bed before returning for a night of laughter, Spanish lessons, discussions about punk, knighting people with a stinky pink ballet shoe, smelling the sweet smell of weed in the air and enjoying a Cow. The Cow is basically a custom where everyone chips in for a beer. Then you stand in a circle and pass the joint, beer and Grappa Miel around until the world takes on a strange light and the world shrinks into the circle. When a third of the Grappa has been drunk beer gets poured into the bottle and this continues until the bottle or you hit the floor, whichever comes first. Note, you do not want the tail of the Cow! A hangover walking tour of the port area of the city and a huge hamburger at the Manchester Diner and you are human again.

While we were having a look at some Mate cups at a street market, a homeless guy standing next to us started stealing stuff off the table and packing it into his jacket, an old man spotted him, and I grabbed the homeless guy as he tried to get away. He looked as if he might turn aggressive, so I raised a fist. In South Africa, a thief is lucky if he gets away with just a severe beating, we have had enough of crime and our first reaction is to strike out at criminals. Uruguayans have a different approach. I was scolded for raising my fist, the homeless guy was scolded, and the stolen stuff put back on the table. This interaction made an impression on me. If the street marketers had reacted with violence then criminals would need to be violent, it is a vicious cycle the only difference I suppose is that South African criminals have always been extremely violent, and an empathetic response does not impress them as much as a few weeks in hospital. A South African policeman once quietly told me that if I catch a burglar in my house that I should not call the cops, but I should beat the thief within an inch of his life or set the dogs on him. Others advised that you should kill the thief then stab yourself in the arm so that you could claim self-defence. Luckily, we had never found ourselves in a position where we would have to make those kinds of decisions.

The shipping agent emailed us to say that the container ship was arriving from Brazil on the Thursday and that we might have the Landy by Friday. We weren't holding our breath. We had been to the agents' offices, handed over a bunch of dollars, had been issued authorisation by immigration for the Landy to enter and had all of our paperwork in order. Another email. The ship is in the port, maybe tomorrow. An email in the morning, they are unloading, maybe this afternoon. Another email, let's go get it! We arrived at the port, the agent's runner did the necessary to and fro and within half an hour, we were standing in front of that container which we had last seen in Port Elizabeth. The seals were broken, the doors opened and there she stood, our precious Landy. She had crossed the Atlantic Ocean and by a miracle of efficient bureaucracy stood exactly the way we had left her, unmolested and ready to roll. Nervously I entered the container while Luisa filmed the moment. I opened the driver door, all seemed fine. I kissed the steering wheel and spoke sweet, reassuring words to the other girl in my life. I slid the key in the ignition, I turned the key. Nothing. Click, click and click. The battery was flat. Not a good start. With the assistance of the dockworkers, we pushed the Landy out of the container and onto South American soil. A great moment in her life and ours. A forklift was called into action and after connecting the jumper cables to the battery under the passenger's seat, the Landy's diesel engine coughed into life. A while later we drove to a checkpoint for the final piece of the paperwork puzzle and then drove out onto the streets of Uruguay, a dream come true. We were pretty nervous to be driving on the wrong side of the road, British is best naturally and headed down to the gas station to fill the tank with expensive fuel.

We drove the Landy up and around the confusing one-way streets and parked in front of the hostel then had a few beers staring down at her from the balcony and watching passers-by take photos of her. This was a moment that we had dreamed of over the last year of preparation, doubt and sleepless nights. I remember being a young adult facing a harsh adult world, completely confused by the simplest bureaucracy. Yet here we stood, looking at our African Land Rover standing proudly on the streets of a South American city, ready to take us anywhere we wanted to go.

WE WILL BE FREE

We arranged a safe parking area because it was too late to hit the road, but within two days, we had packed all of our stuff away and were on the road up the coast towards Brazil. Initially we weren't going to go to Brazil, the response from the Japanese shipping bosses made us think twice, but we were so close to Brazil that it seemed like a huge mistake not to at least try to drive up to Rio, one of the cities in the world I had always dreamed of seeing. Uruguay is tiny and sparsely populated, the drive up the coast passing through small towns and lush green farmland. Each town seemed to have a classic car junkyard and more billboards than the house. As we arrived in Punta Del Este we spotted whales mating very close to the shore and spent a while sitting on the sand taking photos and looking at the other people on the beach. Punta Del Este is a wealthy city, popular with rich Argentines who build large, beautiful houses which stand empty most of the year waiting for the holiday season to be filled with people who have no idea how much their food costs. It costs a lot! With our limited daily budget, we could not afford the huge yellow, Ecuadorian bananas or even the most basic foods. A smaller market far out of town sold locally grown produce at a lower price and it was there that we bought some basic supplies; meat and beer are basic supplies by the way.

Our first camp of this transcontinental tour was the Punta Del Este campground close to the beautiful, modern and very expensive city. The camp was designed to hold hundreds of people with a large field in the centre surrounded by forest and braai areas. At the market, we had our first experience with Latin American butchery, which is very strange by western standards. In the West, meat is cut for storage and transportation. At first, we had no idea what we were looking at in the butchery, the meat is all cut into lumps, no Rib Eye steaks or chops. Our first braai was a great success though; we had some beers, excellent wine and celebrated our first camp under South American skies. Later that

96

night the skies clouded, and the weather changed, rain began to fall while the wind whipped into a gale.

The rooftop tent held out, but the din was terrible as the storm grew progressively worse and we later learned that a cyclone was raging across most of Uruguay. I had zipped on the bottom half of the tent and we all sat inside for the next two days and nights waiting for the rain to stop so that the tent could dry, and we could leave. Only when trees from the forest next to our Landy began to fall did we realise that it was time to move. As we were packing our drenched belongings, the camp manager came over to suggest that it was too dangerous to camp and offered us a room. The road nearby had been closed off by fallen trees and we were glad to be inside the little room waiting for the storm to pass and the road to be cleared. When eventually the rain stopped, we dried the tent with towels, packed up and drove out back onto coastal road north. The cyclone continued to rage as we drove past herds of cows all standing in the rain with their backs to the wind. We were nearing the border town of Chuy and Luisa's research had found a camp called Santa Theresa. The camp was actually a military base within a national park and they had camping areas, a zoo and little chalets. We decided to book into one of the cheap little chalets on a hill overlooking the beach to clean and dry the Landy before hitting the border. The chalet itself had an enclosed garage area with a built-in braai, a view of the ocean, a nice little kitchen, a couple of bedrooms and a fireplace. The perfect place to recharge after those first horrible days camping in the storm. We enjoyed three days of solitude and activity, cleaning, chilling, doing some home-schooling, visiting the little zoo and planning for deep, dark and dangerous Brazil. Anyone who has seen City of God will know what we were expecting to find.

Many people we had met told us not to go to Brazil and a few Uruguayans had advised us not to go. Very expensive and very dangerous they said. One big German Brazilian living in Uruguay had made notes on our Brazil map of all the areas which were extremely dangerous and should be avoided at all costs. He told us not to trust the police and to never drive with the windows open or the doors unlocked, that criminals would stab our tyres as we waited in traffic and that if that happened they would clean out the vehicle and we should not bother reporting it to the police. With that advice ringing in our ears, we headed for the border and drove straight into Brazilian immigration. Where is the Uruguayan border? Back on the road five kilometres. OK, then. We had not seen a border. We drove back and found the little office alongside the road and after being stamped out, the customs officer needing some help with the Carnet, we drove back to the Brazilian border office where a serious-looking police stood with black uniforms and sub-machine guns. The immigration lady, who looked like Shakira and wore high heels and very tight jeans, stamped us into Brazil. Is it dangerous? No, no very relaxed. Enjoy.

14

Brazil!

Entering Brazil, we were as nervous as we had been the first time that we drove into Mozambique. Thankfully the roads were a lot better than they had been in Mozambique and we soon stopped for fuel on a road which was flanked only by farmland, canals and Capivaras for almost two hundred kilometres. We fuelled up keeping our eyes open and our knives and pepper spray handy though the atmosphere didn't feel very dangerous. Driving on we passed little farmhouses and a village or two before coming to an intersection manned by twenty heavily armed soldiers. They looked at us and waved us on with a few smiles, taking the turnoff to a coastal town called Cassino we spotted a supermarket and decided to stop and have a look at the prices and maybe buy a few groceries. We knew it was going to be very expensive and we were already concerned about our budget. Parking as close as we could to the entrance of the supermarket and scanning the area for bad guys, we stepped into the cool air and noticed a few things immediately. One, everyone was very friendly and there was hardly any security. Two, most of the prices were in single digits and a lot of the goods seemed cheaper than South Africa. This cannot be true. We had done the currency conversion twenty times. Two Brazilian Reals (R$2.00) = $1.00 US which = R10.00 (South African). Essentially then R$1.00 = R5.00. No, it just can't be. Damn, it's cheap! Ahh, maybe when we get to the teller they slap on a huge tax. Nope. Shit, that's awesome. So, we bought meat, beer, bread and water and walked back out to the Landy, surprised and pleased that she was not molested and went looking for camping. Because very few Overlanders had been to Brazil there was very little information about where to camp and so began what would become a ritual, the search for camping. Because our GPS was old and useless, we spent many hours at the end of a long drive driving in circles looking for a safe place to camp. Cassino had a few options surprisingly, and while driving on the beach we met a kind 4x4er who led us to a rundown grassy campsite in the middle of the town, but we decided to head back to a campsite we had seen on the road leading into town. That camp did not seem very safe or secluded; only a little fence separated us from the hostile, bloodthirsty Brazilians. We sat around camp with weapons close by and planned the next day. The great news was that Brazil was far cheaper than anyone had said it would be and so far, we had not been raped or even murdered. That Sunday we decided to risk a walk-in town in the afternoon. There were no police, anywhere and stores would put racks of merchandise OUTSIDE the shop, unsupervised. Everyone was chilled and friendly, walking hand in hand, eating ice cream, chatting to friends, smiling at us. What the fuck is going on here? We ate strawberries dipped in chocolate, hot dogs and drank cool drinks and chatted to people who wanted to know where we were from. We were invited to visit a local's restaurant, we made Facebook friends and we exchanged email addresses. Ok, maybe this town is safe, maybe the others are wild?

The Allie's from Port Elizabeth had told us that it was possible in Brazil to camp at service stations which catered to truck drivers. The service stations have complete bathrooms, restaurants and sometimes Wi-Fi. Driving north to Porto Alegre we had read somewhere that there was a camp, but we were struggling to find any camping near the city. We had driven down back roads parallel to the river and had searched for tourist areas which might have camping, but after a few hours, we pulled into a large clean service station almost defeated. If we could use the Wi-Fi, we could possibly find some camping. Luisa struggled to connect while I wandered around asking random people if they knew where I could find camping. The owner of the station said we could camp around the back which I thought was a great idea, but Luisa refused; she was not interested in camping in a service station like a trucker's wife. She would soon eat those words. While we were making a fuss, a lady came over and indicated that her husband speaks English. That was when we met Barry, a small seventy-year-old African American with a deep drawl. Barry took his time to suss us out, white South Africans have a reputation which precedes them and told us that he did not know of any camping, but we were welcome to stay at his place. I don't know why but I decided to trust Barry. We had never stayed with a stranger before while travelling, especially risky with the kids around. Following Barry's silver Chevrolet, we drove rapidly past huge beautiful lakes and green forest. Stopping for a toilet break Barry told us that he had two houses where we could stay, one was his lake house and the other was his beach house. Both sounded promising. Driving past a wind farm we arrived at a scarcely populated area next to a lake. The lake house was Barry's weekend project and he had built it out of recycled materials, Coca-Cola cans, surrounded by a small fence and long green grass, Barry suggested we could stay there as long as we wanted but as Luisa needed the Internet and still unsure how safe Brazil was we instead suggested that we could perhaps stay at his beach house. No problem and off we drove, again rapidly. Nearing the town of Osorio, the sun was beginning to set and spotted a few large campsites, Barry stopped outside one and said, well, there is camping here, and you are welcome to stay here, or you are welcome to stay at my house. There was something about the look in his eyes, I glanced at Luisa, looked back at Barry and told him we would love to see his house. Barry's face lit up and off we went, by now the light was fading rapidly. The conversation in our Landy was a little tense. Shit man, there was camping right there. I know, but I like this guy. Well, you better hope that we don't regret this. Driving into the town we saw Gypsies with horse-drawn carts, hookers hanging around looking for Johns (prostitution is legal in Brazil) and the town looked rough. Gradually the area started to improve, and we drove into a tree-lined neighbourhood, turned a few corners and stopped outside a house opposite a park where teenagers played soccer. The house was a lovely, clean double story with well-kept green lawn. Barry invited us in and told us that the entire bottom floor was reserved only for guests and we had all the conveniences of a modern house at our disposal.

What a relief. We made hot dogs while Barry went to the store to buy beer and pizza and when he returned, we settled in to chat. He had an amazing life as a Marine Engineer and had even travelled to South Africa in the Sixties where, as a black man, he had to have a special pass to be able to explore the city after dark. Barry had travelled the world by sea and he had a respect for people like us travelling by land. We spoke about travel and Brazil while his lovely Brazilian wife, Madalena fussed over the kids. After an excellent night's sleep, we went on a little tour of the area and up to a little mountain overlooking the town. There was a community up on the mountain, an eccentric church with large Jesus and Mary statues and a take-off point for hang gliding and paragliding. It was hot as we stood around taking photos and as Luisa opened a rear door of the Landy to get some water, my brand-new Sony laptop slid off the seat and landed on the tar with a crunch. No point getting angry, just breathe, it's just stuff, no point getting angry, just breathe. I had prepared that laptop for the writing and hugely popular and exciting movies I was going to make. It was the top of the range Vaio, and we had paid half price for it because it had been returned to Sony with a loud fan. The laptop refused to switch on, the screen and the housing had broken in the fall. This was a sign of things to come as, one by one, our technology fell victim to the perils of travelling.

Leaving Barry, we continued to travel north on the insane BR101 where fully loaded trucks barrel along at speeds exceeding 120 kph. We had to keep the Landy running faster than the trucks to avoid being sandwiched. The south of Brazil was a surprise with most towns being quite modern and many European looking people wandering around. In the past there was a lot of German and Italian immigration and the blonde, blue-eyed are very common. Stopping in coastal Torres we found a little grassy camp and set up for a few days. The town was pleasant, and we ate huge hot dogs filled with potato chips, salsa, corn, peas and mayonnaise. A little girl from the camp would play with the kids and scare the wits out of them with her fun ferocity and a group of unfriendly Gypsies set up their informal camp next to our camp. We had seen a few Gypsy camps so far in Brazil and Barry had told us how they would demand money from the ordinary Brazilians who would pay them purely because they were scared of some bad Gypsy Ju-Ju. We felt safe though and decided that, though Brazil may have some dangerous areas, once again we had been fed bad information from people with strange agendas.

We had been having trouble with the battery charging our two 40lt fridges and after much head-scratching decided to take the Landy to a sparky (Auto Electrician) to see if they could find the problem. The Landy created a fuss wherever she went and the sparky's workshop was no different. He poked around in the battery box under the passenger seat for half an hour but could find nothing. The battery was receiving a charge and the alternator was working, so we were all pretty confused that the battery was not holding a charge when the engine was off. The sparky apologised for not finding the problem and let us leave without paying.

After two days we headed for Florianopolis in the Santa Catarina State. Driving into the city, we were amazed to see huge shopping malls and even a Statue of Liberty replica outside the New York City Centre mall. The roads looped, and we had to be careful to follow the correct lane over bridges past splits and while trying not to get sideswiped by speedy

Brazilians. It was getting late, but we manage to stay on course with a bit of shouting and Luisa assaulting my left arm, to cross the Colombo Sales Bridge onto the island of Florianopolis. We can't believe the beauty of the island we are heading to. Clean and organised with large luxurious apartment buildings, wide avenues, green lawns and exercise spaces and expensive-looking restaurants. Why had we never heard of this place? We follow the road to Lagoa de Conceicao, where there is camping. Drive up a steep busy road to a viewpoint then down into a modern tourist village past supermarkets, pubs and sexy people, over a little bridge, almost crashing the Landy as a girl with the most superb buttocks I have ever seen cycles past us, Luisa assaults me again, past a dune trying to reclaim the road, past the police station, the blue lagoon to our left and turning right between two restaurants into the camping area. We have a look around and check-in. There are a few tents and motorhomes; the place is tidy and well run with enough toilets and large open-air kitchens. We just knew we were going to be there a while and made friends with a very sweet French couple who were travelling with their three little boys.

Now, there are two specifically interesting habits in Brazil which I, unfortunately, managed to combine into an awful story. You shall not laugh. It is not funny. Number one is the Caipirinha. A drink made of sliced lime, crushed ice and 40% proof sugar cane. Number two is the rather unpleasant but infrastructurally necessary practice of disposing of your used toilet paper in the bin provided next to the toilet. You do not flush the paper as the countries sewerage system is based on the reliance on septic tanks. How did I manage to combine these two? The French had travelled south from French Guiana windsurfing and having a generally great time. We were having a few cold beers and they introduced us to the Caipirinha. Being a beer drinker, I have never quite gotten used to the idea of sipping a drink and the result was that we spent the evening slicing lime and crushing ice. The evening fast-forwarded, and we eventually floated back to the tent at 3 am. What a wonderfully refreshing drink!

The next day we headed down to the beach. My stomach was doing somersaults from those lovely drinks, but I was sure some sea and sun would sort me out. As a family, we never travel light, even when going to the beach and, after a dip, I set up the towels and cooler bag, picnic box, shoes, etc. while Luisa and the kids went for a very, very long swim. Then it happened. The somersaults turned into rumbling and cramping. I had to go immediately. But I couldn't just leave all our kit on the beach, this is Brazil. Luisa and the kids were far away in the water. I started packing up while my biology screamed at me "Now!" Loaded with four pairs of shoes, four towels, cooler bags etc. I tried to cross the busy street whilst battling to control the beast inside. I made it across, dashed into the camp reception and dumped our belongings then walked very strangely back to the Landy. I grabbed the soap, couldn't find the bloody toilet paper and resumed my strange walk to the ablutions. Luckily, I chose the private bathroom with a shower near the communal kitchen.

There is a twist in this little tale though. In anticipation of losing a third of my body weight, I had packed a lot of clothing a few sizes too small. I had lost some weight and had managed that morning to squeeze myself into a pair of boardies. Now, here I was, trying to undo the wet waist chord which I had double knotted. I couldn't see past my belly. I pulled the wrong chord. I had made it to the ablutions in the nick of time, but now I was imprisoned in my pants. Just as I managed to untangle that damned knot my body betrayed me, and I did what I haven't done since I was six and it was dark, and I begged my Mom take me to the loo in the caravan park, but she was mad at my Dad so said go on your own, but I was scared, and I lost it. Literally.

So here I stood, feeling six and thinking of THAT scene in Trainspotting. I looked around. I had no toilet paper and there was nothing I could clean with except...

I have since been cautious with the Caipirinha and only knot once.

After that experience, I decided to lose some weight and would go for long walks in the morning and try and do pull-ups on the free gym equipment built on the beach. I would get up early and watch the surfers heading for the beach and the sexy ladies working out. It was a good start to the day and we were having such a good time hanging out and exploring the island that we stayed for just over two weeks before convincing ourselves that it was time to move on. We still had a lot of work to do running the remnants of the business and helping out with the smooth transition of our client database to the new service provider. We would take advantage of a good Wi-Fi connection and a comfortable camp to keep our heads above water, never knowing when we would again be able to connect and serve.

But before leaving, I had to try and find a geek to fix my computer. I was supposed to be writing blogs daily, and I had been very serious about sticking to a routine when my Sony was murdered. Luisa found a Sony dealer in Florianopolis city and we set off in the big Landy to find the place. Problem is that road names and numbering in Brazil, and most of South America is completely illogical. Four roads in one city will have the same name and the numbering of buildings seems determined by lottery balls. Driving around in circles in the hot Brazilian traffic for three hours will put anyone in a bad mood. We did three U-turns outside a police station and as we were driving off after the third, a policeman pulled us over. He was a stocky guy with a short-sleeved uniform, under which you could see large, tribal tattoos. Here we go, Luisa. This was going to be our first dodgy Latino cop experience. I was prepared for it having read so many accounts of bribery and extortion by the South American cops. We have never paid a bribe and were not going to start now. The cop came up to Luisa's window, expecting to find a steering wheel but finding only dashboard. Wherefrom? South Africa. No! Si. He then asked us what we were looking for; he had seen us driving around

106

and wanted to help. We showed him the address for the Sony tech and he told us to follow him. It took nearly half an hour for him to find the store and when he did he went in with me to explain what we needed and then gave us a business card and told us to call him should we have any problems! The nerds were unable to fix the highly specked Sony.

Driving along the coast was mostly good fun though we did get stuck in a few traffic jams and were learning to treat the BR101 with contempt. Sao Francisco do Sul was to be our next stop and the dusty little town had camping but only for ground tents. We drove around to the point and spotted a hotel, Hotel Turismar, with a large green lawn so we drove in and asked if we could camp on the lawn and leave in the morning. There are two ways that could have gone, but they said, OK, sure, where are you from. Or in Brazilian English - wherefrom? South Africa. A stroke of two fingers down the cheek (a gesture we now understood meant - but you are white, how can you be from Africa?) and the kind owner led us to the grassy lawn. He offered to let the kids swim in the pool and invited us to breakfast. We asked how much it would be to camp and he just shrugged his shoulders. We swam, cooked while it rained, slept, had a great free breakfast of vienna sausages, toast, egg and cakes before thanking our hosts for their kindness and leaving to explore the area and look for a ferry back to the mainland. There did not seem to be a light vehicle ferry though we did meet some truckers who were queuing, and they told us that there was a ferry further down a dirt road. The road itself was pretty bad, muddy and corrugated, there did not seem to be much traffic and when we eventually arrived in a little town we were surprised to find it there. It was a nice little town and driving down a road, we found a park with free exercise machines where we all had a little workout with our usual chaotic energy before carrying on towards what looked like a port on the GPS. There was not a port but there were the most amazing holiday homes, each with a private garden area across the road and a private jetty where extremely expensive cabin cruisers stood waiting for the holidaymakers to return. We could not believe that this wealth lay at the end of the dirt road and can only imagine that the residents liked to keep the town secluded, a secret getaway. It was also interesting that most of the houses had very little security and no burglar bars. We fantasised about sneaking into one for a few weeks until the owners returned. Having not found a ferry we had little choice but to return to the BR101 and continue heading towards Sao Paulo.

We made our way back to the BR101 by lunchtime and drove a few hundred kilometres to the city of Curitiba which lies quite far inland and is a beautiful city but very difficult to navigate by car. We arrived as the sun was setting and spent three hours trying to find our hostel and tourist information which were both in the city centre. Actually, getting to the centre was easy enough, but the illogical one-ways and split streets were as confusing as hell. We stopped and asked taxi drivers and couples in dark cul-de-sacs. After driving down the same road ten times we found that we had to do a loopback and around and that a road which had a sign saying one way was actually a partial two-way and the hostel lay in the middle of that road. We found the hostel and by some miracle they had an entrance exactly 1cm higher than the Landy, so we were able to park in the courtyard. Too tired to cook we took a walk to a mall across the road, still nervous of Brazil and acting like the KGB was following us we slipped into the bright modern mall and spotted a restaurant boasting The Best Burger in The World. I had to try them. Nice burger. I make better burgers.

The biggest question nagging at us now was whether we should drive into Sao Paulo city. With over 400 policemen killed in one year and a reputation for drug crimes and murders, we had to have a long hard think. Of all the places we had been to or were going to go to, Sao Paulo was definitely the most dangerous. As parents, we need to be very careful which decisions we make. We are brave and daring until something goes wrong and then we are stupid and reckless. Plucking up the courage we decided that we would visit the city, but we would enter early on an upcoming public holiday to avoid the infamous traffic, thereby avoiding being a sitting duck, we would find a hostel in a "safe" neighbourhood and we would plan the route meticulously. Getting lost was not an option. We would also leave the city on the weekend and choose the most direct route out. Valuables would be handed over if demanded under duress, but knives and pepper spray would be on hand in case we had to defend ourselves. We did safety drills with the kids and mentally prepped to enter the city. We drove in. No-one hassled us. A beautiful woman in an Audi sports car stopped outside a bridal shop, confidently carrying all her glittering, swaying swag. People chilled on street corners, smiled at us, thumbs up. What the fuck? After a few nervous lane changes and U-turns, we made it to the Belem neighbourhood where we would find the little Green Grass Hostel. The owners were typically cool Brazilians and they slept under the stairs, waiting for the next backpacker to ring the bell or need toilet paper or the WIFI code. With the help of the young owner we found and parked the Landy in a 24-hour parking garage. The neighbourhood, which was very close to the centre of the city, was a cool, old area where developers were happy to invest in high rise apartments. 470 Helicopters filled the sky serving as a constant reminder of the city's 26 billionaires and a population of 12 million. The hostel was so small that we called it a submarine and flu spread quickly through her small spaces. I was going for my morning walks carrying not much other than change for a cool drink and some cigarettes and although I sometimes felt like I had walked too far in the wrong direction, I luckily never had any problems with the local population. We were invited to a birthday party held by some Brazilians friends whom we had met in the America del Sur hostel in Buenos Aires the first week of our trip. Valentim and Tati are tattoo obsessed and very cool. Their house was only ten blocks away from our hostel, so we drove the Landy to their apartment for them to have a look before taking her back to the night time parking. We were made to feel welcome by all the family and friends and I drank too much beer and struggled to understand rapid Portuguese while the kids and later the adults, played karaoke. Go, big daddy, go, big daddy, they chanted while I squawked Bohemian Rhapsody. A beer, a burger. Singing happy birthday which culminated in shouting kind heartened obscenities at the birthday boy, you're gay and you've got a tiny dick! Then home to the hostel after I had finished all the beer. Valentim offered to do a tattoo for me, he is a gifted artist, but we were not planning on spending any more time in Sao Paulo than we had to and after a week we left on a Sunday, missing all the infamous traffic and headed around the city and down to the coast over a steep green mountain pass. Cities aren't really our thing, naturally. After a few days we become uncomfortable and grumpy surrounded by so much human activity, noise, bustle and pollution. Sao Paulo had been an eye-opener though, as one of the most dangerous cities in the world pales it in comparison to Johannesburg city. And if Sao Paulo did not kill us then we could actually start to relax in Brazil as even in this huge metropolis people were relaxed, kind and eager to be friendly.

So far, we had not been blown away by the Brazilian beaches and had heard that the beach would be nice two hours from the city. We drove down the winding mountain pass, glimpsing the sea and taking video of the forest. We spotted a large town near the coast to the right, but our GPS told us to go through a little town called Bertioga, along the coast past Ilhabela and north towards Rio de Janeiro. In Brazil, there is a camping club called the Camping Clube do Brazil and we were lucky to find one outside a town called Ubatuba. This campsite was very well organised but actually had very few spaces for camping. Most of the "campers" are retired people living in permanently fixed camper homes. Lovely people who spend their days in Speedos down by the beach, which is accessed directly from the camp which has views of an island.

I pulled the Landy up onto a piece of lawn next to the beach fence and we settled in for more than a week. Keelan and Jessica would play with some of the local kids while I worked on the Landy and did my chores and Luisa worked on the internet. School teachers in G-strings would bring their kids down to the beach for a swim, we would swim and suntan and take long walks. There was a natural spring in the side of a hill up the road where we could go to refill the Landy's water tank. We met Ricard, his wife and sister-in-law in the camp and they took us for a tour of the nearby towns and beaches.

There is something innocent and sweet about Brazilians. I think that one of the greatest surprises for me was the Brazilian culture. South Africa is a tough place where you need to be tough daily and soft Europeans find themselves changed if they stay too long. Brazil seems to have the opposite effect on people. There was poverty, but at the same time, there are very clear and definite signs of progress, of a community which is a family and like all families, there are problems and problem children, but the Brazilian family is one of opportunity and, we felt so much love. A love that we did not feel back home. Perhaps it is the language difference, perhaps if we understood more of what people were saying to us then we would have a completely different approach. But I like to believe that I can read people and what I was reading was curiosity and compassion but also a great love for Brazil and a deep concern that we would share that love and love Brazil and tell our friends and family that Brazil is not just favelas and cocaine, and gangsters and violence. And we are here to tell you that she is not. She is a beautiful woman with a huge heart, a bright future and a great ass.

I always enjoy driving around coastal towns and after buying some picnic food we drove down to the bay and around, following a narrow dirt road which led to a small parking area next to a large tree and a pier. Two girls and their friend were jumping five metres off the jetty into the clear blue water. I jumped off the pier and swam with them while Luisa took photos and made us some lunch which we ate under the tree looking out over the perfect little bay and enjoying the tranquillity and people who could take a mid-week morning swim.

Between Sao Paulo and Rio de Janeiro lies the most beautiful coastline in all of Brazil as we were to later discover. Islands dot the coastline and yachts sail between them, the sun shining warmly and a cool breeze blowing. Lush green vegetation lines the quiet coastal road and little towns invite you to relax. A nuclear power plant built into the side of a hill, shadows and residential town built in a strict grid, reminding me of Melkbosstrand where we to had lived only a few kilometres away from a potential disaster. Hopefully, the Brazilians are better at maintaining their infrastructure than our government is. When the Minister of Public Enterprises blames the constant power cuts on a bolt falling into a reactor five-kilometres away from where your children go to bed, you tend not to sleep as soundly.

We managed to get lost driving into Rio. Heading inland, following our ancient and unreliable GPS. Twisting through traffic, sweating, searching for the correct road we drove through a dirty little city and eventually emerged onto a freeway which led past amusement parks and huge shopping malls to an area called Barra Shopping. Then a tunnel and another, a glimpse of the sea, Favelas on a hillside, roads cut into the side of a cliff, more tunnels and we arrive in Rio, Copacabana and Ipanema. To drive my South African Landy into Rio de Janeiro will forever be a highlight of my life. The city itself is without a doubt the most beautiful city I have ever seen, with the most frustrating traffic congestion. Often when I am sitting somewhere wild, all alone with a beer in hand, I think of those poor buggers in Rio and wonder why the hell they don't just buy bicycles.

We had heard through the overland grapevine that it is possible to camp in your vehicle in the parking lot below the Sugarloaf Mountain cable car station. The parking lot sits between a military base and a military school. Military police patrol the parking area 24 hours a day which makes the location very safe. Apparently, all you need to do is roll up and ask an MP if you can camp in the car and they will say yes. Hopefully. The sun was setting by the time we made it to our "campsite" and we found that a graduation ceremony was in progress. We drove up to a very large black MP and sweetly asked him if we could camp. No! Please leave. Shit! Our only back up was a youth hostel or two in the city but they were expensive, and we would have to park our home on the street. More than a little concerned we retreated to the parking area to wait for a friendly-looking MP to arrive. I spotted a smiling guy with lots of bling on his uniform and made my move. Sure, he said no problem. Just wait until the graduation ceremony is finished and you can go park. Excellent, how long will they still be? Oh, two hours maximum. We decided to try and find some food and re-joined the traffic heading up the road. We spotted a buffet restaurant and managed to manoeuvre the Landy into a tight parking area. The buffet was fantastic, and every dish was fresh and tasty. I have never had a really good buffet, but the Brazilians love a buffet and a Churrascaria, a meat buffet restaurant. It was not a cheap meal, but it was satisfying. After a few hours, we decided to return to the Sugarloaf to park. The graduation ceremony was still going on, long tedious speeches, group chanting, fireworks low overhead repeated until after midnight when the cadets eventually threw their berets in the air and the crowd slowly began to disperse into little chatting groups. They had made all the effort to dress in their best clothing and would be damned if they were going home without socialising for a few more hours. I started the Landy and slowly made my way through the crowd, past the security barriers into a parking spot. We confirmed with the MP's that we could open the tent and they said no problem. Wherefrom?

Not only is the parking area directly under the Sugarloaf it also serves a perfect half-moon beach which must have been sublime five hundred years ago when the water was pristine and there were more fish in the ocean than plastic bottles. At night a full moon lit the Sugarloaf and the little bay, and we could see Christ the Redeemer shining in the background. I was watching the documentary Senna the other night and what struck me most, was that back in the Eighties Brazilians described Senna as the only good thing about Brazil. How could it be that such a beautiful country full of such wonderful people has such terribly low self-esteem?

With the rooftop tent opened, we climbed into the tent and soon I was snoring very loudly (I always snore very loudly) to the amusement of late-night revellers who would slap the tent in encouragement. It was a Friday night and the Mariocas were up all night, standing in groups listening to my snoring, chatting loudly, telling jokes and inspecting the Landy.

To get clean we drove to Copacabana beach and parked the Landy in front of a hotel across from the beach. There are these subterranean bathrooms under the sidewalk and for a small fee, you can use the loo and shower. I had to pinch myself. Having a shower under Copacabana beach. Yes, you read that correctly, a shower beneath Copacabana. How could we ever return to a mundane existence after an experience like this? The rest of our lives would have to have some serious highlights to compete with this experience and not suck completely. Good time to be singing some Manilow.

And an early start meant that we could drive almost all the way up to Christ The Redeemer, or Corcavao in Portuguese, without having to queue with all the tourists at the foot of the mountain. I am, without a doubt, the worst person to ever take to a tourist trap. I would rather not see the attraction than spend a morning, afternoon or evening rubbing shoulders with my fellow tourists. I am the miserable bastard who ruins the experience for everyone. This makes Luisa madder than Kim Yong Un, but I refuse to change, you can go, take the kids, I can't wait to not see the photos. My problem is, I watch the people instead of taking the photos and usually the people piss me off. The view was nice though and we got some nice pics and rescued a wooden Jesus who now lives on the Landy's dashboard and who once lost both his outstretched arms in Bariloche in the middle of traffic. They just flew straight out the window. A miracle.

Unfortunately, we spent most of our time in Rio in traffic looking for a store to fix my computer which had been dropped on the concrete back in Osorio. The Barra Shopping area outside of Rio has many malls and is the commercial part of the city. We found a Land Rover dealer and explained that we had a problem with the vehicle battery. They were amazed to see the Landy, they only sold the upmarket Landy's, but their solution was to sell us a new battery. We had established that the problem was not the battery. Across the road from Land Rover, we spotted a Bosch service centre and I approached them for help while Luisa went looking for WIFI. The owner, Claudio, was a tall Japanese Brazilian and he was methodical in trying to find the problem. He tested the battery and the alternator but could not see any faults with either. He tested our power splitting device, which ensures that the main starting battery always receives a charge and never runs flat and even had a diagram for the splitter filed in his office. After two hours of searching, he was stumped and suggested that we go to a battery centre and swop batteries, perhaps that would solve the problem. We drove back into the traffic to find the battery centre Claudio had recommended but found that a new battery made no difference. By now the sun was setting so we returned to our parking lot camp under the Sugarloaf and listened to the Marioca having a good time around our tent. That Saturday morning was fresh and beautiful as we set off to see Claudio again. His mechanic spent an hour digging around in the battery box until he found the problem. Eureka. A simple fix, the positive cable was not connected to the auxiliary battery and because the battery box was such a tight fit no-one had been able to see this. The technician who had installed the battery back near our home in Plettenberg Bay had given me a strange look when I told him where we planned to travel in the Landy. 'It's lekker to be white, hey?' Perhaps jealousy makes him particularly nasty. We asked Claudio how much we owed him, but he did not charge us a cent even though they had spent almost four hours trying to solve the problem. We had also found a company to fix my Sony and they did the work in a couple of hours.

We had camped for two nights in the military area under the Sugar Loaf in Rio city and then camped two nights in a parking lot on the beautiful Grumari beach south of Rio. We had driven south from Rio along the coast looking for more traditional camping. We found a Camping Clube of Brazil, but they were expensive and there was a very excited and over-friendly Englishman who seemed ready to jump in the Landy with us and become part of the family if given half a chance. Driving parallel to the undeveloped coast we eventually arrived at a restaurant with a large parking area. We asked the owner if we could camp and he said no problem. On the second night in Grumari a local lady came to us and said "peligrosa aqui, criminales, cuidade criancas", dangerous here, criminals, caution with children! We hardly slept that night waiting and watching for the criminals to make their move. Around midnight a tall something with long thin legs and a large upper body glided very quickly and un-naturally towards the three beach kiosks 50m in front of us. It slid in behind the first kiosk and after thirty seconds it headed towards the second and then the third kiosk and disappeared out of our range of view into the restaurant area to our right. After about three very long minutes the creature re-emerged and headed back the way it came. It was moving very swiftly with very little effort, but between the second and first kiosk, it seemed to sense us in the Land Rover hidden in a dark corner of the lot. It paused for a moment, seemingly in mid-stride, perhaps to sniff the air and then moved rapidly back onto the beach and vanished. Luisa and I had almost soiled our sleeping shorts! We lay there, in the rooftop tent, staring out the windows, waiting for the beasts return, the howl and the sound of ripping canvas. Eventually the sun rose, and we ventured out to look for tracks. Werewolves wear size 12 sneakers! True story. Exhausted we headed for the highway which loops around Rio to her poor, ugly sister city Niteroi and then up the BR101 to Buzios.

Bridget Bardot described the water of Buzios as resembling bubbling champagne and so, gratefully, they commissioned a statue of her sitting uncomfortably. An upmarket town with a very friendly tourist information, touristy but beautiful if not a bit windy in December. We spotted an area on the beach where we could free camp, but the wind was howling, and Luisa needed to get some work done and for that, as always, she needed the internet.

Rio had been a highlight naturally and we had achieved our goal of reaching the city. We could turn back now and head for Ushuaia. We could. But everyone we met kept telling us to keep going just a bit further. The next town is lovely, the next beach is beautiful. Eventually, we were so far north that we decided to rent an apartment in Natal for Christmas. Ironically Natal means Christmas in Portuguese, so it was a fitting place to be for the season. Getting to Natal was going to be an adventure, but we did not know that driving into the town of Pipa after sunset on a Friday evening. As we drove into the town it was clear that the area receives very few Gringo Overlanders. A thousand eyes watched us drive down the main road. Then sirens and a policeman on a motorbike pulling us over. Wherefrom!? South Africa. No! Fingers tracing down his cheek. A radio call and his partner arrived on his motorbike. We handed over our documents even before the open-mouthed cop asked for them. The partner hardly spoke any English and they were fascinated by the steering wheel on the right-hand side. We were sure that they were going to look for an excuse to fine us, but again the cops in Brazil surprised us. They asked where we were going and escorted us with lights flashing down to the ferry. It is quite a feeling to be escorted by the cops. The ferry, unfortunately, was too small for the Landy and we had to drive through the lagoon to the beach on the other side. It was dark, we had Keelan walk the crossing and a local guided us through the lagoon, which the Landy easily drove through and up the other bank. Driving into the little town we found camping and settled in for the night. The next day we had another ferry crossing, this time across a very deep river. We drove down the beach onto the ferry while holidaymakers sunned themselves. The colour of the sand and water and bikinis was vibrant and electric. Dolphins accompanied us as we crossed the river on the ferry listing heavily from the weight of the Landy. We would be landing on a small piece of beach and would have to drive over rocks, in the seawater to get around to the beach which would lead us to the road to Natal. Luisa had found an apartment online and we settled in for a few weeks in the sky with a strong wind constantly blowing through the barricaded windows. The apartment block was modern and geared for families with a few swimming pools and games for the kids. The Landy was completely unpacked and scrubbed and small repairs were made. Christmas was simple, our first Christmas while on the road and we had to bear in mind that we had very little space for large gifts. Luckily our kids are grateful and happy to receive a few, well-considered presents. We could not find a Christmas tree in any of the supermarkets in Natal, so I made a "tree" out of two badminton rackets and some tinsel. Everyone laughed at my tree; they don't know art when they see it. The Brazilians are crazy about Christmas and the city was decorated with millions of lights, stores were decorated with extremely expensive and elaborate displays and a Christmas market was set up near the city centre.

A Brazilian Overlander we had met just after Buzios told us that it was possible to drive the nearly 600 km's from Natal to Fortaleza on the beach. Having lived in Cape Town for years I had learnt to drive a Land Rover on the sand tracks of the Melkbos 4x4 off-road vehicle facility and now and then driving the Atlantis dunes. So, sand driving is a skill I possess, and I had nice tyres on the Landy which were perfect for beach driving. However, we were concerned about driving exclusively on the beach because of the likelihood of damage to wildlife, such as turtle nests and that we might run into rivers which we could not drive through and which might not have ferries. The decision was made to consult the maps and evaluate the drivability of each stretch of coast before deciding to use the road or the beach. We also decided to sleep on the beach because we had real trouble finding places to camp. The northeast of Brazil is just so far away from most of the population that it is not seriously considered as a holiday destination by most in the south. We did meet a family from Sao Paulo who tailed us for a while then overtook us and pulled us over to give us curios out of the bed of their bakkie. We would drive either on the beach or along the coastal road heading north and looking for places to camp at the end of the day. Driving off the tar onto the beach near Canoa down a slipway, the sun began to set, and we were looking for a quiet place to camp. There were wheel tracks on the sand which assured us that the route was not impassable. The greatest danger of beach driving is tides. If you miss-judge the tides and are unlucky enough to get the vehicle stuck far from any help and with nothing to attach the winch to, chances are good that you could lose your beloved vehicle to the sea. Almost everything we owned was in that Landy. I spotted an area up a slight bank and close to some palm trees where we could park and open the tent. I looked at the driftwood etc. lying on the sand and tried to establish a high tide mark. Unfortunately, it was a cloudy evening and I could not see the moon to verify whether it was a full moon which might bring a spring tide. Just to be on the safe side I attached the winch cable to a palm tree and connected the controls and linked that into the tent. If in the middle of the night, the sea came to get us, I could winch us up the beach from the comfort of my tent. That probably would not work as I would need to steer and have the engine on to power the battery which drives the winch. Going to sleep with the sound of waves crashing a few metres away can be a bit worrying but waking up on a sunny morning to the same sound is revitalising. Without showers or toilets available we bathed in the sea. We had a small toilet for Jessica, but I prefer to go au naturel and a surfers' aqua turd just feels so bloody natural. After a breakfast of cereal and yoghurt we made the decision to keep on driving along the beach to find the next town. As there were already tracks in the sand we could assume that we would not be causing any further ecological damage by driving on the sand. Along we went until we found a point where the tracks ended, and we could see that the beach did not seem passable. A wind farm was twirling to our left and we made the decision to drive up over some dunes and out of the beach area via the wind farm service roads. The wind was howling as we drove up onto the paved road which the sand was fighting to reclaim. The road led in all directions, the GPS had no idea where we were and there was not a soul in sight. Eventually, a pick up passed us, and we turned around to follow him and find out how to get out of the maze. He led us out and before we left the compound we took some time to have a look at some dismantled generators before being chased away by security. We have driven into an unauthorised area and were technically trespassing, but luckily, we were let off. That night we entered Fortaleza and met with an off-roading personality in the city. We had a few beers with Dutchman, Coen and left the city to look for a place to sleep. Our new friend had given us coordinates for a couple of places to park and sleep, but both turned out to be unwelcoming, the first a construction site in a residential area was locked up and the second, a gas station, told us that we could not stay there. At 2 am we parked at a gas station near the edge of the city and tried to sleep in our seats with the windows slightly open, the heat dehydrating us, mosquitoes eating us, prostitutes and drunks disturbing us. I couldn't sleep and neither could Luisa, so we decided to continue driving until we found somewhere where we could rest safely, in the tent. Half an hour down the road we found a gas station with an armed guard who allowed us to open the tent near the other trucks. Within ten minutes we were dead to the world, except Luisa, who was hearing footsteps in Peru.

That was to be our first night of many camped at a gas station in Brazil. The parking area where we slept was full of water and oil. The bathrooms were not the nightmare that we were expecting, but they were gritty. That is just one of the beauties of overlanding. You never know where you are going to land up that night and every night after. One night you are sleeping under palm trees listening to the sea and the next you are tiptoeing through sandy oil, parked between big rigs, surrounded by litter and stray dogs. But you are always headed somewhere, and a good state of mind gets you ready for another day on the road. Many friends and family think that our Overlander friends and we are on a permanent holiday. Well, we are, but it is not the holiday which many work all year round. It is an often-trying existence and it takes a certain type of person to be able to do it for an extended period of time. And the Overlanders I appreciate the most are those who travel with kids. Kids are a full-time job. They require cleaning, clothing, feeding, educating, attention, quality time, nurturing and discipline. I can't imagine what childless Overlanders do all day. All that free time on their hands must be challenging. That said, living on the road has many challenges and often it is simple things like laundry or finding a decent grocer and a campsite which can be the most frustrating. We have met Overlanders who never stay in campsites and only ever free camp. A particularly crazy German couple we met in the German ski town of Gramado, Brazil, only ever stayed in campsites, but never, ever, showered. I could not understand why you would stay in a camp if not for the bathrooms. It takes all sorts in this strange tribe.

We had settled on a final northerly destination in Brazil, Jericoacoara, a national park set amongst dunes with crystal clear freshwater lakes and beautiful beaches. Already we had driven too far along the barren, dry coast of Brazil, but everyone told us to just keep on going, you have to see this you have to go there. We were supposed to be in Ushuaia, the most southerly town in the world, but we were past the equator! Back home in Africa we had driven to within a few hundred kilometres of the Equator and here we were again, but could see no reason to drive up to the Amazonian River city Belem. The seasons would begin to change soon in the south and we needed to be in and out of Patagonia before the winter crept in. We have some relatively cold winters in South Africa, but I have only seen snow once before in my life and it is the one element I have no idea what to do with. I do not know how to drive in it, camp in it or survive in it. Snow on a mountaintop is great, that's where it belongs, while we sit admiring it in a camping chair, by a fire, in shorts, sipping a cold beer. Jericoacoara has not seen snow since before the last ice age, thank God. Touts and tour guides insisted that we needed a guide to drive to the town set on the cusp of dunes, in the middle of the desert. If those guides could drive there in their rusty Land Cruisers then we wouldn't have any problems, we just needed to follow the tracks. We took a lesser-known route which led through a mangrove forest and a rickety wooden bridge before ending on the beach where we would have to drive parallel to the sea and past a dune at the water's edge, our wheels kicking up soggy, salty sand in the high tide surf. Kitesurfers and windsurfers littered the beach and we entered the town full of tattoos and dreadlocks, tourist traps, surf shops and the sticky smell of marijuana in the air. A friend suggested that we could ask a local lodge owner if we could camp in the lodge parking lot. We asked, and they invited us to occupy a spot near the front gate and offered us the use of the staff toilets. They had kids who spent the day swimming with our happy brats in the pool, Jessica disappearing for a dune walk with a visiting family. The kids had grown so confident and outgoing in the last couple of months, we began to feel like this trip was going to be better for them than we had ever imagined. They disappeared with the lodge kids and Luisa and I took advantage of the childfree day to explore the dunes and lagoons with the Landy, swearing like troopers and telling rude jokes, being unrestrained adults without the self-censorship all good parents practice. We lay in hammocks hung from wooden poles over crystal clear freshwater in a lagoon which sparkled in the afternoon sun, swam and hugged in the water, warm wet flesh and soft lips, romantic in the freedom of the day and massage of the water.

We had an almost 4,000 km drive down the BR343 to get from Parnaiba in the far north to Foz do Iguacu in the south. Brazil is simply huge; apparently, it is larger than the USA, excluding Alaska. The drive took us a week of driving all day and sleeping in gas stations every night. North of Brasilia, the capital of Brazil, was horrible driving, single-lane roads, but not much traffic except for the odd farm vehicle and long-distance trucks. We did not visit Brasilia at all instead of driving around the city and looking for camping at a national park which was described by the Lonely Planet as being beautiful, peaceful and popular with weekend hikers. It was also closed when we arrived after dark, and even the attempts of a couple of passing locals could not raise a human to open the gate for us, so we headed back down the long dirt road and onto the BR343 and looking for a petrol station to camp at. This gas station was the worst so far, with drunks and hookers loitering and a bathroom which was closer to a medieval pit than any modern convenience. The lights did not work, and the filth was deep underfoot. This, again, is the Overlander paradox, one day you are lying in a hammock in a blue lagoon, the next you are surrounded by filth, oil and poverty. Luckily there was a little restaurant down the road which served us egg on toast the next morning and allowed us to use the lovely clean loo. The further south we drove from Brasilia the more beautiful the farmland became until eventually we were surrounded by the most amazing rolling green fields and fantastically large blue skies.

The south of Brazil had been populated by German immigrants since the late 1800s and the infrastructure reflected this. The population was taller and blonder and more like us than any area we had been since South Africa. There are many stories and rumours and a few documentaries which have linked the South of Brazil and the North of Argentina with the Nazi's before and after World War 2. And being who I am and knowing what I know, I believe many of the stories. There are apparently hotels and homes and towns which were built exclusively by and for the Nazi's. If I was running away from an international court, this is probably where I go because so few other go there. It is almost as far away from Europe as you can get and with no significant tourist attractions there are few visitors to take the stories back home. But the Germans explored South America extensively before and during the war and there are also German colonies in Bolivia, Peru, Paraguay, Chile and Ecuador. Rudolph Hess was kidnapped from Brazil by the Israeli Mossad and if he was there then who else might be hiding in the bushes dreaming of the glory days of the Reich, eating Wurst and being generally unpleasant?

At a butchery, we had a conversation with a woman in a mix of Portuguese, German and Afrikaans. If the farmers of South Africa could only see the south of Brazil, I believe that most would pack up and head for this beautiful, safe, fertile and prosperous part of the world. I am actually surprised that there has not been a mass exodus, but perhaps that is part of the beauty of Brazil. Her dangerous reputation keeps a lot of people away, but I have a feeling that soon Brazil will be experiencing an immigration explosion, especially after the World Cup and the Olympics. Actually, here is a tip. If you have any real money lying around, go now and buy property along the Brazilian coast. Wait for three years then sell and retire. It happened in South Africa and now only foreigners can see the sea without getting into a bus.

There was another benefit of heading further south. The gas stations began to improve drastically after Brasilia and we spent one night parked in a quiet corner of a gas station which covered the same area as a Rugby stadium. The forecourt had twenty fuel pumps; there was a car wash, a hairdresser and two restaurants. In the morning, the owners offered us a free car wash in exchange for some stickers on the Landy. I agreed but was a bit shocked when they handed over two stickers the size of half a door. I still have the stickers but won't be putting them on the Landy. They will go on the wall of my pub when I eventually settle down.

Foz do Iguacu sits at the border between Brazil, Paraguay and Argentina. There are magnificent waterfalls on the Brazilian and Argentine sides of the river. There are a few camps, but we opted to skip the Youth Hostel full of bloody overland tourists in a bloody orange overland truck. They were drinking beer in the pool and throwing coarse British accents around like litter. Respect your Queen man. The other camp, near the city, was called Camping International and was perfectly run by a German lady who had been in Brazil since just after the war. The lawns were green and perfect, the bathrooms shiny clean as was the swimming pool, there was even a free washing machine and a supermarket a few kilometres away. We parked under a mango tree and small, deliciously ripe yellow mangoes would drop into the lush grass to be scoffed messily after a good rinse. I must have eaten twenty a day in the ten days which we were there, cleaning up the Landy after all that time on the road, catching up with emails and swimming in the pool. After spending so many days sleeping between big rigs, breathing in exhaust gasses and sharing the showers with truckers, who were mostly nice guys and Luisa feeling like she might have married badly, it was good to relax a little and get cleaned up, sleep as late as possible before the sun cooked us out of the tent. The kids made friends with the crowd of kids who lived at the camp or spent their days there. We hardly saw them during the day, they were either riding a tandem bicycle or climbing a tree or swimming in the pool.

15

Paraguay

The initial fear we had completely disappeared within a week of entering, and we had made really good friends, friends we hope to meet one day again. It was decided that we would drive into Paraguay, into Ciudad del Este which lies across the Rio Parnaiba and a complicated border crossing. Ciudad del Este (City of the East in English) is a Zona Franca, a tax-free zone and as such the border crossing from Brazil is extremely busy with taxis and private vehicles carrying hordes of Brazilians, heading across the river to buy electronics, clothing, tyres and basically anything desirable. We managed to find the correct customs office and after almost two hours we joined the traffic crossing the bridge, sadly looking at Brazil in the mirror.

Paraguay is immediately clearly a different creature to Brazil. Poorer, with a far more "indigenous" population and a more Third World feel. Touts hassled us and tried to have us to follow them to shops, then to parking, then to the mall. One stubborn character latched onto us and was determined to make money out of us one way or another. He insisted on riding his motorbike in front of us, trying to lead us to one of his little cash cows when he was trying to lead us right and we turned left he would quickly turn to get ahead of us, a big, ugly, reptilian estate agent smile on his otherwise human face. He feigned friendship, using little tactics to endear himself to us, little sacrifices which would ensure our loyalty. I was hoping his motorbike would explode between his legs causing a horrible, slow torturing crackling, burning, cockless death. The fantasies of a man who has been sitting in customs offices and queues, with restless kids, for the last 5 hours in heat close to 35°C. The Land

Rover looks expensive and we are the picture of wealth sold to South Americans. Almost every billboard has a picture of a blonde or a blonde family selling wealth and beauty, soap, real estate and beer. We pay a gringo tax everywhere and for every service. We are rich, obviously. We should pay more.

Luisa bought a large pink Sony laptop and a no-name tablet. It only took four hours of searching to confirm that the price we saw in the first store was a good price. Hand over cash, check stuff works, head back to Landy, thank God it is still there, buy a few shirts from the vendor who watched the truck, get the hell out of town. The choices were to tour more of Paraguay or head back to Argentina. Our priority now was to get down to Ushuaia. The GPS showed that there was a ferry ten-kilometres south of the city which led back to Argentina. We had spoken to many locals before we crossed the border, but no-one mentioned the ferry, they all said that the bridge was the only way over. We decided to trust the unreliable GPS and follow it down a road which ran parallel to the Rio Parana. The locals waved at us as we passed, and we would stop conversations just rolling by. The Landy really is a superstar on this continent. We found the ferry, no queue and a little customs office. We sent a kid off to buy us some Cola and waited half an hour for the ferry and then waited half an hour for the ferry to leave with only us and an Argentinean family. Paraguay remains on our list of countries to explore. Does a day trip count as being to a country? I don't really know, but we have the stamp in the passport, so we can tell people we have been there and leave out any details. Who will know any better?

16

Return To Argentina

Customs took five minutes, with no inspections and we were again in Argentina looking for a camp, but there was only one camp in Puerto Iguacu. We were shocked when we drove into the camp to see hundreds of campers. Overland trucks and Overlanders of every description, motorbikes, vans, motorhomes. French, German, Dutch, British. In Brazil, we had seen only that one overland truck in Iguacu and in total we met about four other Overlanders. Why on earth were these people not crossing into Brazil? Well, they had obviously heard and read the same crap we had heard and read. It is not true people. Finally, we were heading south through beautiful Northern Argentina. Plentiful camps and little German villagers and a road sign for every bump in the road. German farm stalls supplied us with amusement, cheese, bread and sausages as we enjoyed the vast green spaces. We camped at a gas station before heading to beautiful Gualeguaychu having heard that there was a Carnaval taking place, we booked some tickets and settled into a camp overflowing with Argentine holidaymakers. It had taken a while to find the camp at night and we had been amazed that women exercised alone in a park in the dark, something which is impossible in South Africa. South Africans are also famous for our love of meat, but I am afraid that we are lightweights compared to the Argentines. We would wake in the morning and by 9 AM our neighbours would have a huge fire going. By 10 AM huge slabs of meat would be tossed on the grill, liberally covered in coarse salt and a layer of flattened cardboard boxes to insulate the heat. Five men would spend the morning drinking beer and eating half a cow before retiring for a siesta in preparation for the Carnaval and the other half of the cow. All South American cultures have a huge appetite for beer, meat and music. None like to sleep at night, only between lunch and sunset. That is a gross generalisation perhaps only true on weekends or public holidays.

The Carnaval is held in a stadium built purely for that purpose. Three-quarters of a kilometre long with grandstands on either side of a thirty-metre-wide runway. The best seats are naturally more expensive and are located close to the judges. We bought the cheap seats and settled in for the spectacle. Most people, like me, think that Carnaval is only held in Brazil and while the Brazilians have the largest and best Carnavals they are at the tip of an ass shaking iceberg. Every country we have been to in South America has a Carnaval and the Carnaval in this little town was mind-numbingly fantastic. The most beautiful women with the most perfect bodies adorned floats which must have cost more than most buildings in town. Marie, Marie HEY! Mari, Mari, HEY! Boobs and ass and muscular men, a sea of shaking flesh, glitter and ostrich feathers. Mari, Mari, HEY! I had too many beers before we arrived and soon I was feeling drained by the excitement. Carnaval was made for cocaine and cocaine for Carnaval. This isn't a braai where you down a few six-packs and stare at the flames for a couple of hours. This is a state-sanctioned party; the entire and sole purpose of this exercise is to lose your mind and embrace the inner beast.

17

And Uruguay

We awoke hung-over, packed the Landy and decided to drive back to Brazil. If that is the show, a small Argentinean town can put on what the hell is Rio going to be like?

It was a decision which has become a typical example of our spontaneity. Instead of sticking to a fixed route or program, we tend to be reckless and whimsical. Without considering time or budget or commitments we jump headfirst into a new path if that path is appealing, adventurous and feels right. It is not the way these things should be done. It is exactly how these things should be done. It took two days to drive across Uruguay to get to the Brazilian border at Frontera/Riviera. We chose the shortest, most direct route through the farmlands where mostly only dirt tracks existed. Green parrots flew alongside us as we rumbled over terrible roads past herds of fat happy livestock. For most of the day, we did not see another soul and enjoyed the fresh country air, hoping that a Gaucho (cowboy) would stop us and invite us for a traditional Uruguayan Asado (braai). Uruguay apparently has some of the best meat in the world. We had tasted a few cuts and were pretty sure that South African meat is better but only just.

Eventually, the bad dirt road ended, and we were driving again on tar. The Landy was swaying a bit, which I thought was caused by the strong crosswind and as we were overtaking a motorcyclist our right rear tyre burst. The poor guy almost had a heart attack and I definitely felt my heart jump a few beats as I slowed the three-and-a-half-ton beast down by shifting down the gears and feathering the brakes. The last thing you want to do is slam anchors with a blowout. The tyre had exploded and was completely destroyed. We had not had a puncture in over 70 000 km's of driving with these mud tyres and I had been very careful to take care of them and visually inspect them for cracks and wear. I changed the tyre while balancing on the verge of the windy single lane road. The plan before leaving South Africa had been to change the tyres in Bolivia after Patagonia. The tyres still had plenty of tread when we left home even though they had done about 50 000 kms. We did not plan to tour so much of Brazil and had travelled almost 20 000 km's in South America since that day the Landy arrived in Montevideo. Eighteen thousand kilometres of that had been in Brazil.

The central border between Uruguay and Brazil has to be the strangest border we have been to. Strange because there really is no border in the traditional sense. There is a city and one side of the road is Uruguay and the other side is Brazil. Cross that road and your Uruguayan cell phone won't work, you pay in Reals and people speak Portuguese. We did not know this and only realised when we stopped to ask a tyre guy where we could buy tyres. He told us to go back to Uruguay where tyres were cheaper. What do you mean go back to Uruguay? Where the hell are we now? Brazil. The Brazilian tyre guy then closed up his shop and had us follow him back across the "border" and took us to a tyre shop where we found the correct size tyres and the shop closed for siesta which left us hanging around for a few hours. When the shop eventually reopened we bought one replacement tyre. I argued with Luisa that we should just change them all and swallow the cost, but the replacement tyre was US $209, and tyres were apparently half the price in Bolivia. We argued about it during the siesta, I was worried that if the one tyre went that the rest were ready to go. Luisa dug her heels deep, deep down. She would not budge and eventually, I gave in against my better judgment.

Finding Immigration and customs was not easy, we had to drive in circles to find the Uruguayan bureaucrats and another hour in circles to find their Brazilians, half cousins. Before we officially left Uruguay, we stopped at a supermarket to stock up. A homeless "car guard" came over to do what car guards do but he took the service a step further. He was trying to see inside the vehicle to the point that I had trouble getting out. The kid was probably high on basuco, a paste which is a by-product of cocaine manufacture. He was aggressive, and I responded aggressively. I was not in the mood for a pushy junkie after a day of arguing with Luisa and driving in circles. I walked him back away from the Landy and while I was checking that all the doors of the Landy were properly locked the bastard lunged at Keelan, who was walking away and spat on his neck. I saw red and was ready to rip the kids head off, but Luisa shouted when she saw my intent and I relaxed, remembering how the Uruguayans deal with their petty vagrant thieves. I still have a lot to learn about nonviolence.

18

Viva Brazil!

One of the towns which we had missed the first time in Southern Brazil was the town of Gramado, a German skiing town set up in the mountains above the rainforest. Driving up to Gramado, we had the most delicious fruit salad and strawberries and cream at one of many fruit stores along the road. The owners spoke to us in German, assuming that we were German. I replied in terrible German that we are South Africans. That was the first clue that we were "leaving" Brazil and entering a satellite German state. We stopped outside a very clean house with a manicured garden to ask a very blonde woman which way to go. The higher we climbed the mountain road the further we felt from Brazil until we reached the town at the top. There was almost no sign that we were still in South America. The buildings, signs, restaurants, hotels, street sign, everything was German. The campsite was perfectly clean and organised and comfortable. It was here that we met the non-showering German Overlanders in their Iveco camper. He had a large mop of curly red hair and a large belly and chatted with us for ages about travelling and Africa and Europe. It is one of the sweet tragedies of this kind of travel that you will meet amazing people and will part ways knowing that there is a 99.9% percent chance that you will never meet again. The town provided plenty of distractions and we visited many chocolatiers for free samples and often left with bags of goodies. It was the wrong time of year for snow sports, but a large indoor ski ramp was being built while we were there so soon there will be winter sports all year. Driving back down the mountain we felt as if we were returning to the messy, slightly chaotic Brazil we had grown to love. We managed to get as far as Florianopolis, where we ground to a halt. It was proving to be very expensive to attend the Carnaval in Rio and although we had a friend, in Rio trying to help us out we were not able to find any accommodation or Carnaval tickets which did not murder our budget. It did not help that the Rand had lost almost 40% to the Dollar since we left home. That was 40% of our money gone. The friend in Rio, Allan, was a great guy and fellow Overlander who we never actually met. He had seen us stuck in traffic in Rio while he waited for a bus and took note of our website address on the Landy. He messaged us and became our online guide to Brazil, giving tips on where to go and where to stay. He has also helped out other random friends we have referred to him. And he spends a lot of time helping people find hostels or whatever else they need for no other reason than that he is The Dude. We made some good friends in Florianopolis. It was an interesting time. Marcelo, an Uruguayan and his kids Laila and Gabriel where waiting in Floripa for their horrible little Jack Russell to recover from an illness. Sorry Laila, but that dog is a menace. Marcelo taught me how to braai meat like an Uruguayan, an instruction I sorely needed, he explained the different cuts of meat while spoiling me to a selection of fine imported beers, the kind I simply could not afford on my unemployed nomad budget. Floripa has a huge Carnaval, but it is the country's biggest gay Carnaval. The normal-looking guys walking around the campsite would transform into muscular women at night and would wander around acting camp and flashing their butts at people, stopping cars on the road to give them flowers and blowing kisses to all the men. Our kids were amused, as were we. A lawyer from Rio spent the days and nights walking around in a little white Speedo, disturbing when your chair puts you eye level with the inverted V logo. A dark-skinned man with a large belly and Abraham Lincoln beard spewed fire when we fed him a plate of curry we had made for the kids and an irritating, buzz kill English teacher hung on my ears, trying to impress his future father-in-law and his very young, rubber firm breasted fiancé while the father shot hateful glances at the gay boys prancing around, slapping each other butts and have a water fight.

Finally, we realised that the cost of going to Rio for the Carnaval would be just too much for us, we had enjoyed being back in Brazil though and stopped by Barry's house on our way back down to Uruguay. It was great to see him again and have some beer with his neighbours. Luisa bought a life-size concrete statue of a black girl we had often seen, chin in hand, waiting in many windows and patios for her beau to return. We simply did not have space for a chunk of concrete, no matter how cute Luisa thought it was. But, if you have learnt anything about Luisa, my friends, it is that no-one says no to Luisa, not when she wants something. Luisa gets what Luisa wants and she deserves the best the world and I can give, but why the hell does she never want anything reasonable.

We parked the Landy outside Marcelo's apartment in Rio Grande do Sul that little shit terrier ruining the night by getting sick again and having to be taken for a five-hour visit to the vet. If I have ever met an inconsiderate hound... Within a few days, we were back at our first camp in Brazil outside Cassino. It felt strange to be back in the camp, it felt like years but had only been four months since we had been there. The plan was to stay for two days then head to Uruguay, but Jessica became very ill one night. Any parent of a kid with an active imagination will know that sometimes kids just make shit up. Luisa had a sore back one morning and Jessica soon started complaining about a sore back. She had cried wolf a few too many times and we were not convinced that she was actually in any real pain. Until she vomited and then we had to move quickly. It was raining, and the tent was open and all our camping gear out, to pack up would have taken far too long so I went to the camp owners house and asked his son, Gabriel, if he could call a taxi for us. He asked what was wrong as it was about 23h00 and when I explained that Jessica was sick, he dropped everything, grabbed his car and raced us to the clinic in Cassino. The doctor did not speak English, so Gabriel stayed to explain the symptoms. The doctor diagnosed the problem as the appendix, dangerous; we had to get Jessica to the hospital in Porto Alegre as soon as possible. Gabriel took Keelan and me back to the camp to pack up the Landy while Luisa and Jessica waited for the ambulance. Gabriel then insisted on taking us to the city and the hospital. He stayed with us until the girls arrived and then explained the symptoms to the doctors. Only at 04h00 am after making sure that we were taken care of and asking if we had money, did he leave to go get two hours sleep before getting up to be at work by 07h00 am. Jessica was feeling better after an injection of Voltaren and the doctors booked her into the hospital and ordered every possible test of blood and urine, chest x-ray and an ultrasound scan. Luisa stayed with Jess while Keelan and I slept in the Landy in a car park across the road. In the morning Jessica felt better but the doctors ordered that she stay in hospital for a week to be observed. Though grateful for the care that Jessica was receiving, we were worried about how much the treatment was going to cost. It turned out that Jessica was dehydrated. For some reason, she just did not like drinking water and even though we all drank plenty of fluids, Jessica obviously was not drinking her water. I don't know what she was doing with it, but she was definitely not drinking it. Luisa stayed in a private room with Jessica the entire time and both were fed three meals a day. A group of clowns stopped by to entertain Jessica and returned with gifts and a get-well card. The nurses would pop in every hour and were friendly, gentle and caring. Keelan and I would drive into the city once a day to visit the girls and bring them clean clothing, snacks and whatever they asked for. At the end of the week, Jessica was discharged with a clean bill of health. Now for the moment of truth. We headed to the finance area near the exit and asked a finance lady for the bill. No, no bill. Are you sure? Yes. What about the room and the tests and the medicine? No, no bill. Had this happened in the USA our trip would have been over. But here in Brazil Universal Healthcare is alive and well. We returned to the camp and Gabriel's family had baked cupcakes for Jessica to celebrate her healthy return. Again, we cried when we left Brazil. Beautiful people, beautiful, wonderful, loving Brazil.

19

North to South

We returned to the camp in Punta del Este where the cyclone had threatened to drop a tree on us and while we were registering at reception a green Land Rover Defender pulled in. It had Brazilian plates and inside sat Isabella and Rafael. The Road God had seen our sadness when we left Brazil, so he sent us some Brazilians! They were driving down to Ushuaia and back up around the continent. We decided over some meat and wine that we would drive together as much as possible. They had some people to meet, and we were heading to Montevideo, so we made plans to meet up after Buenos Aires. We were invited by a group of Americans to join an Overlander hang out in Bariloche, which presented us with a bit of a problem. Bariloche is on the west coast of Argentina and we had planned to travel down the east coast. We spoke to the Brazilians, but they did not want to go to Bariloche first, so we agreed to split up and meet again for the drive up north.

Our route from Punta del Este took us back to Montevideo for another wild party with the guys from the hostel then a ferry ride back to Buenos Aires which we drove through and directly onto the road to Bariloche. About 200 km's west of Buenos Aires, a policeman, stopped us at a checkpoint and told us to pull over. He told us to wait and went to fetch a fat policeman. Fat policeman are almost 100% corrupt in my experience. All the problems I have ever had with corrupt cops have been with the fat ones. In Malawi, Mozambique, Tanzania and now in Argentina. Fat cops should be put on a diet and receive moral regeneration training. Criminals are better than corrupt fat cops because you expect the criminal to be criminal. Many corrupt fat cops are criminals in uniform, the worst type of criminal other than a criminal in a suit.

Fat cop called us over to his little white booth next to the road. He told us, in Spanish that our driving lights were off, and the fine was 900 pesos which worked out to almost double in South African Rand. Luisa flipped out completely. She started shouting at the guy that he was crazy. We stood outside his cubicle in full view of passing motorists and had a loud discussion in Afrikaans. Luisa was stomping the dust and refusing to pay a cent. We had never paid a bribe and this time was no different. We would make a scene and wait him out, but there was no way that we were going to hand over any money. Well, we didn't really have much on us anyway. The fat cop tried to get Luisa to calm down and step inside. He asked how much do you have, we said nothing. Nothing? Nothing. He told us to get lost, which we gladly did, this time with the lights turned on. We stopped in a little town full of Catholic statues and asked about a place to camp. The sweet people at the supermarket told us to camp at the IPF gas station just outside of town. Luisa was not really looking forward to gas station camping again, but we were surprised to find that the IPF had trees and a lawn, a playground, a braai area, Wi-Fi and nice clean toilets. It was a campsite with gas and it was free. We had a braai and set off the next morning for Bahia Blanca and the road to San Carlos de Bariloche. A massive storm blew at us; a huge black wall of cloud partly obscured the sun for most of the afternoon. Behind us it was a beautiful day, ahead of us rode the Four Horsemen. We had nowhere to take shelter amidst the grassy pampa. For an hour we drove towards the storm amazed by the theatre in the sky. First, we were hit by huge plops of rain, then the wind tripled its power and hail began to beat down on the Landy. The dry grassland was soon drenched, and the roads emptied as every vehicle pulled to the emergency lane. The area resembles Tornado Alley in the USA and we all had our eyes open for a twister. We had no way of knowing whether this area, did, in fact, suffer from tornados but after a while, we decided that we should keep on going. This is why we travel in a military-grade 4x4, when other vehicles can't continue we can and we should be able to drive through and out of most of what the road throws at us. The storm continued its natural show of power and beauty as we headed back onto the road and drove past cars whose owners had spread blankets and clothing onto the bodywork to protect from hail damage. The upper surfaces of the Landy are covered either in aluminium protection plates or the tent and accessories on the roof and the windscreen is almost vertical so hail damage does not really concern us. Flooding is a greater concern, but the road was built with run-off areas and was higher than the surrounding area. The storm washed us for the next three hours until we reached Neuquén after dark. We could not see any sign of a campsite, so we asked at a fuel station if we could camp and they agreed. In the morning we stepped into the little coffee shop and ordered some very expensive coffee while Luisa went on the internet. Her Mom wished us a happy anniversary. We had both forgotten! It was the 1st March 2013, our tenth anniversary and, thank God, we had both forgotten. We ordered an expensive breakfast to accompany the coffee and sheepishly celebrated our nuptials.

By that afternoon we would have driven through some spectacular lake areas and down into San Carlos de Bariloche, a European inspired skiing town set amongst an incredible setting of forest, lakes and snow-capped mountains. Arriving at camp, we met the group of American Overlanders and settled in for a few days of beer drinking, Asado and great conversation. Americans have always fascinated me.

The mountainous area around Bariloche seems like the perfect place to build a remote off the grid homestead to wait out the apocalypse. There is plenty of water and good fertile land for crops, sun in the summer and beautiful cold winters. We could grow our own food and have a large fireplace in front of a large comfortable bed. We could build and create everything we need; the stars could be our television. Horses and the Land Rover (the Defender is a civilian, military, or agricultural vehicle depending on your need) could do a lot of the heavy work and vegetables, rabbits, chickens and pigs would keep us well fed. We would need a few large dogs and a few smaller hunting dogs. Finding the dogs would be no problem as there are many pure-bred strays roaming the campsites in Bariloche. Our camp with the Americans had Great Danes, Doberman, Saint Bernard and German Shepherds eyeing our Asado hungrily every night.

South of Bariloche is the town of El Bolson and south of El Bolson, you will find a magnificent national park hugging Lago Puelo. I don't know why but the park is not promoted in the guide books and we only decided to drive through the park on a whim. The entry fee was quite expensive, but no limit was stipulated, we could have stayed for a week and not have paid a cent more. There are different types of camps set along the shore of a beautiful clear lake. Some camping is free and has no facilities and we found an idyllic secluded spot with snow-capped mountains in the background and a pebble beach for the kids to explore. I took the axe off the Land Rover and began hacking at a large tree trunk lying near our camp. I felt great, truly manly, bearded, long hair, shirt off, a Viking in his natural environment. An American, who had a terribly violent experience in Peru, had taught me in Bariloche how to use an axe. He had been raised in a forest and was a carpenter and with his guidance, I was finally able to chop logs into firewood like a proper woodsman. A trout would have been excellent on the fire, but I failed to catch one and we grilled excellent Argentinean beef instead. The nights were cool even in February, but we cuddled under our down duvets in our rooftop tent, keeping each other warm, smelling of smoke and eating Toddy chocolate biscuits while planning our route south to Ushuaia.

Ushuaia is the most southerly town in the world and an attractive goal for travellers on the PanAm. But, being that far south and with winter approaching we needed to get down through Patagonia and back up out of Bear Grylls territory before the snow set in and our African bodies were found frozen next to Ruta 40. The Southerly wind blasted us along the entire Ruta 40 south to Ushuaia. A constant headwind in a heavily loaded, brick-shaped truck is not ideal for making good time or saving precious money. In Rio Mayo, we would make a great discovery - Patagonia Lamb. We walked into a small supermarket looking for dinner and asked at the butchery if they had lamb. Well, we did not know the Spanish word for lamb and had left the Spanish/English dictionary in the Land Rover. So, we asked 'do you have BAAAAAAAA?', 'What'? Asked the amused butcher while his other customers giggled. 'Do you have BAAAAAAA?' He made us repeat the question three times before bringing a fresh Cordero out of the large stainless-steel fridge. Yes, they did, and it was very cheap. Luisa bought almost an entire animal and some vegetables which we prepared over a fire that night in a rundown little camp just outside Perito Moreno, the town, not the glacier. Giddy with lamb lust we set out in the morning to buy more, just in case Rio Mayo was the only lamb town in Patagonia.

The road ran parallel to the Andes and was mostly dead straight, dry and windy. A few tough animals grazed along the road and we lusted after their flesh. There is something about the cold, dry expanse which makes you crave grilled meat and the Patagonians have perfected the Asado, which is more than a meal or a method of preparing meat, it is a deeply ingrained part of the culture, a celebration of survival, a reward amidst the cold, brutal beauty of Patagonia. Although Patagonia is split by the Andes between the Argentines and the Chileans, they really are one people, with an equal love of the land separated by politics. The Chileans are more chilled out and friendly though and we would learn to enjoy chatting with the Chilean border officials. There are also large no-man lands between the many borders spanning Patagonia, a clear sign that the two countries have a long history of dispute.

The Ruta 40 between Perito Moreno town and Tres Lagos is mostly horrible washboard dirt. The wind blew violently and the temperature in the shade was close to zero. Our red fuel light came on, 60 km's before Tres Lagos and I had forgotten to fill the reserve tank or the jerry cans. The distances were not too great between fuel stations, but the wall of wind halved our fuel efficiency. As I was driving up a hill contemplating the consequences of running out of fuel the rear of the Landy suddenly bucked out and shook violently. I eased the Landy to a stop and climbed out fearing the worst. The left rear tyre had disintegrated as badly as the right rear tyre had done in Uruguay. Completely beyond repair. I secured the vehicle with rocks behind the three good tyres and jacked the vehicle up with the eight-ton bottle jack. I replaced the wheel with the spare which I carried on the bonnet, the icy wind making my hands numb in the shade of the Land Rover. A Chilean Wicked Camper carrying two bearded Swiss brothers stopped to ask if they could help. A few other vehicles had just rushed by covering me in dust and stones. I thanked them, but we had the situation under control, it was just a blowout. I threw the destroyed tyre onto the bonnet and carried on, without a spare tyre and running out of fuel. As the sun set, the fuel needle sunk to its limit and we eventually rumbled into little, dry and desolate Tres Lagos. There was one gas station, just outside of town and we pulled up, relieved and thirsty for a celebratory beer. The bearded Swiss brothers were parked by the pump, looking concerned. Do you have money? No, but we have some wine. Do you have food? No. Ah. We paid to fill their tank with enough fuel to get to El Chalten, the town at the base of Fitz Roy Mountain and invited them to stay with us at the camp in town, an invitation they gladly accepted. We paid for their camping and invited them to dinner. A French cyclist had already erected a tent in the camp and he was also in need of help to repair his broken bicycle. Luisa cooked pasta while we organised the "rescue" of the Frenchman with the Beards who had room in their camper to transport the Frenchman and his bicycle to El Chalten. The Beards drank the red wine they had given us and shivered. They were both wearing short pants and thin jackets. Do you have long pants? No. Do you have winter jackets? No.

Perito Moreno Glacier lies almost 60 km's east of El Calafate, a beautiful town full of tourists and horribly impatient Argentineans. The fee to enter the park to view the glacier is not pocket-friendly and we had heard that there are ways to sneak into the park. Apparently, you could either drive in through the un-gated access road after 7 pm or before 6 am. If you drive in at night you camp in the park but run the risk of being booted out if caught. We decided to sneak in at 6 am after driving to the gates at 5 pm and getting a map from a ranger. The first left before the park leads to a dirt road and we drove this road looking for a place to free camp amongst the grassy fields. Fifteen kilometres of searching and finding nowhere suitable a little house loomed on a hill. A sign outside said camping. The little farm was run by leathery old Patagonian cowboys who hung out in the kitchen of a surprisingly modern little establishment with huge windows facing the Andes, a display cupboard full of fossils and antiques and a little pub which did not serve any drinks. A woolly lamb bounced around us and begged to be scratched. It sniffed at our feet and apparently passed the time pretending to be a dog. The little lamb and her Mom slept under the Landy that night when they realised that they could not climb the ladders. We had a small meal and went to sleep early, dreading the 4 am wake up and cold. The glacier is spectacular, and we had it entirely to ourselves. The sun was still trying to climb the Andes as we hurried down the deserted tourist walkways until eventually, we were face to face with the frozen blue river. With no-one around to pollute the air with noise we could hear water running inside the glacier, ice cracking and we waited, hoping for a large chunk to break off and entertain us with its demise. Luisa and I stripped down to our undies and Keelan took some photos of us posing near-naked and ice-cold, this action needs no explanation, getting your kit off in inappropriate places is entirely appropriate.

Our first border crossing into Chile was at Rio Turbio, a soul-less industrial town which we struggled to drive through because tyre burning factory workers had blocked the only road in and out. There were campsites along the road, but Luisa decided that they were not nice enough and, as it turned out, they were all closed. Driving around looking for a place to stay for the night, we eventually found a fuel station with very slow internet and searched for a campsite or any sleeping recommendation from other Overlanders. None. The sun was setting, and we decided to take another stab at driving through the town towards the border. The tyre burners had gone home for dinner, we drove through and up towards a hotel the GPS insisted was next to the border. We found an abandoned ski lodge and decided to camp in the parking lot, but then we saw movement inside the building and a lady came out to ask us if we needed something. The hotel was open and inside everything was as it should be. We stood behind our sad-looking kids and asked if we could camp in the parking lot. The poor lady looked completely confused that these gringos would be living the tramp life. OK, she said. No problem. Now Chile has very strict laws about fresh produce, meat and seeds being carried over the border. We pulled out our little braai and began cooking the remainder of our lamb and chicken. A group of workers arrived, Argentineans contracted to build roads, they were staying at the hotel and were very amused by us making Asado in the parking lot. They went to dinner and came back to drink wine with us and offer cocaine which we politely refused.

20

The Great Patagonia Rubber and Rim Fail

Our new friend and hostel owner Eduardo had kindly taken us to six stores and the local Gomeria (tyre repair) in the hope of finding replacement rims for our Landy. The business was being run out of a little old couple's backyard, old tyres and rims were stacked in every available space, and four very dirty men were doing what tyre guys do. The sweet old man said "sure, no problem, I can get those, come back tomorrow at 3 pm". What a relief.

We had come to Punta Arenas with the promise of a duty-free area, Zona Franca and dreams of cheap rubber to re-shoe our trusty Defender.

We drove into the Zona Franca early on a crisp blue morning singing along to Queens Bohemian Rhapsody. All smiles and headbanging. At first glance, it looked as if we were in for a short morning of rubber shopping, perhaps another night in the town and then on down to Ushuaia. All the major tyre brands logos were blowing in the breeze and we ran into the Brazilian couple we had not seen since Uruguay. They too had a couple of blowouts and by the end of the day had their new tyres, a couple of new sleeping bags (they had frozen their Brazilian, we have never been below 15' Celsius, butts off in Ushuaia) and were back on the road the next morning. We were not so lucky.

The tyres I wanted were found in the Goodyear shop. 33 x 12.5 R15 Mud Terrain beauties. Big, badass tyres designed to crawl over everything and make you and your truck look legendary in the process. Easy, cheap. OK, put them on. No sir, I think there may be a problem. What problem, no problem, Tranquilo, put them on. No sir, your rims are too narrow, it's dangerous. Here, take these 31's they will be fine. You don't have 32's? No sir and neither does anyone else. Here, take these 31's they will be fine.

A quick poll on the interwebs and those in the know different things. What about load rating they say, you need an F rated tyre not a C. This is starting to get complicated. We say OK, let's sleep on it. The next day we decided to go hunting for steel fifteen-inch Land Rover rims. How difficult could it be? We searched for two days down every back street, scrapyard (where Luisa stood on a rusty nail which went straight through her boot and 1 cm into her foot) Gomeria and parts dealer in town. We heard about a scrapped Land Rover down the road next to the DVD shop and drove around for 2 hours trying to find it. How is this possible? It should take no more than a quick web search and a phone call to have the size you want, in the colour you want to be delivered to your door at the price you want. At least that is how it works back in sunny South Africa. But they don't speak rapido Espanol back home and they don't take a bloody siesta for half the day and there are a lot more Land Rovers roaming SA's streets.

Eventually, I admit partial defeat. Luisa says take the 31's and let's get on with our lives. No, I say. They are small and weak and not worthy of my Landy. OK, the second choice is a set of 7.50m X 16 truck tyres, the kind they use in the military and the Camel trophy. Able to carry three Landy's on one tyre, a kickass pattern and half the price. Great, now we just need to get some 16" Land Rover rims. Enter the sweet old man. Sure, no problem. Come tomorrow at 3 pm. We go see him at 3. Come back at 6. We return at 6. No, not yet, come back at 8. Actually, come back tomorrow at 10, 3 and 6 and 8 and repeat the next day for best results. By day three of this, I was ready to explode. Sunday afternoon and Luisa and I take a taxi to the local supermarket for dinner. Hey, that Gomeria is just down the road, let's go see if they have the rims. What do you think our chances are? 10%? So, I walk, and Luisa hobbles two kilometres down the road. Shit babe, sorry, I was sure it was a lot closer. We arrive at the old man's prepared for disappointment but, believe it or not, there they are, being painted, ready to be collected the next day and looking OK. We return in the morning. The sweet old lady fleeces us. I cannot stand in her kitchen and negotiate; the smells are just too awful. We say our goodbyes at the hostel and drive to the fitment centre. Great news, two of the rims are too out of shape to be balanced. $@#@&@*^!!!! Luckily an English-speaking local (who we should have met on day one if the Gods were smiling on us, which they obviously weren't) directs us to a professional engineering firm in town who can shave and balance the rims. The kind of engineering firm who could easily have modified our original rims to fit the 33" tyres. We return the next day, collect the repaired rims, drive to the fitment centre and they balance and fit the wheels and tyres. All good, let's do a quick test drive and hit the road. We get out onto the road and the Landy is shaking and making horrible clunking noises. Please, not the diff!! It turns out that the rims are old Chilean Military and are just too small to accommodate the Defender brake callipers. Tyres off and back to the engineer who says manana (tomorrow). The fact that Luisa and I have not murdered each other by now is a miracle. She turns to me and says the words I have been dreading. "31's"!

The road from Punta Arenas to Ushuaia involves a ferry crossing, 280 kms of tar and over 100 kms of bad dirt road. The new "biscuit" 7.50 x 16 tyres seemed to be coping with the road and load, but it will take a while to get used to the whine of the tyre as opposed to the hum of the mud terrains. The Landy felt nimble but not as surefooted and definitely not as beautiful as she was on the fatter tyres. About 60 km's out of Ushuaia the rear of the Landy began to vibrate very badly. We stopped to check the tyres and rims, but there were no obvious signs of damage or punctures. I cautiously drove back onto the tar and 50metres down the road the Landy shook violently and the rear right tyre let out a loud hiss, the Landy slumped and shuddered. I carefully braked and pulled over onto the shoulder which was unfortunately banked. On closer inspection, we found that the rim of the rim had sheared off and the tyre had deflated. I climbed under the Landy and weighed up our options. Eventually, we decided to unload the rear load area and drive with the flat tyre 20 metres further to a more level area of the shoulder. Squashed me would not be popular with the kids; maybe even the wife would not be pleased. Keelan slowed traffic by waving an orange t-shirt and I struggled in the dirt to replace the wheel.

An hour later we rolled into Ushuaia, Fin del Mundo, The End Of The World, the capital of Tierra del Fuego and the most southern city in the world. Instead of joy, I was feeling irritated and disappointed. Trying to save some money and some bad decisions had put us in a very horrible position. We now had tyres I hated, wheels I could not trust and a long way to go before we could replace them. I also had the almost impossible task of finding a replacement wheel in the most southern city in the world where Land Rover parts are extremely rare and extremely expensive. While other travellers were off exploring the mountains and national parks or planning trips to Antarctica I was driving around searching for a Land Rover needle in a Toyota haystack and after three days, we were no closer to a solution and Luisa was giving me the evil eye. Our options were running out. I had been to a tour operator who ran Land Rovers and he had some spare wheels and he might have sold me one for about US$300 as a last resort. The price was very high, but it was the replacement price and he was not trying to rip me off. I was considering our options and drove to the Supermarket to buy some groceries. A Defender 110 was parked outside, and we parked next to her as is the Land Rover custom. When we emerged from the store we found the owner David, who had just completed a world tour in his TD5, packing his groceries away. We chatted about the Landy's for a while and I mentioned my dilemma with the wheels. David had come across a British run classic vehicle rally on the road south and he knew that they were in town, that they were supported by Land Rover Defenders and that they were soon shipping out. I invited him to stay with us at an apartment we were renting at a hostel and after dropping off his bags we set off to look for the Brits in his 110. It was a stroke of luck that I had run into David and another bit of luck when we entered a hotel as the rally head mechanic, Charles, was leaving. Sure, he said. 'We are just leaving to put all the vehicles in shipping containers, an hour later and you would have missed us completely'. David and I followed the convoy up to the loading area outside town. One of the Defenders had a puncture, but the wheel was in perfect order. How much do you want for the wheel I asked? Well, the replacement cost is GBP30.00 so you can give me US$40.00. I gave him US$50.00 for the wheel and tyre, thanked them deeply and earnestly for saving my butt, and my wallet and David and I returned to the hostel for a very bloody steak and a few too many celebration beers. Thanks to the Land Rover community I did not have to brave leaving Patagonia without a spare tyre. The Land Rover community is an unofficial backup team and I have learnt that these passionate guys and girls will always be there for a fellow Landy driver. They will help wherever and whenever they can and if they can't help they will know someone who can.

21

North Bound

Heading north was a relief. The snow was getting thicker on the mountains and we now had to retrace our steps to Bariloche. We continued to get punctures as the standard Land Rover rims were tubeless and the bloody awful 7.50 R16 tyres were tube type. It felt like I was changing tyres every few hundred-kilometres and searching for tyre shops to repair the tubes daily. I dared not drive faster than 80 kph for fear that the tyres would fail and send us either into the path of an oncoming truck or down the side of a cliff, or even just rolling, destroying our truck and probably ourselves. I derided myself daily for allowing our safety to be so terribly compromised. And each puncture was a sharp blow to a very sore spot.

In Puerto Natales, we put on our hiking boots and climbed Torres Del Paine. The 20-kilometre climb is done in three stages. The first is a long, slow, torturous climb up a hill then down a steep path to the first base camp. At the first resting spot, we had lunch with an Argentinean couple, geologists, who we had met at a camp in Puerto Natales. Together we climbed the second wooded stage which reminded me a lot of the Skeleton Gorge route up Table Mountain from Kirstenbosch Gardens. The third stage was a steep section of grey rocks and a muddy path. Then a stumble over enormous grey boulders and around a corner to the pool below the fingers of the Torres Del Paine. Again, Luisa and I stripped down to our swimming costumes and posed for Keelan, a hundred eyes asking their brains what the hell we were doing. I resisted the urge to go for a swim in the frigid water and tried to protect Luisa's remaining honour while we re-dressed. The kids had handled the climb without any problems, and Keelan had done half of the route without shoes on. We started calling him the Hobbit when he started to do all the hikes barefoot even over sharp rocky terrain. The geologists schooled us and the kids about the rock formations and the erosion which created the fingers. It was one of the best classes the kids have ever attended and an example of the type of learning we could achieve outside of the traditional classroom. Here they could see and feel the subject and had earned the right to enjoy what very few kids can.

Heading back onto the Ruta 40 in the Landy, our legs wooden from the climb, a hitchhiker stood with thumb in the air at the turnoff to El Calafate. The bearded man was wearing a black cowboy hat and Luisa recognised him as Rob, a fantastically irreverent and humorous New Zealander who we had first met in Punta Arenas at the hostel and again at Puerto Natales. I gave him the "sorry we are full" signal but Luisa then told me that it was Rob. Are you sure, I asked? If we go back and it isn't him, we will have to give the guy a lift anyway. No, she was sure. We turned around and drove back to find a grinning Rob and his girlfriend Fallon. The sun was going to set, and they had been standing there for hours. We managed to squeeze their huge backpacks into the rear area and loaded them in the back with the kids for the drive to Tres Lagos and the camp where we had fed and clothed the Beards. In the morning we strapped the backpacks to the front of the Landy and headed back up the horrible dirt road to Perito Moreno town. Again, we almost ran out of fuel. When will I learn? For 80 km's the fuel gauge showed that we were completely empty, I slowed down to 60 kph, we freewheeled downhills and tried to drive as economically as possible and just when I thought we would grind to a halt, when Rob was offering to hike to the next fuel station, we rounded a corner and there stood our salvation. Cheap, lovely, golden diesel. We were low on cash and I accepted some money from Rob for fuel though I felt like a proper dick taking money from hitchhikers and I promised him that I would repay him with a bottle of booze. As far as I can remember, I still owe him that bottle.

That night we reached the little camp in Perito Moreno and slept soundly knowing that the worst of the Ruta 40 was behind us and that soon we would cross into the Carretera Austral. I would have enjoyed Rob and Fallon's company through the Austral, but we just did not have space for two extra people and their luggage for an extended period. In the morning they walked off to hitch a ride or catch the bus and we drove past them feeling terrible for not taking them with us. I almost stopped for them, Luisa knew this, and she gave me THE look.

22

The Carretera Austral

One last day in Argentina and the weather in the little border town was serene, shining spring, the colours electric autumnal leaves and blue skies. Luisa and I were having a debate. We knew how strict the Chileans were about the food being taken into the country, but Luisa had eight kilograms of lamb and she was insisting that she was going to smuggle it into the Carretera Austral by freezing it, folding it in newspaper and hiding it in the rooftop tent. I was dead set against the idea. The fine if caught trying to smuggle lamb into Chile was about US$1,000. Luisa called me a pussy and told me to grow a pair. Now apart from the fine I actually do respect and understand Chile's efforts to protect her agriculture, but Luisa is a lamb addict and a bad person. Short of tempting physical violence, there is not much that will change Luisa's mind when she channels the stubborn beast within. It is no longer about the lamb or being right, it is a matter of winning, a battle of egos. Fine, but you will pay the frikken fine. We approach the border. I am trying to be cool, but I am as nervous as a Pakistani heroin mule. We fill out the immigration forms while I scan the area for sniffer dogs. We lie on the declaration forms, nothing to declare. The lovely lady asks me to open the Land Rover. Do you have any meat? I twitch and blush, I try to act cool, but her training kicks in. Jessica was not told about the lamb because she would definitely snitch, Keelan knows, but he has been told to sit and wait until we leave. He is not even allowed to look at the Landy. Paranoia is a terrible thing. The customs lady digs around and finds some firewood on the roof of the Landy. She confiscates the wood and, presumably she thought I was trying to keep the wood hence the weirdness, she let us go. Luisa was victorious as we drove into the Carretera Austral. It is official though. No matter how much I need the cash there is no way that I could ever pretend to be that Pakistani mule. I was brainwashed very well by the conservative masochists who designed and implemented the Apartheid education system.

Driving into the Austral, we pass little crowds of European hitchhikers lining the road. Sorry, we are full. Onto a washboard dirt road and down along a winding, dusty road to tough Cochrane, a town built for harsh weather and inhabited by people who know how to survive the Patagonian winters. The supermarket sells shotguns, beer, camping equipment, cheese, milk and LAMB. Cheap, fresh delicious lamb. And plenty of it. I give Luisa THE look. Luisa pretends not to notice. She is too busy buying more lamb. A fellow Overlander had told us about a camp 60-kilometres south of Cochrane at a place called Rio Nardis. We arrived at the gravel road to the farm as the sun was setting, crossed a swaying suspension bridge and drove past a few farms, doubting that we were heading in the correct direction, until we reached a sign saying Rio Nardis. Eventually, the road led into a farm where a pack of dogs and a young farmer met us and led us across a field to the camp which turned out to be the most beautiful secluded camp we had ever stayed in. That far south most of the camps have a Refugio, a little building providing shelter should the weather turn nasty. This camp had a Refugio with a wood-fired oven, large windows for admiring the mountains and books and board games to keep the mind busy should you be trapped indoors. About 20 metres in front of the Refugio there was a fire pit surrounded by log chairs and about 20 metres behind the Refugio there was a beautiful wooden structure with a large fireplace and an Asado area. We grilled some lamb, drank Austral beer, chatted happily and awoke the next day to blue skies and green lawn. I spent the day cleaning the Landy with Luisa and listening to the Dave Matthews Band. We did not want to leave. I planned to go fishing the next day, maybe we could grill something other than lamb, but that night the weather changed, and we spent the next two days cooped up in the Refugio, playing Rummikub, hoping that the rain would not become snow. The Landy was refusing to start and I was starting to worry that we might be stuck with an electrical problem very far from any type of modern workshop. I tested the batteries which were fine and was confident that the starter was doing its job. Luisa, being less mechanically sensitive, managed to get the Landy going by pumping the gas pedal and turning the engine over for half a minute.

The Carretera Austral is mind-numbingly beautiful and, heading north, we would often round a bend to be amazed by a beautiful lake and a sheer drop. Set along the lower spine of the Andes where the tail of the submerged serpent reaches the sea, the Carretera Austral is a rocky mountainous route where blue glacier water rolls over grey rocks between green forests. The area faces an ecological disaster if the government and corporations of Chile go ahead with their plans to build dams, or represas in Spanish, which will flood the valleys and destroy the homes and farms of many. Streams and rivers which have carved their way to the sea over millions of years would become submerged and lost to history. The love of the soil and land lives in the bones of these secluded, hardy people and their opposition to the dams is resolute and, I suspect, they would likely take to guerrilla action against the authorities if the building of the dams is approved. Patagonia Sin Represas! Patagonia Sin Represas! Patagonia Without Dams!

The weather continued to be wet and cold; often we would wake in the morning with ice stalactites hanging inside the tent, ice which would melt with the rising sun and drip ice-cold into our sleeping faces. We continued to have punctures, the inner tubes becoming a patchwork of repairs. Our progress was slow, and we were surprised to reach an excellent tar road and little towns where we could stop and watch a rodeo or stock up on supplies. Being late in the season, we were finding that many camps were closed, and we were spending a lot of time in the evenings trying to find a place to sleep. A very well rated camp outside of the little city of Chaiten was closed, and as the sun was setting we doubled back to a national park camp we had seen along the road. The camp seemed closed. Luisa lifted the heavy boom, and we drove in to find unlocked Refugio's and, as the rain began to fall again, decided to camp next to one of the Refugio's and leave a note and a few pesos for the ranger. I started a fire which smoked out the entire Refugio and while I was swinging the door to get the smoke out I heard a hissing sound and turned in time to see the Landy slump on yet another fucking puncture. With a few beers in my belly, a smoking fire, falling rain and a growing anger, I jacked up the Landy to change the tyre. As soon as I removed the bastard tyre the jack slid out in the mud and the Landy fell onto her axle in the mud. Had I been under the Landy I would have been crushed. I took the spade off the side of the canopy and dug a hole in the mud deep enough to attach the spare wheel to the hub, then engaging low range and diff lock drove the Landy out of the hole. When we eventually ate I was exhausted and covered in mud. It is in those moments when everything is going wrong, that you want to throw in the towel and that it is the most important to remember why you have chosen this life that you are loved and love in return and that, eventually, all will be just fine. We woke in the morning to the ice and the dripping to find that there was a ranger on duty and instead of being livid that we had broken in, he had opened the bathrooms and turned on the geysers. After a good shower and packing up we drove to the ranger station to ask what we needed to pay. The ranger told us that the park was closed, and he could not give us a receipt, and therefore we did not have to pay. That wonderful man was exactly what I needed to re-motivate myself and return to the road.

Just south of El Bolson we crossed back into Argentina, and as we entered El Bolson we saw a Land Rover Defender 110 parked next to the road. We stopped to chat with the owners, Overlanders from Austria who never stayed at campsites and only ever free camped. They had hacked into some free WIFI, and we chatted while their emails downloaded. A few kilometres down the road we spotted another Defender 110 belonging to Paul and Helen, British Overlanders who had driven across Russia (where they had hit a horse) and were driving south from the USA en-route to Ushuaia. They were having problems with a shredded turbo hose, and we suggested that they camp with us at a camp we knew of on the road to Bariloche. They needed WIFI and we invited them for a braai. They followed us, and we drove into the camp to find a Land Rover Discovery belonging to a member of the Land Rover Club Argentina parked outside the brewery. The driver came to look at our Defenders, and when he heard that Paul was having problems, he made a few phone calls. Within twenty minutes a very tall, thin man in a Defender appeared, looked at the hose, disappeared and re-appeared with a replacement hose. Land Rover people. Amazing. We braaied and solved the world's problems. I was inspired by Paul and we wished each other God's speed before heading our separate ways. Paul had terrible luck in Patagonia and after two accidents spent the winter in Puerto Natales rebuilding his rear axle in a frozen Patagonian campsite.

We continued north, smitten by the landscape just north of Bariloche, eventually arriving in Mendoza and reuniting with our precious Brazilian friends and an American couple, Luis and Lacey, who we had met in Bariloche with the other American Overlanders. We partied with the Brazilians and Americans, drank excellent red wine, beer and tequila, I fell off my chair and someone fell out of a hammock, Luisa made Southern Fried Chicken and we gave the American a hard time about his Toyota while he secretly lusted after our Defenders. For reasons which do not make any sense, Defenders were not sold in the USA after 1997 and the British trucks are as sought after as G-Wagons. I did some work on the Landy and after a few days we left, the Brazilians taking a Northerly route and us taking an easterly route into Chile.

23

A High-Altitude Breakdown

The road between Mendoza, Argentina and Santiago, Chile traverses one of the most spectacular mountain passes in the world. The road winds like a 100-kilometre snake down the Chilean side of the mountain and, luckily for us, we were driving up the Argentine side and down into Chile. At the base of a long mountain pass, we stopped to put in fuel. I was waiting in the wrong queue and quickly reversed into an eighteen-wheeler which had snuck up and parked me in. The impact broke the sunglasses on my head as I head-butted the ceiling and tore a gash in our aluminium canopy. Had the angle of contact been 5°C different we would have smashed our propane gas tank against the truck and possibly caused an explosion at a gas station. Nice driving Graeme. We were rushing to get to the border before the sunset and because the road is so treacherous the Argentine side is open during the day and the Chilean side open at night.

We pulled into a large customs building at about 3300 metres above sea level. The place was large and modern but deserted; an official told us to continue on the road and as we returned to the Landy Jessica noticed that the right rear tyre was flat. I changed the tyre, sweating and cursing, then we drove and upwards through the barren mountainous landscape. There were a few little towns along the way, but mostly the freezing, dusty landscape was devoid of any animal or plant life and seemed completely inhospitable. I don't know why but I turned to Luisa and told her that we need to be prepared for any bad luck and when something happens we must stop, drop and roll. Assess the situation and react calmly. We were ten kilometres from the border, struggling up a very long and steep hill when a loud alarm sounded. The alarm was from an engine management system, the Little Black Box, which I installed when I bought the Landy to monitor the coolant, oil and battery. I pulled to the curb immediately. I actually do not want to relive this moment but will suffer through for your sake, dear reader. The coolant was pouring out of the elevated water tank at the back of the engine. If I had not installed the LBB the standard Land Rover temperature gauge would only have alerted me when the engine was hot, not when the coolant was low, and I would have cooked my engine. We looked back at the valley while we assessed the situation. We had a few litres of water with us, do we risk trying to get over to the border, or do we head back into one of the small towns to look for shelter? As the sun would soon set we choose to head back down. I topped up the water tank with 5litres of water and managed to get the sluggish Landy back onto the road and heading downhill. Within five kilometres the alarm sounded again, and I pulled over into a large emergency area. We looked around and saw only an abandoned farmhouse and dry red mountains surrounding us. I took the blue water jerry can off the roof and told Luisa that Keelan and I would go looking for more water. I told her to hoot repeatedly if she had any problems and I would run back. As I turned to leave a huge explosion shook the valley. Spinning around I saw a huge plume of dust and smoke rising from the side of the mountain 500 metres away. Unseen road workers had seen that we had stopped for a while and had begun demolition work. The dust and smoke hung in the air, and I was reminded of Salvador Dali painting. When our heart rates returned to normal Keelan, and I set off down a hill and across a rocky field, over broken rail tracks and to the edge of a mountain where a red river ran back to Mendoza. We searched for a safe path down the steep bank and noticed footprints and the cattle hoof prints. The water was freezing, and I tried my best to fill the jerry can with clean water. Stretched over rocks, my muscles burning from the exertion of balancing and filling the jerry can, within ten minutes we had thirty litres of water and began the walk back to the Landy. I filled the water tank and we headed back down to the next town. What we needed was the internet which would give us access to opinions about what was wrong with the Landy and what we could do to fix it. I suspected that the problem was the thermostat which is supposed to open and close according to the temperature of the coolant and thus regulate the cooling of the coolant. If the thermostat was not opening, then the water would not flow or cool. At the first town, we found a horrible hotel and small backpackers. Neither had the internet, and both were expensive. I remembered passing another town on the way up to the border and we decided to head there to seek better luck. The Landy was now behaving and the coolant stayed in the system as we drove into the next little town in complete freezing darkness. Luisa spotted a blue sign. Penitentes. A light was burning, and we parked outside. The manager's name was Mariano, luckily, he spoke English and we explained the problems that we were having. I asked him if they had internet and he said yes. I asked him how much the rooms were, and he told me it was roughly US$150.00 for a room. We asked him if we could sleep in the parking lot and pay him to use the internet. He looked at us for a short while. No, you can have the room for free, it is no problem. We could not believe our luck. The kids were deposited in the room with some sandwiches and Luisa and I began searching the internet for clues. I suspected that the problem was altitude related, but unfortunately, most of the Landy gurus on the internet never get to explore high mountain passes and most told us that the head gasket was gone, which would have been very bad news. I did not believe that the head gasket was the problem and so the next day we searched for a way to bypass for the thermostat. (Two years later I realised that was the day the Mass Air Flow sensor failed which reduced the Landy's power output at altitude significantly). In many cars, you can remove the thermostat from the housing, but in a TD5 the housing is sealed. We would need to remove the thermostat housing, carefully cut it open and glue the housing back together after removing the thermostat. I lay underneath the Landy and fiddled with the awkwardly angled hose clamps holding the thermostat while Luisa knelt on the bonnet, providing resistance and encouragement from above. Mariano had made us eggs and hot chocolate for breakfast and called us in for a lunch of cheeseburgers and milkshake. An old man across the road supplied us with some magical poxypol glue and Mariano and I glued and reinforced the hollow housing with large hose clamps and duct tape. Penitentes was a ski lodge but had not had snow for three years. A maintenance crew were the only other inhabitants of the hotel and they spent their days working on the ski lifts. That night the workers invited us to an Asado and Mariano supplied us with large cold beers. Luisa helped the workers start a fire, and they tried to act cool while my Ginger Ninja schooled them in fire-making. The next morning the thermostat housing was replaced sans thermostat and we left Mariano with gratitude. He did not ask us for a cent and had taken very good care of us. The reward for being a great human is great Karma, and one day I hope to have the opportunity to repay his kindness.

Nervously we drove back up the mountain towards the border, past where the workers had shaken the valley, up past where we stopped for water, up past the customs area where we had the flat tyre, up past where we broke down, new ground, past haunted dilapidated corrugated rail tunnels hanging onto the mountain, through a rock tunnel and down to a long queue of trucks and cars at the shared Argentine/ Chilean border. I was relieved to have made it up the highest point of the pass without losing any more coolant. The repair was working and ruled out a head gasket failure. Luisa went ahead to figure out the exit/entry procedure and within an hour we were sitting in heavy traffic on the serpentine road. Luisa had booked an apartment in Concon, a Chilean coastal town and we were going to spend two weeks there, getting our lives back in order and working on the Landy. In 180 km's we went down from 3500 metres to sea level. The Landy was running cool but very well and we reached the apartment with a huge sigh of relief and a deep swig of beer.

Concon is a grey little town on the Pacific coast and was typically Chilean rustic, built poorly of wood and strange angles. I took the bus to Santiago to search for spare parts while Luisa caught up with work and the kids did schooling. Santiago has some very beautiful neighbourhoods, and I enjoyed the opportunity to be alone walking instead of taking a cab, looking at the pretty girls, enjoying the architecture. The Landy spares place had very little stock and I was only able to buy filters before taking a very expensive taxi ride to the Land Rover dealer who fleeced me for a thermostat. Neither business had a replacement water cap, which I suspected might be faulty, but I had a spare in my spares crate, which would have to do for now. I also went to the Bolivian embassy, where very short people tend to hang out. At 1.95 metres tall I was a bit out of place and had to duck through archways and doorways. I like feeling like a giant, and the Bolivians kept a shy eye on me while I waited to be told that I needed more documentation.

I spent most of my days in Concon working on the Landy in the stony parking area next to the apartment while Luisa worked, Keelan went surfing and Jessica read books and coloured in pictures. Keelan was bitten by the surfing bug in the cold Southern Pacific, and I would have to walk down to the beach at night and shout into the black ocean until he emerged, dressed like a seal in my wetsuit, telling me he was going for just one more wave. No. Get your ass out the water.

I cleaned out the entire cooling system, put in the new thermostat, cleaned the entire vehicle and tried to sell the mud tyre which we had bought in Uruguay. The other mud tyres were old, and we left them in

Punta Arenas, but I could not leave this almost new tyre behind. I had also kept the tyre which the classic rally guys had given to me in Ushuaia. In total, I had seven tyres on and on top of the Landy. I decided to dump the one. With the Landy running well again I drove her to a gomeria (tyre repair store) to have two five-foot-tall women repair the punctured tyre in a shed next to their house. They worked intelligently and without power tools, using experience and leverage to do a very tough job. I felt bad making them work so hard but had to respect that they needed the work to survive until they charged me double what they should have, and all sympathy drained swiftly.

Luisa prepared the documentation for the Bolivian visas and Keelan and I drove the Landy the 80 km's into Santiago. At the embassy, I was asked for but could not provide a photo of Luisa or her signature on the application form. I searched our packs of paperwork ten times. The signature I could improvise but the photo I could not, she looks nothing like me and wears no beard. We spent a few hours driving around trying to find an internet cafe to download and print her photo, but there were no internet cafes, and we ran out of hours and drove back to Concon in a grey mood. My fault, I should have checked the paperwork before I left the apartment. The good news was that the Landy was driving perfectly and had been up and over some big hills with no problems at all. I was confident that we would have no more problems with the cooling system. Little did we know that our problems had not yet begun?

24

Enter Sandman

Back in the late 90's, Luisa and I had owned a powerful little Mazda bakkie. We lived on a farm at the end of seven kilometres of dirt road and had a great time playing rally driver. Luisa was fearless on straights and over large bumps, but I knew how to slide the little Mazda around the corners. We would time our "laps", but the outcome as to who is the fastest driver is still hotly contested. Luisa does, however, have the dubious honour of the greatest, longest, highest air ever achieved in a little white Japanese pick up. She achieved this with my brother lying in the back and she landed the vehicle like a marshmallow on a feather bed. It all happened slow-mo and I will never forget looking over, first at her growling and focused and then back at my brother who had floated a meter in the air with a look of pure panicked pleasure on his face.

The little Mazda had to cross a submerged bridge every day and during the rainy season, water would flood into the cockpit. On hot summers days, we would block up the drainage areas in the bed and drive down to the river, park on the bridge and fill the back with water. A mobile pool. Why not? We also used the little Mazda to move house a few times, overloading her stupidly, she would haul manure to feed my green lawn obsession and was our daily driver. We worked her quite hard. Rednecks.

We started having starter issues after a few months on the farm. With no financial backing and a limited income, it was decided that I should repair the vehicle. We made a few calls to Luisa's brother, Elmar and he suggested that I should remove the starter, clean it, let it dry and then replace it. Without the internet or a manual or any inkling of mechanical knowledge, I tucked into the engine with the few spanners I had lying around, removed the starter, cleaned it with petrol, replaced it, started the engine and blew all the fuses. WTH. Another call to Elmar and he took some time to drive out to the farm to check what I had done. He asked me to show him what I had done. I pointed at the starter and told him that I had taken it out, cleaned it and replaced it. He asked me to tell him again what I had done; only this time, he had a huge grin on. I repeated … That's the alternator, you idiot! Ah, that explains it. So where is the starter?

Poor me, I was unlucky enough to grow up without a Dad to teach me these things. I had a few bicycles and could repair those with my eyes closed, but the internal combustion engine was a complete mystery to me. I could demolish an apartment in a couple of days, landscape a large garden and was pretty handy with most major power tools, thanks to my time doing manual labour in Israel, but a 1.4L Mazda engine was a complete mystery to me.

Eventually, we had the Mazda running, and I had learned all there is to know about a starter motor. A little while later the Landy bug bit thanks to Brazilian friends who lived in a dry little town called Randfontein about twenty kilometres from my own teenage home. They owned a 1989 V8 Defender, and it was the coolest machine I have ever driven. It was especially cool filled with cool Brazilians on a mission. Inspired, I bought a 1980 Series 3 bakkie for R12,000. Luisa had a pot business on the side (garden pot, people) and my new Landy's first job (immediately after purchase) was an 80-km round trip to collect a giant cement pot in a rural area, then drive it out to the CBD to show to half pissed ladies during their Friday night drinks. On the way there and back the gearbox sounded like someone had dropped a handful of coins in it and two days later she ground to a halt. And no, Luisa did not sell any pots that day.

Again, it was decided that, due to our precarious financial situation, I would repair the gearbox. How difficult could it be? With my previous mechanical failures still fresh in my mind, I went out and bought a manual. I took the seats out of the Landy, removed the floor panels, released all the nuts and bolts and removed the gearbox. I had forgotten to drain the gearbox, but that is a minor and messy detail. Over the next week, I stripped and scrubbed the box, sourced the replacement parts from Warren at Liemers Land Rovers, struggled for two days with one bloody circlip and eventually started to rebuild the box. There are so many stories within this story, but, for the sake of brevity and lower beer consumption, I will focus on the pertinent. Lucky you. My biggest problem is that the images of the rebuild in the manual did not really gel with the parts I had on the kitchen table. The 1st, 2nd, 3rd gear and synchromesh just did not seem to fit back together logically. I found a specialist and drove the box to him. After a progressively heated discussion, we eventually established that the image in the manual was of a Series 2A box and not a Series 3. He slid the gears back onto the shaft in the correct order and sent me on my way. Armed with new knowledge but no digital camera to record the correct layout of the gears, I rebuilt the box and reinstalled it on a Sunday at 2 am because I had a meeting the next day and would have to take the Landy.

She drove like a dream. I decided to take the shorter off-road track over the mountains that muddy Monday morning (I had overslept) and made it to my clients at Lonmin Platinum Mine without any problems. Ok, the exhaust had fallen off, but I had managed to put that back on en-route. Once the exhaust was semi-professionally repaired (in Magaliesberg on the way back home), the Landy did not give me another day's trouble. Except for the time I overfilled the air filter with oil but, again, that is another story. We used that Landy daily and moved house again, fully loading her and a double axle trailer, making three trips of over 60 km's per trip on mostly dirt and hilly back roads from

Randfontein to Hartebeespoort and the gearbox never gave us the slightest problems. OK, she dripped oil, but she is a Landy and a bit of oilage is to be expected. I spent all my free time and money on that Landy, scrubbing, cleaning and painting. I made seat covers, put in a sound system which hurt my brain and scrubbed and Formula 40'd the chassis. Eventually, Luisa forced me to sell her, for R24, 000, which paid for our wedding, a few months' rent and part of our relocation to Cape Town. It was not a Charles and Diana affair, but we married on the beach 1600 km's away from home and, apparently, the paperwork is valid.

Again, we have decided that all repairs on our current Landy, on our current adventure, should be tackled by me. But this time around I have a few positives. I will not be rushed, I will take my time and, hopefully, make the correct decision, I will clean and polish every nut, bolt and removed the part. I will slowly trawl the internet and find pictures and guides and notes and blogs. I will have a few beers and consider my options. I will mentally prepare, and I will take my bloody sweet time. I also have Luisa. Luisa is not afraid of grease, mud, dust, dirt, or getting her hands dirty. She will crouch on her knees on the wings of the Landy and talk incessantly. She will research, learn, support and instruct as she sees fit. Not that I ever listen, but it is the thought that counts.

On the day we left Concon we had to return to Santiago and the Bolivian Consulate where, eventually, our visas were issued. Our Brazilian Land Rover buddies were heading north to San Pedro de Atacama, and we were going to meet them there and then travel Bolivia together. First, though, we had to travel a few thousand kilometres of sand, mountains, desert and more sand. Camping at a fuel station near Bahia Inglesa and then into Antofagasta up to Calama and up to 4000m and dry, dusty, freezing San Pedro de Atacama built of mud in an area without water. It is the driest desert in the world and we could feel it in our bones. The Brazilians were waiting for us, and we hugged, kissed and drank to celebrate our reunion. I prepared a fire, and they mocked me; apparently, I don't know what vegetables taste like. In the morning we all climbed into Rafa's Landy and visited the salt flats, swam in the 30m deep water-filled mine shaft and arrived back at the camp as the sun set. The next morning, we drove up to the El Tatio Geysers at 4500m. Waking at 4 am we dressed warmly and closed the tent then followed Rafa up the wrong road, a road so damaged and steep that we had to engage low range. The geysers "switch off" naturally at 9 am and we arrived just after 6 am to temperatures of -7° C and ice hanging from the bottom of the Landy. Luisa and I got our clothes off and paraded nearly naked while our sensitive bits were bitten by the frost and Keelan took photos to document our insanity. Clothed again we toured the geysers and Keelan swam in the hot pools while Luisa and I fought the nausea of altitude sickness. I was glad to leave the beautiful mountains and volcanoes and begin the drive back down to the town and a mid-day siesta. Keelan started to vomit as we drove back down on the correct road and sympathetically the Landy began to vomit cooler out of the water expansion tank. The alarm beeped, the child vomited. We stopped on the side of the road and found that the water tank contained a mix of oil and water. A very, very bad sign. We asked Keelan to relax, breathe and sip water. The Brazilians stopped their Landy and we discussed the options. Because the engine was not hot we decided to drive my Landy back down to the camp and work on her there. It took a few hours, but we only had to stop a few times before we made it back to the camp. By now Luisa and I feared the worst and were definitely not having fun. The camp owners suggested that we should call a mechanic, but I knew exactly what they would say - head gasket. Then they would haul the Landy away for some very expensive repairs which would not solve my problem and would actually create more problems. No. I would stick to my original decision and would do all the repairs myself. I would not fail. I was going to fix this. I stripped out the radiator and intercooler and took them to Calama to be re-cored and cleaned. I searched the internet and sent a few emails to friends back in South Africa. I suspected that the oil cooler had blown a seal and Jakes, a mechanic in Cape Town who I had never met, confirmed the suspicion. Almost everyone I spoke to told me it was the head gasket. The Brazilians were waiting for me to fix the Landy so that we could drive to Bolivia together as planned. The border was only twenty kilometres away and we would be able to tour the Salar de Uyuni. I had to tell them that we would not make it, that we needed to get back down to the coast and repair the Landy and that if we went with them to Bolivia there was the risk that we would be a liability to them, we would only damage our Landy further and they would have to tow us around. We also knew that there were no Land Rover parts available in Bolivia and there were strikes taking place across that country which was shutting downtowns and cities and trapping travellers in the unrest. I felt terrible, every time we made plans with Rafa and Isabella, I let them down and although we had originally planned to travel most of South America in convoy we had actually only spent a few days together. We made the correct decision. We nursed the Landy to Calama where we camped in a sports area, then left the next day for the road down to Iquique, a coastal city with a duty-free zone where we could do all our repairs and maybe buy some new tyres and get rid of these terrible, skinny, puncture-prone rubber bastards who sapped the joy out of my soul every time I looked at them. I had to stop a few times and top up the chocolate muck in the expansion tank, but the Landy soldiered on. She has never left us completely stuck and this very long day proved no exception.

In total, we spent one-month camping in a paragliding school campsite waiting for parts to arrive. I ordered a Nanocom (a diagnostic tool for the TD5 ECU) and a replacement oil cooler from Jakes, a helpful mechanic based in Cape Town. I also wanted to order a new set of rims for the Landy but luckily, we did not as DHL screwed up our invoice and did not stipulate that we were tourists which would have provided us with a tourist invoice allowing us to reclaim the 80% import fee that we had to pay on top of the couriers' invoice. I stripped out the cooling system and removed the aircon unit, the exhaust manifold, radiator, turbo and the water pump. When the new parts arrived, I replaced the water pump and the oil cooler with the new modified version and replaced all the exhaust manifold bolts. When I originally drained the coolant, it had looked like chocolate sludge. I drove the Landy down to the beach and around the block a few times then back up to the camp, then drained the coolant and was relieved to see perfectly clean green coolant in the bucket. The head gasket was not the problem. Leaving Iquique was bittersweet. We had made friends with Dutch Overlanders, Joop and Adrie in their big Man truck, we had ridden the buses to town so often that we knew many of the bus drivers, we knew where to get the best rotisserie chicken and French fries and Completo hot dogs (Chilean speciality full of avocado, mayonnaise, small potato chips and mustard). Keelan had rebuilt an old bicycle and taught Jessica how to ride a small bicycle without training wheels, we had many braais watching the sunset over the Pacific and felt the earth tremble from frequent earthquakes.

We asked the German owner for a discount since we had been camped there for a month. He responded by telling us how many millions of dollars the ground was worth, how soon he was going to buy an olive farm up the road and that he never had to worry about money again. And no, we could not have a discount.

Jessica in Melkbosstrand, Cape Town

Family hug in Bolivia

Parque Nacional Los Alerces, Argentina

Rollerskating rink in Iquique, Chil

Dakar Rally in Uyuni, Bolivia, 2015

Chilling on a ferry on the Amazon river

The Oiapoque River, French Guiana & Brazil

Keelan at the Dakar Rally in Bolivia

Camping in gorgeous Brazil

Gauchos in Neuquén, Argentina

Camping in South Africa back in 2010

25

Peruvian Peaks and Troughs

The road out of Iquique was steep, and we were all relieved to reach the summit without any bloody beeping from the LBB. Our destination was Arica and the border crossing into Peru. The Landy was running perfectly, and we made good time heading into Arica where we camped in an area with more camping areas than we had ever seen before. A Land Rover Chile member, David, met us outside his electrical workshop and we took a few photos. He had a set of aluminium Discovery rims (called llantas in Chile) which he was willing to sell to us for only US$200.00, a bargain but he did not have the nuts needed for those rims and we needed to have a chat to a Land Rover Peru member, Oscar (who spoke hardly any English) said that he had llantas to sell us in Peru. The next day Oscar sent us a message asking me to bring him the arroz from David. It was all becoming a bit confusing. We had hesitated when we had the option to buy the rims, and now we were loading them into the back of the Landy to transport over the border which could not have been done legally, without paying import duties, by Oscar. We booked out of Chile and as we approached the border my mind began to race. What if I was being set up? What if the rims had been hollowed and filled with drugs? What if the customs guys had dogs who would smell the drugs then an x-ray would spot the powder then I would be spending the next fifteen to twenty years getting my big blonde ass traded for bubblegum and cigarettes in either a Chilean or Peruvian jail!? A paranoid mind is a terrible creature. A hard-nosed customs agent told us to unpack the entire vehicle for x-raying. We told him that the Landy is our home and that it is full of many uninteresting things. To avoid unpacking we left to take care of the immigration process then returned to find a kinder customs official who told us we could leave after completing the last paper hurdle. All this time I am sitting there trying to act cool, but this was even worse than The Great Lamb Smuggle in Southern Chile. I was sweating bullets. Stamp, stamp, wherefram? South Africa. Stroke of the cheek. Si, si, blanco. Free at last, we drove into Tacna and found a smelly little hotel with a parking area large enough to accommodate the Landy. Many Peruvians are dark, and many are grumpy, Tacna is full of elaborately decorated tuk-tuks transporting everyone and everything. A favourite decoration motif is either Batman or Spiderman inspired, with many lights and things which shimmer and reflect. We ate a street dinner of chicken and rice which had been waiting for us for a few days. Delicious. Luisa disappeared into an internet cafe for a few hours and contacted Oscar who said he had been waiting by the Mosque at 7 pm, but we had not driven past any Mosque and I was not going to go look for one at night after such a stressful day. I also secretly believe that the narcs might be waiting for us there. I needed to get those bloody rims out of the Landy ASAP. I took the rims out and inspected them for signs of manipulation. Seeing none we agreed to meet Oscar the next day. We met outside the post office in town while Luisa was trying to send the black concrete Brazilian girl back home, which she did not do because the postage was too expensive. Oscar, a sweet man, took us to a restaurant where we had a chicken dinner. After chatting for a while we realised that rims are called llantas in Chile and arroz in Peru. Llantas in Peru are tyres. Oscar had some tyres for us which we did not need, and since we did not have the nuts for the Discovery rims we handed them over reluctantly. The next day we went fishing with Oscar and his family. We followed his Landy through the mist to a misty beach where my Landy bogged down as soon as I drove onto the sand. Those tyres were pathetic. Oscar's light 110 bounced along over the sand on street tyres with absolutely no problem. I was almost down to the chassis. Oscar offered me a tow recovery. No way Jose! Luisa took the spade and cleared the sand around the tyres I was busy deflating. Low range, second gear, diff lock. Nothing. I grabbed the spade and cleared out more sand before throwing wood and palm fronds in front of the useless, bastard tyres. I had my guys and Oscar push the Landy and feathered the throttle which freed the Landy. Luckily, we were not going very far, and we set up for a misty day of eating Asado lamb and doing some fishing. I caught two small, flat sole which Jessica made me release even though I planned to grill them for dinner. The wind put paid to any ideas of camping on the beach and we returned to Tacna for another night in the smelly hotel and left the next day for Arequipa, a city at almost 3000m en-route to Cusco and Machu Picchu. An image of Machu Pichhu had been my screen saver for the last year and it was the image of that glorious ruin and mountain which had helped to keep me motivated when it felt like we would never actually leave for this adventure.

Arriving at Arequipa at night we found terrible drivers stuck in arrogant traffic. I used my bullbar to push the noisy little cars out of my path and battled around un-marked streets to find The Hotel las Mercedes which had space for us to camp. Rafa and Isa were there waiting for us, and we were eager to see them again. If Keelan had not spotted the hotel hidden next to a double lane road, almost under a bridge we were driving on, we would have continued searching for who knows how long. We manoeuvred around a confusing network of one-ways and avoided being tailgated while waiting for the staff to open the large blue gates. We parked next to the Brazilians Landy and rolled around on the perfect green lawn as we had not seen lawn since we had left Southern Argentina. There were even a few flowers and a little stream running next to the lawn, behind a fence. The altitude and dry air was uncomfortable and not conducive to enthusiastic beer-drinking, but I gave it a good go anyway. Rafa and Isa had already been to Machu

Picchu and we only had one day with them before they left, and I fell ill. The day they left another Landy showed up, this time a white 110 driven by Bill and directed by Rosemarie. Bill and I were instantly good friends, but it would take Rose and me a while to get used to each other. Our route to Machu Picchu would be through Chivay, with its Colca Canyon and Condors where we would choose a route to Cusco. We left the camp and immediately got lost driving up the side of a volcano instead of out of the city. The Landy had not been running well at altitude since our troubles in the mountains between Argentina and Chile, and I really have to work the gears and revs to get the turbo working like it should. The turbo lag was ten times worse at altitude than it was at sea level and I would have to rev her hard and drop the clutch to get the power I needed to climb the many steep Andean mountains. After an hour of screwing around, we found the road out of Arequipa. A 180-kilometre climb from 3000m to 5000m before dropping back down to 3700m in Chivay. Bear in mind that 3000m is as high as the highest peak in Europe and we would be driving to 2000m higher. The Landy handled the climb without any problems once the traffic thinned and at one stage we were driving at 100 kph at 4500m. The dry grassland populated by Alpacas and leathery brown people, surrounded by peaks. Jessica started to cry out from an altitude headache and, as had happened when Keelan started to vomit at El Tatio, the Landy joined in and vomited her fresh green coolant out over the engine. The piercing beep, beep, beep of the LBB raped my ears. It is now the sound I hate the most in the world.

Luisa tried to calm Jessica as I stepped out of the Landy to scream expletives under my breath. The 60L drinking water tank was full of water and I gave the Landy a five-minute break before topping up the coolant, relieved that there was no oil in the water. It took us four hours to travel almost 25 kilometres to the 5000m viewing point, or mirador in Spanish. Chivay is in a valley and I knew that I just needed to get past the mirador and I would be able to almost freewheel to salvation. But first, we had to reach the mirador. Every few kilometres the LBB would scream, I would stop, let the Landy cool, top her up and drive on. We used the Nanocom to give us an accurate reading of the coolant temperature, which should hover at 87°C bout would jump to 106°C just before the water rushed out of the expansion tank. For the last few kilometres to the mirador, the road was surrounded by steep slopes and hanging ice. This could be a very dangerous place to spend the night with temperatures plummeting once the sun sets. Up we climbed and often we would stop to repeat the beeping, cooling, top-up process. Breathing was laboured, Jessica still whimpering from the headache, everyone on edge. The sun sank behind the mountains in front of us and the beeping sounded on what I guessed must be the final approach to the downhill pass. I opened the 60-litre water tank. Empty. We had milk for the kids to drink, but we were all out of water. I told Luisa to wait and I walked up the hill to see if I could find water and the route down to Chivay. By the time I reached the mirador, the sky was black and the only light I could see was the Landy's flashing emergency lights. A pick up passed me walking in the dusk. I watched as it climbed passed the 4995m mirador sign and a little higher, around some obstacle in the road then disappeared. I waited for ten minutes to see if the red tail lights re-appeared, but they did not. This must be the summit. Breathing heavily my feet dragged me back down the hill to the Landy. As I returned a bus pulled up, locals asking if we need help. Yes, por favor, we need water. We gave them two plastic bottles and they drove up to a stream to fill them with water. The one guy really made an effort to get clean water, the other guy was happy with watery mud. We thanked them, asked about the road ahead, topped up the coolant and set off for what was hopefully going to be the last uphill stretch of this nightmare. The road climbed, we reached the mirador, drove around some rocks lying in the road, then a twist and the road climbed some more. We might make it! The LBB screeched at me, I muted it, Luisa checked the coolant temperature, 95°C, we kept going, the road levelled then, painfully slowly, the nose of the Landy began to dip and down we went, the coolant temperature dropped to 89°C, 85°C and 80°C and down we went to Chivay.

The only fault I could think of was the water cap. The thermostat was a new original Land Rover part. The oil cooler repair held there were no signs of a cracked head or broken head gasket. I had left South Africa with two water caps, the one on the expansion tank and a spare. I had put the spare cap on in Iquique and it had done well until 4500m. We booked into another stinking hotel and researched our problem. At first, I went looking for parts to repair the water cap. Bill and Rosemarie who we had met in Arequipa drove into Chivay and found Luisa and I wandering the streets looking for plumbing parts to bypass the thermostat. Our thinking was that the pressurised water cap and thermostat worked together to regulate the flow of coolant. If we bypass the thermostat, the coolant will flow without building pressure. I had stupidly thrown away the old thermostat housing we had used to get down to Concon, and now we needed a new solution. Bill and Rosemarie agreed that waiting there for a new cap to arrive from Lima would take too long and would be very expensive. If we waited a day they would travel back to Arequipa with us as our back up team after they had visited the Colca Canyon. In Bill's words- we will not leave without you. Land Rover people! While they visited the Condors and the canyon Luisa, and I removed the thermostat and searched the little hardware stores for plastic plumbing pipes with the same diameter to accommodate the coolant pipes. We thread together a combination of three pipes and installed the MacGyver into the cooling system. The next morning Bill and Rosemarie joined us, and we drove out of Chivay and back up to 5000m on the edge of our seats. We had bought a few cans of oxygen before leaving the town but only when we were almost at the top of the pass did we realise that, in all the excitement, I had forgotten to fuel up the Landy. Luisa monitored the coolant temperature with the Nanocom. Everything was working as it should, we climbed slowly and after a tense thirty minutes we reached the mirador, it was all downhill from here. Bill gave me ten litres of diesel when we reached the toll gate before the drop-down back into Arequipa. We only had to top up the water once due to leaks in the plumbing pipes, but we made it back into the cities horrible traffic, followed Bill as he straddled lanes and looped around to the hotel entrance. The gates opened, we drove in, I kissed the Landy, I kissed, Luisa, I kissed Bill and lay down on the grass.

It took five days for the new US$10 water cap to arrive from Lima, five days during which I had the flu and Keelan turned fourteen. That faulty water cap had been the cause of two of the most frustrating breakdowns we had ever had, and I was particularly pissed off with the situation because I had included a spare in my original spares list, I had done my job, but the supplier back home had given me a faulty spare. What can you do? Live and learn, perhaps.

26

The Great Rip Off In The Sky

The route to Cuzco took us back up to the road to Chivay and then over the top of the Andes. We were confident that the water cap replacement, an original Land Rover part full of springs and rubbers, would solve our problems. If not, I would lie down and slit my own useless throat, my altitude thinned blood racing the coolant down the pavement.

We had no problems that day and climbed back up to 5000m, a long slow slog where I decided, on Bill's advice, to use low range even on the pavement when the Landy was struggling. It was a great bit of advice and would save my clutch. Instead of struggling to get the turbo to kick in, I could just use low range power, then change back to high range for the straights and downhills. It took almost thirteen hours, but at 11 pm we rolled into the Quinta Lala campsite above Cusco. Driving into the city I realised that the tight twisting up hills required low range and I switched over which made the climb up to the well-hidden, un-posted camp that much easier. A group of Overlanders were sharing a fire when we arrive. Dutch Coen, who we had met in Fortaleza, Brazil and his partner Karin-Marijke, a Belgian, Hendrik (who later offered us beer and put it on our tab) and another Dutch couple, photographers Wim and Pauline whose modern VW camper had travelled across the length of Africa and half of South America but still looked in showroom condition and I have never seen Wim clean or work on the camper. He must do the maintenance after dark when everyone is sleeping. Of all the Overlander rigs I know, that shiny soccer mom VW camper has been the most reliable. The very friendly Belgian was very grumpy the next morning, and his large black Mercedes G Wagon camper was refusing to start. At 8 am on a very cold morning I started the Landy, evicted my sleepy family, tied up the tent ladders and dragged the big German and her Belgian up and down a wet, grassy slope, four or five times until the German coughed back into life with a massive belch of black smoke.

Cusco is by far the touristiest town I have ever been to. It is beautiful and while walking around the Plaza de Armas, we spotted a WWII era Willys Jeep parked outside the cathedral. A crowd had gathered a few metres away and was snapping away at the Jeep's only occupant, Lorena. We approached the pretty celebrity to ask if they knew where the camp was and gave her directions. Lorena was travelling with her boyfriend, Julian, who was searching the town for the friend of a friend who had promised them a place to stay. They had driven down from Colombia and were heading to Ushuaia in a vehicle without a solid roof or closable windows. A few hours later they spotted us walking outside the market, they could not find the camp and were looking for us to give them directions. We caused a traffic jam, hailed a taxi and Lorena and Julian followed us up to the camp where we grilled some meat in the icy air.

We began planning the trip to Machu Picchu and we had been through hell to get there. It had better be magnificent.

Well, if you put enough people in one room, intelligence of the individual gives way to the dynamics of the group. The loudest idiot is the correct idiot. "Do I look stupid!? We are four here, first in the queue! Yes, there are four tills, but we want one each! Shut up little man, or I kill you!"

Perhaps that is why I hate rooms full of people or queues or tourist attractions. Perhaps that is why I really, truly loved Machu Picchu and hated the Machu Picchu Experience. The location itself is amazing, sublime and heavenly, out of this world. The weather was perfect, the grass green, the rubble unruined. People talk about the energy of Machu Picchu and how after a visit, you will have strong dreams. I had no dreams at all. We had left behind the independent exploration and relative tranquillity of overlanding and becoming one of the shuttled, harassed, begged, ripped off great white herd, as an American friend calls the Machu Picchu crowds.

There are a few ways to get to Machu Picchu from Cuzco. You could fly to the ruins by helicopter, land where you choose, enjoy a three-course meal, a private viewing and deflower a few local virgins in the Sun Temple if you throw enough cash around. You could pay hundreds of dollars to take the nice train, the OK train, or the shit train from Cuzco. Regardless which train you choose, you will pay hundreds of dollars. Even though Machu Picchu is only 80 km's from Cuzco, if you decide to save some cash by not taking the train you will be forced to endure a 6-hour nightmare drive around a 280-km detour of mountain passes in the care of an angry 5-foot man behind the wheel of sixteen feet of unroad-worthiness and bad suspension with a penchant for overtaking trucks on blind corners. Or you could self-drive with eyes wide open. We self-drove.

The Peruvian government has only one use for the glorious ruins of the great Inca's – cash cow. And to control the cash cow, you must control access to the cow and her delicious milk. The road stops ten kilometres short of Machu Picchu and thereafter access is by train or by foot. Whether you drive or are driven you will run out of road somewhere near a dusty town called Santa Theresa. There are a few hostels, and you could even choose to hand your life over to a local for some fun adventure sports. There is no guarantee that he will hand it back in the same condition, but you are on holiday – so have fun.

We camped at a place called Cola de Mano with a great German couple, Lukas and Eva. The place was run by a really friendly guy who turned out to be a bit of a windbag who also ran a zip-lining business, The Safest in South America. As part of the weeklong celebration of Keelan's birthday, he and I went for a bit of almost airborne fun. There were six lines in total and the first five did not even kill us even though we were flying a few hundred metres over the valley floor. The last stunt was the Superman when the harness is put on backwards and you hang, facing the ground and fly over the treetops. The camp owner's son, who we named Rupert because he reminded me of a good friend back home, took care of Keelan's harness. The other, over-friendly, guide attached mine. It is a bizarre feeling stepping off a platform into thin air. I had done the world's highest bungee jump in South Africa, and even though this was tame by comparison, it was still a horrible feeling. And that horrible feeling became terror when I began rolling forward out of my very loose harness. Keelan was screaming happily, so I focused on trying to prevent my own demise. I held onto the harness as tightly as possible and tried to straighten my body to prevent slipping out of the harness. We flew over the trees and the camp, I spotted the Land Rover waiting below and wished to be with her, I wished to be anywhere, but where I was. We reached the end of the line, and I shouted at the guide to get me off the line. I was now hanging upside down and my hips had rolled out of the harness with only my upper thighs holding me in. The little Peruvian was too small and weak to haul my heavy body in and he strained like a child playing tug of war with a bull. I shouted at him to hurry up as I felt myself slipping further. Rupert and Keelan climbed up onto the platform, and Rupert reeled me in. The little Peruvian gave me a big nervous smile before I grabbed him and threw him headfirst to meet his death in the deep valley below. This is what I might have done in a world without consequences.

From Santa Theresa, you will need to take a collectivo (5 ft. man 16ft...) on a terrible dirt road to Hydro Electrica. Here you can wait for a few hours in the sun with the plump of your herd for a train or you could follow the skinnier herd for a ten-kilometre walk to the town of Agua Calientes which serves as the milking station at the base of Machu Picchu. Aguas Calientes gets its name from an imaginative bureaucrat who thought well, we could call it The Milking Station and the great white herd would think Ah how quaint but let's be nice to the poor rich bastards and give them a town with a name which promises the one thing they probably won't get unless paying five hundred dollars a night. Aguas Calientes – hot water.

I liked Aguas Calientes for the less obvious reasons. There are a couple of schools in the town where cute, little, uniformed, dark-haired mountain Peruvians learn life skills and milking skills. You can even volunteer for a milking! Just call 0410916. They wander around town banging on drums and blowing trumpets washed in a fountain. They are not on a day trip silly they are outside school walls because YOU are outside the school walls and you are economics 101. Then there is the opportunity for me to study my herd. I am aloof because I drove and walked here, I am from South Africa and I brought the kids along. No fly-ins or trains for this hard bastard. Naturally, you will find all the nations of the world in Aguas Calientes. The Japanese with their weird clothing and humour, the South American backpackers with tattoos, hot girlfriends and strange facial hair, the sexy young blonde Americans and the old fat talkative Americans, the world travellers, dressed in local clothing and leather shoes, sitting on their haunches, chewing coca leaves, acting cool, looking ridiculous. Almost as ridiculous as I dressed in a wetsuit, snorkel and mask on top of a mountain.

So, we wake up at 3:50 am to catch a $20.00 US pp bus up to Machu Picchu. We push into the front of the queue then spend a cold hour glaring at others who try the same trick until eventually you are whisked up a winding pass. You could walk up the pass and about 3000 steps and save some money. But that is torture; the Peruvians know this, so just hand over the cash and take the bloody bus. Reach the gates to paradise, watch a big loud Italian pick on a small stubborn Indian, protect the flanks from queue skippers ("hey, how are you man… so you made the walk from Cuzco…?"). The gates eventually open and after a stampede and a climb, you are witnessing the most beautiful sight in the entire world. Peace, tranquillity, beauty, power, history! The kids start whining, a lonely English backpacker decides that you sitting there quietly, will be his new best friend and even though you are trying to absorb and study and feel this glorious place you worked so bloody hard to get to, he wants it to be like his pub back home and you are his mate Brian, so let's talk footy. Bugger off.

After three hours of stumbling over other excited, disappointed, grumpy, irritated, tired

people, being shouted at, lied to and instructed by little people you decide to leave. You have taken a thousand photos of three thousand people, some rubble and a big rock. You want to get back on the bus, have some lunch, catch a train, get back to your camp, have a beer, some chicken would be nice and get back down to the beach.

Machu Picchu is a glorious, beautiful, statuesque, proud, dignified lady reduced to prostitution to pay a bad husbands bad debt. That said, I feel honoured to have been there and richer for the experience.

We left for the long winding drive out of the jungle, up over another mountain and down the winding road to Cusco. Rob emailed to say that he and Fallon would be in Lima for a flight out to the UK. Would we be able to meet them there for a few beers? We had hung out with the Overlanders in Quinta Lala for a bit too long and needed no more encouragement to hit the road to the coast, sea level, oxygen, seafood. Before we left Julian and Lorena handed us a blender, a backpack, some books and a hat to take back to their parents' house in Chia outside Bogota.

I remember fondly driving between Johannesburg and Durban back in South Africa. There is a pass called Van Zyl's about mid-way between the two cities was a chapel has been built at the summit so that truck drivers can stop and say a little prayer before descending the Highveld. I have seen many trucks come to an end there, but after driving the

Peruvian passes, I realise that Van Zyl's is what Peruvian drivers would consider a gentle slope.

The Andes were spectacular, and I have nothing but respect for the tough Peruvians who etch a living out of the cold, dry soil. The road builders in Peru must certainly be the world's best and I personally recommend them for that colony on Mars. They have toiled with little oxygen to carve near-perfect paved arteries over and through some of the highest peaks in the world. The expense must have been staggering and there is so little traffic that there hardly seems reasonable for such effort but if your country is split down the middle by massive peaks and all you have is a LOT of sand on the one side and a massive jungle on the other, you have to find a way to connect the two for the economy to survive.

Many of the roads in the Andes consist of endless switchbacks and hairpin bends. As the crow flies two destinations maybe a couple hundred kilometres apart, but the road connecting them will be almost five times that distance. As soon as you get over one peak you see another then another peak gradually leading you up into the rarefied air at over 5000 meters. Eventually, you start heading downhill, feeling a little proud of your vehicle for coping with such continuous torture, only to reach a valley and another huge climb up the other side. The views are mind-blowing and the little villages and sheer toughness of the villagers are humbling. When these people go on holiday and breathe the thick moist oxygen of the coast, they must bounce around like Duracell bunnies.

27

Goodbye Andes, For Now

At the Nazca Lines, we climbed a tower to view a monkey and part of a tree. Eight metres in the air Luisa lost all her courage and splayed out on the floor of the steel platform while Keelan and I took photos of her misery and pretended to jump out of the tower. Luisa has whittled her phobias down from fearing absolutely everything to only fearing most things and we believe that mocking her is the surest route to a complete cure.

Before leaving Cusco, Luisa had emailed the Backpackers Hostel in Mira Flores, Lima and booked a parking space for the Landy. We arrived in misty Lima to find Bill and Rosemarie parked behind Canadian Mark and a very strange German with dyed red hair and a large, badly decayed Man truck. Bill and Mark shuffled their trucks to make space for us while the German evaded capture. A quiet Estonian, Tarmo, had parked his little Toyota bus in a corner. Tarmo had been around the world in that Toyota and we had met him in Punta Arenas and Puerto Natales. MiraFlores is a great part of a horrible city and I enjoyed walking around Kennedy Park, munching on the wide range of excellent food available. Rob and Fallon arrived with a few bottles of Pisco, the Peruvian plonk of choice, a list of cocktail recipes and a bag of limes, sugar and other ingredients. Bill, Mark, Luisa, Rob, Fallon and I made merry until the red-haired German lost his mind about the happiness and then we made merry for a few hours more. Rob and Fallon's flight was leaving at 9 am and they had to be at the airport by 7 am the idea being that we would party all night and they would sleep all the way back to the United Kingdom where the real world awaited them. We left the hostel for a raucous walk back to their hostel to fetch their bags, then had a cheeseburger at a restaurant full of hip young things at 5 am and found our friends a taxi just before 7 am. It was one of the best nights we had being adults in South America.

The next evening a member of the Land Rover Club of Peru came to hang out with us. Land Rovers and Land Rover drivers are a breed apart. I know of no other marque where complete strangers will wave at each other when passing in traffic, or will stop to talk or help a driver of the same brand. We each modify our vehicles to our own needs and taste and will spend hours inspecting other guy's trucks. When parking at a supermarket we will search for the Landy's and park next to them, we will take photos and leave little notes under the windscreen wipers. We will form instant friendships based on this shared passion and will drink beers together and maybe plan a trip off-road. Our vehicles may be 5 years old or 50 years old, but we can see the similarities and envy each other's rides. Often, we will forsake logic and buy more Land Rovers than we can afford, maintain or drive but will love each one and spend nights dreaming about what we will do to them and with them. It's a love affair, others don't quite understand.

Since we began travelling in South America and since we have had a few problems with the Land Rover, we have been reaching out to the Land Rover Clubs of Peru, Argentina, Chile, Colombia, Brazil and Ecuador for assistance and moral support. And believe me; the South Americans have off-roading in their blood. I have a huge amount of respect for these guys and their vehicles; they take on the toughest terrain without missing a beat and are confident in their abilities without arrogance. The Land Rover Peru Club had been chatting with us for a while on the internet and we were lucky enough to be invited to a club meeting in the dunes 40 km's outside of Lima for some braai and dune driving. We met on Sunday morning and drove south to meet the rest of the club at a gas station. A Chilean, Jaime, also joined us in his vegetable oil-powered Series 3 109 which he had driven from his farm in Chile to Venezuela. His Landy was nicknamed Gordo Fritangero - deep-fried fat in English. We deflated our tyres and surprisingly our 130 did not get stuck in the sand though Jaime and a few others did. I just powered through and did not take any chances.

Nik knew of a guy in town who's Dad used to own the Land Rover dealership in Peru. He might be able to help us get new rims and possibly tyres. Unfortunately, he was able to help, but we could not afford his asking price. We would have to continue as we were. I had found that after reducing the tyre pressures in the Carretera Austral and since we were driving mainly paved roads, we were no longer getting punctures, the tyre guys in Punta Arenas had told us to run the tyres at very high pressures and, like an idiot, I listened.

Negotiating the constipated traffic amongst Lima's hooting bullies and madmen in taxis took as long as expected and not long after leaving the city, we had to find a camp. The goal was to get out of Peru as soon as possible as we had all seen enough ruins, sand and mountains to last an entire lifetime. The average Peruvian was not the friendliest guy and who could blame him. He had grown up struggling to make ends meet while rich gringos flew in and drove around in big 4x4's, nose in the air at the litter, poverty and pollution, interested solely in the remains of a proud ancient, invisible culture and mostly completely disinterested in the current inhabitants of Peru. Those making a living out of tourism will go to the ends of the earth to please you; the rest of the population just wants you to get lost for a while. Our Land Rover friends had been very good to us but had they not reached out to us I would have had an almost completely miserable experience at the mercy of the Peruvians.

Except we were not done with Peru. Driving north through the sand and litter we reached Chicama, the longest left wave in the known universe except there was no swell, so we hung out with a Swiss couple and drank beer. Lobitos, a little rundown surf town and a haunted hostel on a hill was our last stop before we drove into Mancora and found the Laguna Surf camp and were seduced by Belgian Pepe's hamburgers and pastas. We stayed in Mancora for almost a month as I did an online English teachers course which would enable me to work anywhere in the world where English teachers are required. We had a real adventure so far and even though the travelling had been very difficult since Punta Arenas, we decided that we would just keep on travelling as long as possible before returning to South Africa to rebuild our lives. I passed the course with 84% even though I had studied in front of the pool on an uncomfortable wooden chair while an endless stream of traveller girls frolicked in the water. One particularly curvy, Land Rover owning English girl lost her bikini top, the poor clips did not stand a chance and popped off with an audible sigh of relief and I had to throw in the towel for the day. Will I ever get a break?

Mancora also had great snack food, cheap litre bottles of beer and a nice rotating group of backpackers to hang out with. Wim and Pauline stayed with us for a while, the Swiss-made an appearance and we had a completely vegetarian, completely delicious braai with a group of salty Argentineans.

197

28

Ecuador!

Crossing into Ecuador was complicated with customs and immigrations being far separated on both sides. The Ecuadorian customs procedure was especially strange, but we noticed that within a few kilometres of the border that there was green stuff growing out of the ground and soon there were even banana trees, palm trees and sugar cane. After many thousand kilometres of shades of brown, we were finally back from Mars. Ecuador uses the US Dollar, and the fuel is subsidised. We had not filled our fuel tank in anticipation of the cheap fuel but had to drive at least twenty kilometres from the border before we were allowed to put in fuel. One hundred litres for US$20.00! Fuel is one of our largest expenses on the road, ironically though Ecuador is one of the smallest countries in South America, so the opportunity to cover ground and save money was not great.

We had crossed the border at noon and by 3 pm we were driving up into the jungle, marvelling at the change of people, geography and scenery. That night we washed Peru off our bodies and settled into our new reality, planning a route down along the coast to a small coastal town called Canoa where we stayed for a while in a great camp by the sea. Keelan surfing, me working on the Landy and cooking prawn dinners, Luisa working and Jessie playing with the animals and her toys.

I awoke one morning to hear Luisa swearing. I have learned by now not to get too excited when Luisa gets excited because she has exactly the same over the top reaction when losing a bra or the taxman takes all the money out of our bank account. Unfortunately, this time, her bras were safe, but our money definitely was not. The South Africa Revenue

Service had sent us a letter informing us that they were going to clean us out, but the recipient of the letter decided not to tell us. We had no opportunity to avoid the financial tsunami heading our way. One day we had money in the bank the next day it was gone. All of it. We jumped down our accountant's throat who assured us that it was a mistake and that we would be sorted out in no time. With absolutely no response from Mr Seepasahd, we managed to reconcile the accounts and prove that the money was confiscated in error. SARS confirmed that they will refund the money, when they feel like it, maybe after going into our great grandparent's tax records to see if there are any ancient debts which need settling with interest.

Jessica turned nine in the camp and even though we had travelled to the nearest town to buy her a new Barbie we had only been able to find terrible cheap Chinese toys. The poor girl awoke to presents of beach jewellery, sweet and a couple of jars of olives. We promised to make amends when we reached Quito, a city up in the Andes which we drove up to not long after her birthday. The only camping we could find was at a German hotel where we again ran into Bill and Rosemarie. The nights were cool, and the traffic woke us early every morning as they screeched to a stop before the speed bump built just outside the fence, four metres from where we were camped behind a curtain of leaves. Luisa took the kids shopping and returned with some art supplies and a new doll for Jessica. Our planned route was going to take us back along the spine of the Andes, south to Cotopaxi Volcano and Banos, a small town surrounded by Volcanoes. In Banos, we just missed another South African couple who had been stuck for a month waiting for parts for their broken Land Cruiser. South Africans are very rare on the Pan-Am and I had to laugh when I heard that he was sick of mountains. He was heading south from the USA and unless he stuck purely to the coastal road, he would be spending the next month or two in the mountains. Ecuador is a developing nation which I found to be more advanced than both Chile and Peru. There are many American retirees who settle in Ecuador because they are able to stretch their Dollars a lot further and perhaps theirs is the influence which has helped to modernise the country. After Banos we drove down towards the Ecuadorian Amazon and skirted along the world's greatest jungle and back up to almost 5000 metres, at night, over a tight steep pass and down into Quito again to visit the Equator, standing either side of the line kissing, jumping, kung-fu fighting, but somehow managing to keep our clothes on. Colombia was calling, and we camped at one last mountain top camp before heading to the border.

29

No Marching Powder For Us, Thanks

We had been warned that the Colombian border crossing is extremely difficult and that we should be very careful as Colombia is racked by crime and has been enduring a civil war for many years. The border crossing was actually one of the easiest we had experienced, and we were very surprised to soon find ourselves in a town trying to buy Colombian insurance and a bite to eat. The Colombian women are very pretty, and a perfect example was bursting out of her uniform while helping us to buy the insurance. The problem was that our vehicle registration number had too many digits and not enough letters and the computer kept kicking us out. Somehow the breathless lady managed to bully the system into accepting us and we hit the road for Pasto, a southern city where a member of the Legion Land Rover Colombia was waiting to meet us. We were due to meet Santiago at 7 pm outside a hotel, but the traffic had been quite bad, and there were many roadworks to slow us down. I asked a motorcyclist at a traffic light where I could find the hotel and he said follow me. He led us straight to the hotel and our concerned new friend. Santiago was waiting for us in his perfect light green Series 3 88, and after initial introduction and apologies he led us up to his house on a smallholding outside the city. We had to drive quickly to keep up with him, but soon we were driving out of the city and onto a gravel road. Bumping along we came to a stop at an unsuspected obstacle. A road maintenance team had dug a huge hole, big enough to swallow a small car, on the side of a cliff and had left two planks of wood as a bridge. Santiago went first and easily cleared the plank bridge. I followed the front of the Landy made it over, and as I thought we were going to make it the rear of the Landy broke the wood, we slid halfway back into the hole and tipped towards the cliff before coming to a rest. Luisa was making a huge amount of noise at this stage but was able to get out onto solid ground. With nothing to attach the winch to, we called in Santiago's Landy and attached the winch to her bumper. I placed the Landy, who was resting on her chassis, into low range, second gear, diff lock and spun the wheels, but made no progress. Santiago changed the angle of his Landy and we tried again, this time I feathered the throttle while Luisa activated the winch and Santiago pulled. The Landy slid forward, gripped and the rear rose up out of the hole. Keelan was given the camera and told to take photos and video of the excitement but he was too excited by the action and took a photo of a headlight and a blurred photo of the top of the Landy. After introducing us to his kids and Brazilian wife, Santiago invited us to join him to a rotary club meeting the next day. We accompanied Santiago in his Landy, the fastest Landy I have ever been in and met the Pasto rotary club, ate Chicharron (pork crackling) and Arepa (a maize bread), potatoes and drank Agua Diente. In Chile and Argentina, they have wine, in Uruguay, they have Grappa Miel, in Brazil, they have Cachaça, in Peru they have Pisco, and in Colombia, they have Agua Diente which is basically Greek ouzo just not as sweet, but just as dangerous. A chilled bottle sat in the doorway, and a shot would be swallowed by each person through the door. The drinking of Agua Diente continued throughout the afternoon and my head was swimming by the time we left for a rapid drive through the gravel back roads to the beautiful home of Dr Santiago Schumacher.

We were warned to be very careful on the way to Popayan as the road has a reputation for bandits and FARC activity. We did not feel threatened, but the drive took a very long time because of a fleet of very slow trucks and the narrow mountain passes. Popayan itself is a very nice town, and we attracted a lot of attention driving around looking for a supermarket to stock up on food and drinks. While we were walking in the modern supermarket barefoot and in our, by now old and worn clothing, Keelan and I noticed two teenage girls giggling and following us. Keelan was now accustomed to girls fawning over him, but we were both surprised when they plucked up their courage and approached me. Do you know Justin Bieber? Giggling, showing me there Justin Bieber armbands. Sure, we had dinner last Thursday. Silly, silly girls.

The amount of military patrolling the road was both alarming and comforting. Kids in full combat gear manned sandbagged checkpoints and gave us the thumbs up as we passed. Eventually, we came to expect the soldiers and realised that their presence on the major routes was routine and not a response to any new extreme military action by the FARC. With only 115 km's between Popayan and Cali we decided to head there for the night and meet another Legion Land Rover member, Edward. Edward had recently been to the UK and had carted back a 20-kilogram box of spares which we had delivered to him from Paddocks, the Land Rover spares provider.

Arriving as the sun set, we arrived in Cali, once again breaking the golden - never drive at night-rule and headed up to Pance, a little town up in the mountains overlooking Cali. The camp we stayed at was at the end of a steep broken road and had no internet or flat ground, but it did have a very sweet camp dog, a very mean camp dog, a few horses and hammocks, a fish farm and a freshwater swimming pool and fresh air. The nearest internet cafe was only a kilometre down the hill and Luisa went down the next morning to keep our world organised and contact Edward. Driving down into the town took a while but it was a nice, slow, bumpy drive in the cool shade of the mountains.

While parked outside a supermarket in Cali, a lovely lady came over to chat with us, intrigued by the Land Rover and the Malaria stickers stuck on the front wings. She worked for in laboratory nearby which studied infections and transmitted diseases and invited us to do a presentation, about our journey and about Malaria in Africa. We gladly accepted and spent the next two days putting together the presentation. Luckily, most of her colleagues spoke English and we were able to present an interesting and informative presentation. They were particularly interested in the similarities between the threat and treatment of Malaria in South America and Africa. At the end of the presentation we encouraged the audience to go to the Malaria NGO website and donate directly towards the fight against Malaria in Africa. We informed the NGO and sent them a copy of the presentation suggesting that perhaps there may be some scope for co-operation between the two organisations. There was no response to our email from the NGO and no response to follow up emails over the next few months. We had noticed that there seemed to be a lack of enthusiasm about the spokesperson program, particularly on social media where a group had been created for trained spokespersons to communicate, but there had been no engagement from the NGO with the page for almost a year. I suspected that part of the problem may have been opportunists, particularly in Africa, who enrolled for the free training then used the certificates to apply for lucrative positions in other aid agencies. We took the lack of response as a possible end to our co-operation.

Edward was a great guy and an African like us except Edward was raised in Kenya. The Kenyans were quite badly oppressed by the British and the Mau Mau revolution of the Fifties was terrifying for every colonial soul in Africa. The Mau Mau had used a heady mixture of politics and witchcraft to scare the tribes into aggression and many white farming families were slaughtered on their arguably stolen land. Kenya won their freedom, kicked out the British but kept Rugby and Cricket, by far the greatest export of British colonialism. As Edward loves Land Rovers, Cricket and Rugby, we were instant soul mates, no need to argue. Edward invited us to visit him and his girlfriend in the city for the weekend. He told us to be there at seven on a Friday night and we managed to get lost after sitting in traffic for three hours then had to engage low range to get up the hill to his house and when we did eventually see him I asked him if he was frikken nuts! I hope he did not take me seriously, but maybe we should have driven through the next morning when it was bright and breezy, and all the good people of Cali were not in their cars trying their very best to get in our way. But Edward cycles twenty kilometres to and from work every day and therefore does not really know what traffic is. Crazy African.

Edward had organised an apartment for us to crash in for the weekend and after finding a parking garage for the Landy, he and Alex made us comfortable, we drank beer, burnt meat, did magic tricks and had a great time until I employed my favourite party trick and snuck off to bed leaving my cigarettes and almost finished drink on the table as a clever decoy. By the time anyone realises I am gone for good, it is too late and I am snoring down the house. I awoke to a strange scene. Luisa was sleeping curled up in a corner fully dressed, Keelan was sleeping on a matt on a patio pathway in full sunlight and Jessica had disappeared. I freaked out, woke Keelan, who had not been drugged, drunk, or beaten, he just decided that he liked the idea of sleeping on the path. He pointed at a bundle in a hammock and I found Jessica. Later I would learn that after finishing all the booze and my cigarettes Luisa and Alex headed off to a seedy side of a dangerous city to score more contraband. I should have stayed awake. Edward, the kids and I went cycling and ate ice cream while the girls slept the day away. That night we ate a curry made by curry experts Edward and Alex then headed for the coffee region and to meet yet another Legion club member, Cam, who had been following our journey since Brazil. Before we left, Edward told me about La Nyapa which is a great local secret for budget-conscious travellers. Basically, if you ask for La Nyapa at a butchery or vegetable market or a juice store you will get a bonus, a little extra and a good laugh from the person serving you, who doesn't expect a gringo to ask for La Nyapa. Prices also improve as they realise that you are maybe not as dumb as you look. I also found out that I would only be able to source the brake pads we needed in Bogota. Bad news. Between Cali and Bogota, we stopped at Salento in the beautiful coffee-growing region. At the camp, we met a few Overlanders and relaxed. I took the tyres off and had a look at the brakes, but there was not much that I could do until I found replacement pads.

We arrived at Cam's home much later than anticipated, the Land Rovers brakes were grinding, and I had to drive slowly up and down La Linea, Colombia's highest mountain pass, before reaching Cam outside Bogota. The brakes were so bad that I drove the entire mountain pass in low range using engine braking as much as possible and taking my sweet time. The pass was extreme by South African standards, but only a bump in the road compared to Peruvian mountain passes.

We were so late that Cam was not at the fuel station where we had agreed to meet and after driving around looking for an internet cafe we managed to message Cam, and he came to fetch us in his 88 Santana Land Rover. Santana is the Land Rover assembled under license by Spain and older Land Rovers in South America are Santana's. We followed Cam, who we nicknamed Cabbage, up a twisting road and down a very steep driveway into his parent's yard. After meeting everyone I ripped up the Lawn parking the Landy and as I sat down for my first beer my chair slipped off the patio and I fell backwards to my death, laughing in disbelief as I went. Some rocks and plants stopped my body and I was only dead of embarrassment. The weekend was spent going to the local market, chatting and eating expertly prepared Colombian dishes, playing with Cam's twin babies and getting to know his parents and wife Carolina. Colombian hospitality is incredible. If a Colombian opens his home to you, then the house is yours and you should feel as comfortable as you are in your own home. We feel that the only respectable way to show gratitude for such hospitality is to relax, get to know your host and cook more food for him than he could possibly eat.

Cam drove us into Bogota from his parents' home, our brakes grinding terribly and took us to meet Memo, another Legion member who would allow us to camp in his driveway while we sorted out the brakes. Memo, an intelligent man with a friendly honest smile, invited us into his home in Chia outside Bogota and introduced us to his wife Cecé and three daughters, Lucia, Juanita and Anna. We did not realise it at the time, but Memo and his family would become as close as our own family, and in the short time we had together they would change our lives.

The first day together, we planned an elaborate meal for Memo's family. Memo had an outdoor cookers idea of paradise. A fully adjustable two-metre-wide braai (parrilla in Colombia) and an oven which I have only ever seen in Colombia and is constructed of three parts. The oven is built of brick and clay and the first lower section is a fire area where a hot, hot fire is made, and once the fire is ready a steel door is locked trapping the heat inside. The middle section is the oven area which is a sealed by another steel door with a rubber seal and screw knob to keep the heat inside, and the top section is the chimney. I started the fire just after lunch and had the oven nice and hot within two hours. We had bought three large chickens which we prepared in the South African beer bird style. A can of beer minus one sip stuffed in the chickens' butt and stood upright. All three chickens were given the beer can treatment, covered in olive oil, herbs, sea salt and ground pepper and place in the sealed oven for six hours. An hour before the chicken was ready we placed a tray of potato wedges under the birds to cook in the fat and served the feast with a big garden salad. Luisa prepared milk tart for dessert and our two families ate and laughed and drank together.

In the morning, I set to work trying to get to the bottom of the brake problem. I removed the tyre and saw that one of the pads on the left-hand side was completely flat, the other was OK. I had inspected the brake pads when they had started to grind and had seen that they were thin, but did not expect them to deteriorate so quickly. The brake disc was wafer-thin and rusty and junks broke went poked with a screwdriver, proof of severe heat. I had been told when I had the discs skimmed back in South Africa that I would probably have to have the discs replaced with the next pad change, but this damage was extreme. The mountains of Argentina, Chile and Peru had taken their toll on my brakes which is not surprising considering that for the last two months the nose of the Landy had either been pointed up at the sky or down at a valley.

I needed to get the hub nut off to be able to take the disc off, but the nut was fixed tight and I needed a special tool or socket to remove it. Cecé drove me into town to see if they had the socket, but it was too big for a small general hardware store to stock. Memo said I could use his perfect green Series 3 Santana, but I did not fit in the Landy and could not change gears, so poor Cecé had to drive me around. We spent the day searching for the tool but left every store empty-handed. That night Memo arrived home from work, the girls returned from school and university and two more Legion members arrived to have a look at the brakes. Chameleon and Miguel tackled the hub nut with a hammer and chisel. They discovered that the reason that my brakes pads were so worn down was that the brake pistons which push and release the brake pads had seized in the open position which basically meant that I had been driving with the brakes on. I asked Chameleon and Miguel how much they were going to charge me for the help and they just laughed and told me to pay in hot coffee. I was breaking my own golden rule by letting someone else work on my Landy, but these guys knew what they were doing and completely took over. A few phone calls were made while I basically stood around wondering what the hell was going on. Chameleon was there at 5 am the next morning and we followed his old

109 into the city. The mechanic, Alejandro, took us for breakfast in his gangster Mercedes and we spent the next 13 hours driving around looking for spares, hanging out with legion members who visited us and Alejandro at the workshop, eating lunch and getting worried as the minutes ticked by and the sun set. Only after 10 pm was the Landy finally ready to go home, we had been ready to leave a lot sooner. Now the moment of truth. We asked Alejandro for the bill. He said don't worry, you don't have to pay me a cent, just pay the spares guy for the parts, the Legion has got you covered for the labour. We were floored. The parts were not cheap, but thirteen hours of labour could have and should have been very, very dear. We took a few photos with the Legion members who had come to meet us and drove back to Chia in awe of the Land Rover community.

Unbelievably the family of Julian and Lorena, the crazy Colombians in the Willys Jeep we had met in Cusco, had a house on the same road as Memo's and less than 500 metres away. We went to chat with his Dad and drop off the belongings which they had entrusted to us. Using the miracle of the internet, we had a video chat with Julian who was down in freezing cold Ushuaia. He and Lorena had split up and she had flown to see family in Costa Rica. He was going to return to Colombia the next Friday and we made secret plans with his Dad to return and to collect Julian from the airport in the Landy.

By now we were part of Memo's family and it seemed as if Keelan and Lucia, the youngest daughter, were planning to elope. They were a cute couple and I was proud that Keelan's first love was such a sweet and intelligent girl, but we all knew it would end in tears. Unbelievably we had already been camped in the parking area for a week and decided it would be best for the family if we went up the Villa de Leyva to wait for Julian's return the next week.

30

Me Importa Un Chorizo

Colombia was proving to be quite a surprise and the most modern and progressive of all the Spanish speaking countries we had visited. If anything, the Colombian cities were on par with the Brazilian cities in terms of modernity, but both countries struggle with a large, poor rural population. I could happily live in either country, but the truth is that the weather is better in Brazil and there are very few places where you need to wear a jacket during the day. The Brazilians and Colombians would be equal if not for the language which sets them apart; in both countries, we had felt loved and welcomed.

During the week we received news that Julian had decided not to return to Colombia yet and would instead drive up through Brazil and Venezuela to get back home. His best friend Diego flew down to join him and the two set off north through the Patagonian snow and ice. We could now head to Cartagena, but the Legion had organised a large braai on the Sunday, and we were reluctant to stand up the people who had been so good to us. We returned to Bogota and Memo's family welcomed us warmly. We drove up the mountain which overlooks Bogota to meet the assembled Legion members, we had bought a few cases of beer and Luisa had baked our now famous South African Milk Tart and Koeksisters. There was a large crowd and Memo, and I made the fire and we took time to have a good look at each Land Rover and get to know the owners. Cam was my guide and he knew the age and detailed history of every Land Rover present. The Legion dearly love their Landy's and are a very tight community who spend much of their free time together. They come from all walks of life from professors to mechanics, civil engineers and English teachers, photographers and architects. And these guys know more about Land Rovers than anyone I had ever met. Their knowledge is broad and includes the entire range of Series and Defenders, they don't suffer fools, and they treat each other with respect.

Shortly before we left Memo's house, Cecé found out that she had breast cancer. We were devastated, but amazed by her good humour and courage. She had felt the bump and had an examination before the cancer had a chance to spread much further. Our job now was to keep the wheels rolling while the family took care of Cecé. The family needed their space and we did what we could before reluctantly saying goodbye. We all had tears in our eyes especially Keelan and Lucia, but we promised to return one day, and it is a promise which I intend to keep.

One of the characteristics of most South American countries which amazes me is the spread of wealth. Cities are a huge, modern, glittering gaggle of phallic symbols and rapid transport systems, coffee shops, burger joints and designer stores. With the exception of some, the majority of towns seem to not be maintained by any sort of municipality and the lack of well-funded and managed municipalities is holding the continent back. With regular street sweeping, refuse removal and recycling, landscape and road maintenance even the poorest town can be lovable, and the residents can feel pride for their homes and that may inspire them to improve their lives. It is one aspect of poverty which confuses me the most; the filth. Poverty does not prevent a person from raking his garden, finding a solution for litter, maintaining his home, cleaning his house, washing his clothes. If a person makes an effort to do that every day and a community joins in, then poverty will soon become history because poverty truly is a state of mind. I know.

Colombia is one of the cleaner countries in a continent plagued by litter and litterers, but even Colombia has a long way to go. There is a section of road in the north between Santa Marta and Cartagena where the road runs along a small strip of land which separates the Caribbean from large beautiful lagoons. Where there should be holiday resorts and a national park the road is lined with an impoverished community swimming in a sea of its own filth. Litter is the multi-coloured plastic lawn of the soggy landscape and children play in it while the adults ignore it, with a few notable exceptions. It is one of the most beautiful parts of Colombia but also one of the most lawless; we were stopped by a commotion in the road and young men carrying large bags of food into the bush, many with their faces covered by cloth. A few stood near the road and stared at us with hateful eyes. We could not see what the cause of the holdup was, but when we were directed past the truck we noticed that the windscreen and windows had been smashed and rocks lay strewn across the road. A few minutes earlier and they might have decided to rob us. It was a shocking experience which we did not expect in a country we had grown to love. And we were discussing whether we should head to Venezuela next, a country with far more pressing social problems.

31

A Change Of Plans

But first I was going to through a big pile of money at our tyre and wheel problem. Our truck was not happy on those skinny tyres, and I was miserable. We could not go exploring deserts or beaches without fear of getting stuck without a way to get unstuck. The tyres had done well in the dunes outside Lima, but we were with ten other Land Rovers and the sand was wet and cold, which makes it a lot firmer. I went onto the Legion Land Rover page and saw that there was a guy in Pasto who was selling fifteen-inch rims for a Land Rover. By now I had realised that Land Rover parts and rims are extremely rare in South America. I emailed the seller and asked a few questions. He responded that the rims were in very good condition. He said that they had been widened professionally and that they had no problems. After much debate, we paid him for the rims and the transport, and we waited in a camp in a town called El Rodadero for the rims to arrive. I went looking for a set of tyres which I had been coveting and found a set, a small miracle because we had been searching for rims and tyres since Chile and had not found this brand in this size 33 12.5 R15. Ideally, I would have liked to put on sixteen-inch rims and 285 75 R16 tyres because they have a higher load rating, but I had never had a problem with the fifteen-inch tyres (until they started exploding at 70 000 kilometres). The rims arrived three days late which is on time by South American standards. I inspected them, and they looked OK, not great, but OK. I sprayed them matt black and then had the tyres fitted. Two of the rims were unbalance-able and I soon found out that they were constantly leaking air. After a short row with the seller then a long row with Luisa, we decided to order a new set of rims from the UK and have them shipped to Cartagena. Luisa searched for and found a nice apartment where we could enjoy Christmas indoors and we drove to the old colonial city to wait for the new rims. Carlos, a Legion member and a great character, needed to ship some parts from the UK and we had them sent with our rims to spread and lower the costs and Carlos could also help us with the logistics and customs. The Legion was again coming to the rescue and when they heard the cost of bringing the rims in from the UK they began a collection to help us pay. I had to reassure them repeatedly that we were OK and would just have to drink less beer and they stopped the collection which I would have a problem accepting. It took a month in a windy, dusty, daytime feeding mosquito campsite in El Rodadero and almost a month in Cartagena for the new rims to arrive from England. We were again bent over a barrel by the courier and by customs, but eventually, I was able to fit the new tyres to the new rims and roll out of town. We are actually very good at getting "stuck" in one place for a long time. It gives us a sense of security and community because locals eventually realise that we are not going anywhere, and they become friends. The supermarket staff get to know you, you find the great street food and good pizza places, you find the deals and the steals and the places to be, you meet people you would never have met, and you become part of the local scene. While camped in El Rodadero Luisa and I chatted about the road ahead. The plan had always been to ship the Landy to Panama from Colombia and we had spent the last few months contacting shipping agents, arranging dates, searching for shipping partners and trying to save a few bucks. At Luisa's urging, we made the decision to circumnavigate the entire South American continent. We would put our direct northern path on hold and instead head east to Venezuela and to the three countries in the upper right-hand corner of the continent - Guyana, Suriname and French Guyana before returning to Brazil to witness the spectacle of the World Cup, hang out with new old friends and perhaps teach English to raise money for our travels. The decision was spontaneous and insane which suits us perfectly.

32

Those Africans Are Mad!

The decision to enter Venezuela was based on the spirit of adventure and the experience we had in Brazil. Everyone told us not to go to Brazil and we fell in love with the country. Just after we had made the decision to cross Venezuela, a former Ms Universe was slaughtered along with her British husband on a road which we would have to drive across coastal Venezuela. Her young child was also in the car but luckily survived the bullets shot by thugs who had blocked the road and stopped their car. We were nervous and had many discussions about safety and planned a reaction to imminent threats. We would drive over any obstacle placed in the road which was not higher than 50 centimetres, we would not stop if we had a tyre blow out, we would never travel at night and we would keep a decoy wallet stuffed with a few dollars and various South American banknotes which we would immediately hand to the gun in the window. No hero stuff. Hand it over and keep moving. In the event of a rock-throwing party, the kids were drilled to drop down low behind our seats and cover their heads with pillows if told to.

The border crossing into Venezuela was the worst we have ever had to suffer through. Our last night in beautiful Colombia was spent in a parking lot in the less than beautiful Rio Hacha where we ate street food and enjoyed fresh fruit smoothies. We awoke before the sun to drive the barren 70 km's to the border and arrived to find a long queue of people waiting to exit Colombia. We were attended to by at least ten Colombian customs officials in an air-conditioned office. Money changers pestered us to and from and in the Landy while we waited amongst the many ugly

1970s and 1980's American V8's, choking on their fumes. The Colombian side took only half an hour. The next five hours would be spent waiting for one harassed man behind a small, low, cracked and tinted window to serve about two hundred people who queued in a funnel of crying children, sweaty fat, stale air and competition. When order vanished completely, Luisa sent Keelan to fetch me, waiting in the Landy parked in the sun breathing V8 fumes and I muscled past the sad woman and the fat man whose low belly uncomfortably massaged my sweaty buttocks, a softly constant, unwelcome pressing from behind. Before the unlikely marriage was consummated I managed to elbow an old, sick lady out the way and trample on a suffocating child, have our passports stamped and led my unhappy family back to the Landy for a ten-kilometre drive past some soldiers and a boom gate in search of customs and the road to Maracaibo. Before we had left the border, I changed US$5.00 with one of the money changers, he had offered me 50 Bolivars (Bs) to the dollar, but I heard that we could get more. The official exchange rate to the dollar in January 2014 was six to one, on the black market, the exchange was hovering at sixty-five to one. And since fuel is essentially free at about US$0.50 for 100 litres of diesel we had not filled our fuel tanks in Colombia. The country with the largest proven deposits of oil and thus an OPEC member was going to be very interesting.

We had travelled back in time, or maybe to a post-apocalyptic future. The only cars we saw were the horrible old rumbling V8's, the road very poor, the countryside is strewn with litter and old wrecks, colourful ugly houses, stray dogs, vegetable stands and roadside fuel vendors. Stalls and weathered stores cluttered dry, treeless towns. Queues snaked around supermarkets and booze selling "bodegas" claimed each intersection. We were tempted to turn around and drive screaming back into the arms of Colombia, but we pressed on and arrived in the western city Maracaibo with its pleasant neighbourhoods, clean streets, modern cars and malls.

WE WILL BE FREE

Our first real interaction with Venezuela was going to take place in the one large 70's era mall. A kind lady at a fast food joint chatted with us in English and we asked about changing dollars on the black market, a highly illegal activity which the government was apparently cracking down on. The owner of the store said that she would give us sixty Bolivars for a Dollar, and we sat down to eat a huge, cheap meal prepared behind closed doors by a chimpanzee in a fire suit, while the proprietor went to the bank to withdraw a large stack of paper to exchange for a small stack of paper. We took a walk around the food court and did a few quick equations. With a fist full of dollars and a high black-market rate, we were going to get nice and fat in poor Venezuela. That night we checked into the five stars Hotel Venetur which was certainly five-star back in the fifties when it was built and probably after its last refurbishment in the '70s, but now she was a ghost hotel run by a staff amicable enough to pretend to care and the faded veneer of age and cigarette smoke. Our room was comfortable and musky and R600 (US$50.00) including breakfast. Venezuela has a huge crime and murder problem and the decision was made not to camp if we could find cheap accommodation. We headed over to the mall next to the hotel, a mall which was presumably built while her neighbour was being refurbished. Many stores selling exactly the same thing and we were looking for another food court for a decent fast food fix and maybe someone to buy some dollars at a good rate. I asked at a few places where I could cambio (change) dollars and most referred me to the official bureau de change. To avoid arrest and any softer Venezuelan bellies against my behind I had decided that I would casually ask store owners where I could change dollars. If they responded that they would buy I would ask them how much and if they answered with an amount higher than the official exchange rate, then they would technically be breaking the law by initiating the exchange at an inflated rate. A squint guy at an American sporting goods stand made a few calls and over the course of the next few hours arranged two buyers for our greenbacks, the one buyer a seller of silk shirts and ties and the other a doughnut and cake vendor. We exchanged nervously at sixty to one in the middle of the food court with the doughnut guy then hidden by clear glass and a mannequin on the third floor with the silk shirts guy who had only ten, twenty and fifty Bolivars notes. The kids waited at the food court while we went off to change money and I realised that we had been very stupid to leave them there while we went off to do the exchange. Had some cops burst in and arrested us we would have a difficult time explaining that we had two kids waiting for us and no-one to take care of them. My blood went cold at the thought. With a striped hippy bag full of money, we went to fetch the kids and then hurried back along the well-lit night time street to the hotel and the safety of our room where Luisa had me take photos of her swimming in a large cash puddle on the bed. The next day the kids swam in the pool and that night we enjoyed a steak and ribs dinner for less than we would pay for KFC back home. Then the next morning after a buffet breakfast we went looking for diesel and the massive bridge which would lead us to Coro, our next stop on the bleak Caribbean coast. We drove through the first of many "free" toll gates which the police have converted into checkpoints. Venezuelans apparently refuse to pay for anything which oil revenue can pay for, which, it seems, is everything. The police stopped us and wanted a look at all our documents which we handed over begrudgingly. To distract their minds from wandering into the weedy garden of corruption we asked if they knew where we could buy diesel. The documents were returned, and the directions are given. Over the magnificent bridge, we drove to find a petrol station which at first said they had no diesel then decided that they did and filled our tanks. The store sold us Magnum ice creams and cold drinks and potato chips for prices so low we could not believe our good fortune. Back on the road, surrounded by V8 passenger cars, V8 delivery pickups and every American brand vehicle ever manufactured. The dry road led us to Coro which has a surprisingly pleasant cobble street colonial area and a few cheap posadas (bed and breakfasts). We would soon learn that beer is extremely cheap and on our first visit to a supermarket we were surprised to find many rows of toilet paper which we had been told was very scarce in Venezuela, so we had brought plenty of our own two-ply. The shelves were stocked with most things you need, but only one brand of each product. If you want tomato sauce (ketchup) you can have Heinz in either the large bottle or the small bottle. Washing powder, toilet paper, shoe polish many rows of few choices. And Venezuelans do not seem to be too concerned about sanitation or cleanliness or bacteria in general. The butchery had the smell of old green meat, chunks of animal lay on washing powder cardboard boxes in cracked glass, uncooled display cases. Chicken preserved in bleach lay limply in clear plastic bags with runny blood leaking on the floor. It was then that I decided that we would be vegetarian for most of our time in Venezuela. We decided to visit the island near Coro, a Zona Franca (tax-free zone) to see if we could find anything we needed in a 70's mall at 70's prices. We found very little, but I lost my heart to a curvy blonde so naturally beautiful that Luisa had actually called me over to meet her. I dreamed of being able to live true to my African culture, to have that second wife I so richly deserved, to save that voluptuous angel from that decrepit town, dusty windswept island and undeserving country. I told her she was beautiful. She thanked me shyly and carried on working. Luisa had to hit me, really hard, to break the spell. Reluctantly we left her there to languish in her sandy hell and we returned to the mainland after driving around the island to watch the wind throw litter across the sand. The posada receptionist introduced us to his professor when we asked if he knew anyone who wanted to buy dollars. A sweet elderly lady, the professor stood in bank queues for an entire afternoon to withdraw a huge pile of her pension to swop for two American notes.

Chichiriviche was our next stop, a town surrounded by islands and full of inflatable toys, beer, drunks, litter and a strange charm when viewed from a boat on the ocean. The suggested posada was closed, but the owner made a call to a friend, David, who ran a posada on the other side of town. Men in pickups tried to divert us to their establishment, but we kept on looking for David's place, Arena Mar, which we found locked and were about to leave when David and his wife returned from buying supplies. The posada had a white-walled Mediterranean feel, with comfortable rooms surrounding a rectangular pool. David had built the posada with his own hands and a couple of helpers. He rushed us into town to buy beer, bread, good meat, eggs, juice and water. He introduced to his family, and we would often chat over a beer and occasional cigarette. David's place would be our home for the next week and we were friends by the time we left. We visited an island before we left Chichiriviche but were disappointed by the litter of the island and were plagued by flies. There were a few more islands in the area, and we soon learned that the further the island was from the mainland the nicer it became. We drove into the Morrocoy National Park and were lucky enough to meet a local park ranger, Rodrigo, who ran a little posada with his family. His work ethic reminded me of David and that set him apart from most of the lingering population. He offered to take us to Sombrero Island in his boat for a very reasonable price. We agreed to go after he assured us that we would find no litter or flies on the island. What we did find was a sparkling blue water white sandy beach paradise. No loud music and none of the good-natured drunkenness and filth we had seen on the other island. Vendors sold ceviche (raw fish "cooked" in lime juice), we lazed in the sun, admired the golden bodies socialising in the water and snorkelled in the clearest water we had ever seen. Venezuela and Colombia both have a reputation for cheap plastic surgery and large circular breasts and strangely protruding Bushman butts are en-vogue. Natural beauty is a rare treat for the eyes, especially on the beaches of Venezuela. A bottle blonde with oversized sunglasses, toothpick legs and bulbous butt and a gay, Speedo friend, stood in the water sipping a beer and chatting with some butt loving Argentinean boys. The girl looked good from behind but like this P from the side.

Rodrigo came to fetch us after a few short hours and because of his status as a ranger, he was able to enter restricted areas and beaches and take us along for a private tour. We went to a rocky outcrop where local fisherman had shrines dedicated after their deaths, we visited a protected beach where turtles came to lay their many, mostly doomed, eggs and I stood on a sea urchin while providing a base for Luisa to step on and slip off repeatedly while trying to climb back into the ladderless boat after snorkelling for Starfish. I don't know what I did wrong, but Luisa waited a week before removing the urchin spines from my foot and toes.

33

The Maduro Dilemma or You Left a Mess Chavez

Arriving back at the little posada we were sunburnt and satisfied. We had seen many thousands of coastline kilometres on our tour around South America, but here we had found a true paradise in close proximity to a political hell. Socialismo in Venezuela is a fraud disguised by a thin thickly pasted veil of patriotism, historic pride, hero worship and bullshit. The first drop of oil discovered in Venezuela was the first of many billions to lubricate the countries descent into poverty, ignorance and theft. The middle classes are mowed down in the streets, tortured in jail and repressed by an upper class which bribes the majority lower classes with social grants, essentially free fuel, food subsidies, free inadequate education and healthcare. Chavez is a god to the poor and Maduro, the fat little boy with the fat moustache who Chavez chose as his successor, spends countless hours every day sitting next to an enormous poster of God Chavez preaching a gospel of socialismo and warning of the gathering Fascists to a gaggle of well dressed, well paid co-conspirators, broadcasted across government-controlled radio and television stations to a population who should be burning the parliament to the ground. But, as in South Africa, the poor and poorly educated are the majority manipulated by the corrupt minority; though South Africa is a political nirvana compared to poor, wealthy Venezuela (I love Mandela but loathe the current version of the ANC). Most Venezuelans cannot and do not travel, those who do, come back with either a better understanding of how politically retarded the country is or with a fistful of dollars to exploit the cleverly devastated economy. A German by birth, Trinidad raised, Venezuelan permanent resident English teacher in central Venezuela asked my opinion about Venezuela after he had helped us secure a hotel room in a full hotel. I told him what I thought. He compared God Chavez to Mandela, I laughed, sang and translated the chorus of Johannes Kerkorels' song, 'Sit Dit Af' (sit dit af, sit dit af, want dis a helse straf (turn it off, turn it off, because it is a hell of a punishment - referring to PW Botha's long, finger-wagging Apartheid-Era televised speeches) he shook my hand and walked away. An hour later, after a cheap and surprisingly tasty dinner, two young men were hanging out by my Landy and they wanted to chat. The one was friendly and polite, the other angling for an argument. Good thug, bad thug. I did not take the bait, they told me they were English students and I knew exactly why they were there. The bad thug was stoned and impatient, good thug was choosing his words very carefully. I played stupid and friendly, finished my cigar and chatted to the security guard for a while before heading up to our uncomfortable fluorescent-lit room. Defusing a situation is much more important than defending either your pride or your opinion when you have a family to consider and a long way to go.

We left Morrocoy and took the dangerous road through Caracas to Puerto La Cruz and another run down five-star Venetur hotel. Travelling the Caracas road was a gamble, and we were very lucky not to be held up by protests, tear gas and bullets of either rubber or steel. Caracas seemed quite modern and the excellent highway ran in the shadow of an incomplete elevated rail system. Venezuela really is a sad contrast of rich and poor, development and stagnation.

Luisa had negotiated a month's rental of a house in El Yaque, a gringo town on the Caribbean Venezuelan Island, Margarita. We bought ferry tickets for the Landy and us and woke up at 4 am to catch the ferry at a secondary harbour ten-kilometres east of Puerto La Cruz. Arriving at the port before sunrise we were told that the Landy's ticket was incorrect and we would have to travel back to the city and the ticket office to amend the ticket. Rushing back through dawn traffic we arrived at the ticket office to find they did not open for another two hours, impatiently we waited, searched for information, eventually upgraded the tickets and rushed back to the other port in time to sit in the hot equatorial sun for five hours while we waited for a fuel truck to deliver eight tons (a few hundred dollars' worth) of diesel to the ferry. Idiots. Isla Margarita is not a Caribbean paradise but rather a grassy windswept importation of Venezuelan culture and Europeans and Americans looking to make a buck. The lady through whom we had rented the basically unfurnished house was kind, attentive and doting until she discovered that she would not make any more money out of us no matter how hard she tried to guilt us into paying US $700 for kite surfing lessons for Keelan or introducing us to everyone on the island with who she had a commission agreement. Skinny Canadian idiot.

The month was spent working, writing, fixing the Landy and kicking a 28-year-old smoking habit. One hot, windy morning I awoke with a hangover to find that Luisa had smoked every cigarette available and left only one old wrinkly menthol which I smoked and decided would be my last cigarette. I knew that if I continued to smoke that eventually, Keelan might start smoking and maybe even Jessica would be tempted. I was never really a heavy smoker unless I was drinking which was every third or fourth night. I enjoyed smoking but had made the commitment to stop when I was forty. Why wait? I stopped that day and have not smoked commercial cigarettes since, but I do allow myself a cigar every other night. In that house, we ate mostly vegetables and drank fruit smoothies, and once I stopped smoking I realised that I had been possessed by the spirit of either a hippy or a Buddhist. I even drank less! A very sad state and I resolved to continue my happily unhealthy but smoke-free lifestyle as soon as we left Venezuela and proudly I have succeeded.

225

WE WILL BE FREE

Despite the dry wind and endless dust, El Yaque was a respite after almost fifteen months of continuous camping. We made lists of chores and set about clearing the list. We left the island having made few new friends and eager to get back down to Brazil. I had fattened up horribly while spending my days writing and snacking every time I craved a cigarette. I hate ferries, and I particularly hate open ocean ferries run by incompetent government agencies. I can swim, the family can swim, and we choose our seating close to emergency exits and do private evacuation drills. But my Landy can't swim. We need to do something about that.

Back on the mainland, we headed east of Puerto La Cruz to visit the mountainous coastal region and found a beautiful posada run and built by a French carpenter who cooked us delicious meals and treated us with kind respect. The sea and island views from his posada were fantastic until the poor farmers began to clear land by fire, after which the views were a memory and we spent a week in a fog.

We visited a town called Caprice en-route to Roraima and Brazil. The town was the cleanest, best organised and most sober town we had visited in Venezuela, but the schools' yards were overgrown and full of litter. Viva Socialismo. There are caves close to the town, and after staying in yet another 70's hotel, we went for a five-kilometre cave walk, led by a little rapid Spanish speaking man and dive-bombed by birds with whiskers who squawked and shat and had more in common with bats than birds. The road was wet and the Landy was making a few noises when we drove up out of the jungle and muddy towns full of Amerindians driving raised and dangerous-looking gold digger Toyota Land Cruisers, up to the savannah and the tepui, flat-top mountains and a grassland region of free camping and beautiful isolated waterfalls which should be managed by Brazil. Throughout Venezuela, we had seen expensive, very well equipped 4x4's but we had never come across any camping areas. In the Roraima, Venezuelans can escape to an area free of Maduro's rantings, pollution, poverty and litter. They can drive far into the peaceful grasslands to enjoy rivers packed with monstrous fish and pre-historic vistas.

In the southern town of Santa Elena, we stocked up on sugar, rice, pasta sauce, beer and cleaning products before leaving for the border where, apparently, we could buy cheap diesel before crossing into Brazil. Venezuelan fuel is the equivalent of Methamphetamine. It is cheap and dirty and leaves you wanting more. As Overlanders our largest expense is fuel with beer a close second. Leaving we found that yes, you can buy diesel, but no, it is not virtually free, but instead, it is $1.00 US per litre, an exorbitant amount by Venezuelan standards. I could almost hear the Venezuelan immigration officials mocking me as I turned the Landy away from the pumps, confident that we could reach Boa Vista on what little fuel we had left. Filling at the border would require changing dollars at terrible rates and we had dedicated the last three months to finding the best rates possible and changing money on the black market which, as it turns out, is a blonde housewife in a black Renault behind the putrid McDonalds where we met the great guy who gave us the free navigation software.

34

Viva Brazil

I was relieved to leave Venezuela and re-enter Brazil. Anticipating armed robbery around every corner does not make a great road trip and I knew that Brazil would be infinitely more comfortable, though I had no idea what to expect once we crossed the border. The kind muscular Brazilian Policia Federal stamped us back into Brazil and a good omen oversaw the immigration procedure. A South African flag sat anonymously above a filing cabinet and rejected any enquiries as to why, here in the middle of nowhere, our flag sat waiting for us.

Luisa wanted to drive through Boa Vista and head directly to the Guyana border. Our Brazilian Land Rover buddies had told us that they had a friend who we could stay within Boa Vista. The friend, Elmer, ran a workshop and we could camp in his yard. I suggested that we stay for a few nights, but Luisa was adamant that we should continue, but the Landy had her own ideas. Stopping for food, we heard a loud clunking coming from the suspension. I thought that the noise was coming from the rear, but could not find the problem after inspecting the suspension. Luisa descended into a foul mood. For some reason, she believes that I can create mechanical failures at will just to piss her off. The reality is that we were facing an almost 600 km muddy jungle track in Guyana and Land Rovers are famous for getting you home and then breaking down. This time the Landy was telling me that she needed some TLC before we hit the jungle. We went looking for an internet cafe so that I could find Elmer's address, but Luisa was in a pitch-black mood. Regardless, we found Elmer and the workshop his father had built, we settled in and I tried to replace all of the suspension bushes lying in the dirt at temperatures close to 50° C. I know that Elmer would not have declined if I had asked to use the ramp, but I could see that the workshop was busy. The use of the presses and some advice helped me to replace all the rubber bushes with polyurethane bushes in three days of blood and buckets of sweat. Elmer's workshop is full of Jeeps and Toyota Bandeirante 4x4's which he and his Dad rebuild from humble agricultural vehicles into larger than life kick-ass go anywhere modern beasts. Boa Vista itself is a low-rise Sunday city with a one-kilometre stretch of free sports facilities which were built by the Ayrton Senna Foundation. It was good to be back in our second home.

Our mission was to circumnavigate the South American continent, and in order to do that, we would need to cross three tiny nations which lie in the north-east corner and which most people do not know exist. British Guyana, Dutch Suriname and French Guiana are colonial relics, almost completely isolated, difficult to reach by road and expensive to travel. Our first hurdle after leaving the kind hospitality of Elmer and his friends was the road from Lethem to Linden in English Guyana.

35

Fish Fry And Lime, Mon

There is not much in the way of tourism in the three Guyana's (Suriname is referred to as one of the Guyana's) and there are very few roads. British Guyana was made famous by the Jonestown massacre in the 1970s when almost 1000 religious nuts committed suicide after killing a delegation at the airstrip, including a Senator, which was sent from the USA to investigate the cult run by Mr Jones. Most of the Guyana's can only be navigated by air, and the interior of all three countries consists of mostly virgin rainforest plagued by logging and illegal gold mining. The roads which are not paved are not really roads, they are a muddy mess.

British Guyana sees itself as culturally Caribbean even though the country is South American geographically. Illegal gold mining by the Brazilians in the Guyanese jungle has led to strained relations between the Guyanese and Brazil and as a result, the road from border Lethem to Linden close to the capital Georgetown is an unpaved jungle track of almost 600 kms. The rainy season was due to start mid-April, and we entered Guyana on the 15th of April. That road is one of, if not THE most, difficult road in all of South America. Essentially a track through tropical rainforest it is difficult to locate on most maps. Rob, my Kiwi buddy, messaged me when he heard we were driving that route, 'but there is no road mate', 'there is a track, apparently'. I like to impress people with the girth and shimmer of my bowling ball size nuts, but that's just bravado, roads like this make me very nervous. If we suffer a breakdown or have a medical emergency, we are very far from any form of civilisation. I have to trust my Land Rover and myself, my navigator and our planning. We had enough provisions to last at least 10 days and would have to improvise if the proverbial shit hit the fabled fan. This is our Camel Trophy, unsupported and with a couple of kids along for the ride.

At first, we were relieved to enter a country where we could speak English and drive on the correct side of the road. But that relief was short-lived. The bureaucracy was simply silly. A man who would not speak louder than a whisper informed us that the supervisor, who was on lunch, would need to phone Georgetown for clearance to give us a three-day permit to drive to Georgetown. The Indian supervisor had either been shot in the jaw or had been a very unlucky cricketer, mumbled that we needed insurance before we could enter. But we were allowed to enter the town to buy insurance before returning after his siesta when he would phone someone who might or might not be A- awake B- playing cricket C- liming. As it happened the twelve-year-old, who sold us the insurance at the Bank of Guyana was enduring his first day on the job and naively neglected all the administrative nuances warranted by an officious bureaucrat and an ABC in Georgetown. The supervisor then asked us if we would stay for the huge rodeo in town that weekend. 'How can we, you have given us only three days to get to Georgetown!' That night, after finally clearing immigration and customs, we camped, I had a "leave me alone" episode and the Landy had to pull a Bedford 4x4 truck and an ungrateful driver out of a muddy little hole. All night it rained cats and dogs and more muddy holes. We started down the road to Linden clean and shiny, but within ten kilometres the Landy was covered in mud. The Savannah road reminded me of a Tanzania populated by ant hills and huge Iguanas. We bumped along and camped that night at an "oasis" run by a man who would rather not extend hospitality to even those who were friends of his best friend and who had children living in their homeland. Dick. We met a Landy nutter called Sebastian who lived on a farm near the Oasis and whose Dad we would probably meet on the road to Georgetown. That night we shared living space with a courageous and unlikely Argentinean couple who were travelling in a little French van on terrible roads but had by some miracle drove the worst section of the jungle before the rains turned. I truly do not understand people who drive 2x4's where 4x4's are necessary; you ruin both the photos and the fun. I refuse to pull your adventurous ass out of any little mud puddles and if I do you owe me a year's supply of beer because you don't leave home in a little van to tackle huge roads unless you are prepared to rely on someone else to pull you out the shit. That said, I really liked these Argies and might even exempt them from the 'wait for help' wall of shame.

The rain fell in sheets all night, savannah gave way to the jungle and the road became more muddy and slippery and I was grateful that I was in a fully equipped 4x4 with large mud-terrain tyres. Unfortunately, the tyres were a bit too wide for the mud spats, and we had to drive most of the road with the windows closed and the lame aircon blowing cool air onto our knees. The air conditioning in a 2003 Defender is as powerful as a parrot fart; the kids were sweating in the back seat surrounded by hot, humid jungle. The windows were covered with so much mud that eventually the Landy's interior was dark and we could not see the jungle to our left or right. Sections of the road would be wide and corrugated where vehicles were able to accelerate and make up some lost time caused by the narrower mud pooled sections where you had to choose your line and gear carefully to ensure that you did not slide either into the jungle or into a huge pit in the middle of the road. Surprisingly we passed a few sedans travelling the road in convoy accompanied by a couple of large 4x4's which would drag the sedans on their bellies through the worst sections. We later learned that these were second-hand vehicles headed for sale in Lethem or Brazil. A few trucks and buses managed to get stuck on the road and churned the mud in an attempt to get out. At the end of the second day of driving, we arrived at a compulsory police checkpoint at Mile 53. The police struggled to believe that we were South African but told us that we could ask for camping at a restaurant next to the road, past the Chinese restaurant. The owner of the diner served us beef and chicken curry and a very Jamaican sounding accent, we slept next to a hut where travellers and gold miners arrived during the night to hang hammocks and join in the snoring chorus I led from my rooftop tent. It was Easter weekend and we awoke to an offer of coffee or tea and six large and delicious hot cross buns. We did not need to pay for camping either. The Guyanese are very proud of their hospitable reputation, which we would soon enjoy in large doses. The last third of the road was to be the easiest as much of it had just been graded. We met some more Land Rovers on the road and the owner of a Defender TD5, Deo, told us where we could buy Landy parts in Georgetown. Driving at a maximum of 20 kph we were making very slow progress. A ferry had to carry the Landy across a very large and swift-flowing river, and there were very few inhabited pockets where we could purchase cold drinks and reassurance that we were on the right road. Swarms of green carnivorous butterflies populated the road and fed on little mounds of Iguana roadkill, fluttering across the roads as we approached. Visibility was restricted to a maximum of 100 metres up the road and five metres into the jungle in most places. The excitement was soon replaced by impatience, when will this bloody road end? Because there was a rodeo taking place in Lethem that weekend convoys of taxis and 4x4's were heading towards us from Georgetown, chewing up the road surface as they struggled through, blocking the road with a queue of vehicles as 4x4's winched and dragged the stricken vehicles out clinging red holes.

Emerging from the jungle in Linden we were excited and covered in mud. The Landy was power washed almost white and drove us to Shipman's, the only official campsite in the entire tiny country. There were plenty of creeks (pronounced cricks by the Guyanese) where we could park and free camp, but we planned on camping for a while, while we sorted out the visas for Suriname. I am lucky enough to have been eligible for a British passport and I travel with both that precious European passport and my precious African passport, but my family does not qualify for a First World passport until they have lived in the UK for five years.

Immediately we noted a few similarities in Guyanese and South African culture which made us feel comfortable. Everyone seemed obsessed with Cricket, curry and beer. We found products like Crème Soda and Marmite which we had not had since we left South Africa eighteen months earlier. We arrived at Shipman's on a Friday and negotiated a rate with the Indian camp manager, Mr Kumar who was a retired Guyanese Army sergeant and was very particular about how his camp should be run and he ensured that the music level never reached Brazilian, Venezuelan or Colombian levels. We had seen many signs advertising, Fish Fry and Lime and when asked, Mr Kumar explained that lime is not a citrus eaten with a fish, but to lime is to relax, to chill out, or to hang out. Some stores would have a sign saying No Liming which meant no loitering. We awoke on the Saturday to a camp filling with day campers and overnight campers, a lady asked if she could use a pot and returned it full of rice and chicken. Another group offered us lunch and refreshments and, yet another group brought us dinner. This generosity continued on the Sunday, and we spent the public holiday Monday with a group of new friends who fed us the most delicious pork ribs, chicken, salad and cold beers. We swam in the dark water rumoured to be home to Anaconda, Piranha and Cayman, Luisa jumping on me every time something (usually one of my feet) brushed her leg. There is almost nothing better than a scared girl in a bikini, Hollywood knows this well. On Tuesday we endured constipated single lane traffic, in order to enter Georgetown and reach the Suriname consulate which was only open to the public for a few hours in the morning and a notice on the gate informed us that there was a strict dress code and a long list of documents required, meaning we had to return the next day to Georgetown and submit our applications which may or may not be free and which may be for a week or two. Sitting in the sweltering heat in long sleeves and trousers we waited while Luisa went into the consulate and discussed our visas with an official who told us that we would have to pay US$160.00 and come back in a few days to receive either a transit or a tourist visa. Meanwhile, we had to report to the Guyana Revenue Authority to extend the vehicle import permit. An angry little policewoman was waiting for us at the end of the road once we left the GRA with our vehicle extension. She wanted to know if we had extended my permission to drive, which I had no clue I needed, and she did not make an effort to explain. She also bust us for not wearing seatbelts. She was aggressive and kept telling me to shh while I was overheating and losing my patience with the bureaucracy and this uniformed midget's bad attitude. She called a male cop to explain what we needed and told me that I could get the renewal once we had gone to the station to pay the fine for not wearing seatbelts while Luisa and I pointed out every single car which drove past with an unseatbelted occupant. Under different circumstances, we could have been pleasant to each other, but I had enough of stupid policemen and she probably did not feel that I was treating her with sufficient respect. The male cop told her to calm down and go away and he explained exactly what we needed and how we could get it from the GRA. Three hours of queuing later I had a one-month driver's permit to compliment my one-week temporary vehicle import permit.

Georgetown is a strange city of overgrown green grass, double story wooden buildings, Rasta's, Indians and very few white people. A little blonde girl walked into butchery with her Mom and could not take her eyes off us whities sitting in the Land Rover. We never experienced any aggression or insult, but we did feel unique and conspicuous. The butchery was excellent, and the meat was cut in the Western-style, which is far superior to the Latin butchery methods. We bought a few beef sausages which, when barbequed tasted 97% like the boerewors which we consumed in large amounts back home. The Landy parts store had a few awesome Land Rovers parked outside but unfortunately were very expensive compared to the quotes which we had received from the Land Rover official dealer in Suriname. We were beginning to tire of the campsite when we received word from the consulate that our tourist permits had been approved. A drive back into Georgetown, hand over the dollars, receive the stamps and drive down the coast past wooden houses on stilts, farming communities and two zombies, one a well-dressed man and one a grey old woman dressed in black clothes faded grey and arrived past sunset at the ferry crossing to Suriname. We parked in front of the gate and opened the tent for a night of free camping and bad pasta while a drunk labourer wandered over and had a discussion about respecting the working man with the security guard who had moments earlier been explaining the procedure for getting out of Guyana. It turned out to be a complicated procedure with a focus on vehicle insurance and fleecing us of US$195.00 for the ferry.

36

Nou Gaan Die Poppe Dans

The immigration procedure was intentionally dogmatic and uncomfortable, and the guards would have been welcome in any oppressive regime. My vehicle was the first on the ferry after a large truck and we sat in the Landy wondering if the Surinamese were going to confiscate all of our delicious beef sausages. They didn't check the truck for food and chatted to us in Dutch once we had queued in the express lane and a taxi driver and I bullshitted our way to the front of the queue past fainting children and cripple old ladies. I am by now a seasoned traveller and I understand that only the fittest survive an immigration queue in a hot, stuffy room and decent behaviour does not have a place amongst the accumulated exhalations and body odours of a travelling herd. I have my own kids to worry about. We had a problem, the immigration official refused to enter me into Suriname on my British passport because I had entered and exited Guyana on my South African passport. There was no way we were going to get sent back to Guyana on that expensive ferry and go through the whole visa process again. We did not budge, but spoke to the official in Afrikaans and promised to be good tourists and leave Suriname within a week. After half an hour and a few discussions with the big boss, the officer reached for my British passport and stamped me in.

Entering Suriname, we drove past many acres of rice paddies and jungle, a worker greeted us from a roadside hut with his genitals pulled out of his underwear, a glare and his hands-on his hips. The towns were much cleaner and more organised than neighbouring Guyana and we passed abandoned vehicles being eaten by the jungle and a house with swastikas incorporated into the fence. Every store seemed to be Chinese, and we drove through Paramaribo, the capital city which houses most of the population and which is actually dirtier and less organised than the rural towns which are in direct contrast to the South American norm. We drove through the city and searched the road for free camping en-route to the only established and very expensive campsite in the country where we would spend two nights in the jungle before heading back into Paramaribo to apply for the French Guiana visas. Our first stop was at the Land Rover dealer, SEMC, where we met Peter and the cutest and maybe only, redhead in the Guyana's. Peter suggested that we head down to the shared Land Rover/Ford workshop where we might be able to find an area to sleep and where we could buy parts. Our ball joints were starting to go and particularly the rear A-frame ball joint, and the drop arm steering ball joint was definitely dead. The workshop was so well equipped that I asked Ray, the workshop manager, to do the work for us replacing the ball joints while we tried to put together all of the paperwork required for the French Guiana visa. Again, as a UK passport holder, I did not need a visa, but we had to provide travel insurance, photographs, bank statements, marriage and birth certificates, business documentation and 135 Euros for the Africans. It was found that the engine mountings would also need to be replaced, SEMC had stock, but the genuine Land Rover parts were US $217.00 each. With all the visa costs and ferry costs, the price of the replacement ball joints and the labour we were stretching our thinning budget too far. The dealer took pity on us and, because we were the first Overlanders they had ever met in Suriname, they gave us one engine mount for free. Hallelujah. Unfortunately, they could not fit the new engine mounts as it was late, the next day was a public holiday, and we needed to head for French Guiana as our visas were effective from 01 May. Before we left though we had a visitor in our little camping area, a Frenchman named Bernard who was also a Land Rover fan (we had spotted his Landy in the city) and who had friends in French Guiana, who we could possibly stay with. We met Bernard again on the road between Paramaribo and the border where we had a pow-wow. He was heading back to the city from the jungle with a wobbling front end and I was heading away from the city with the same problems. His problem was that his suspension rubbers were gone, I had half tightened front left wheel nuts, and the alignment was out. It was good to meet Bernard again; Land Rover owners have a special bond especially those in very remote places.

37

Of Course, We Have Insurance Monsieur

We purposely left Paramaribo too late to catch the early ferry to French Guiana and arrived an hour before the late ferry departed. We waited in an overgrown urine scented parking lot while Luisa sorted out the immigration stamps and the tickets for the ferry. A few tourists and many locals wandered in and out of the rundown building and took water taxis over to French territory. We were nervous because we had faked our vehicle insurance papers. The French insisted on European insurance which would have cost E185.00 for one month. I am a careful driver and since SARS had not yet refunded our money, we were still running low on funds and abusing our credit cards. A German Overlander we had met in Colombia and again in Paramaribo told us that he too had faked the insurance, but had nearly been unsuccessful. He advised us against trying to duplicate the green European insurance, but instead to create South African documentation. Luisa went to work and after a couple of days, we had authentic looking paperwork with the words French Guiana strategically scattered in all the right places. We had planned the crossing to fall on a South African public holiday, late in the day, so that if the customs officials tried to phone South Africa to confirm our insurance the fake telephone numbers we had provided could not be answered by fictitious people. Waiting for the ferry I was having visions of my Landy being seized and destroyed while we stood around crying and blaming each, waiting to be deported at a huge expense. At times like these and especially during dodgy ferry crossings, the kids love to make loud banging noises and completely inappropriate comments which our nervous brains over-interpret. We approached the little riverside border post apprehensively, waited for the ferry to dock and drove up to the immigration office where two officials studied our passports and our insurance documents. We joked and tried to act natural. The kids who had strict instructions to behave were making a scene, Keelan terrorising Jessica and Jessica whining continuously to get our attention. My eyes shot daggers and the promise of swift death at my beloved children. They knew I was playing nice guy for the officials and waited until I asked them acid sweetly to behave. The officials stamped and waved us through. We asked for customs, and they told us to leave and stop if customs told us to. Driving out our hearts were in our throats. Little hidden fist-pumps and huge smiles. We made it. The Landy was not going to be destroyed and we were not going to be deported and in my joy, I forgot my earlier plans to murder the children.

French Guiana can only be entered legally by expensive ferries in the south and north or by air. The tiny colony is surrounded by jungle and water and is home to the French Space Centre which accounts for a third of the country's GDP. The colony has a very dark past as a penal colony and it was here that Henri Charriere's, Papillion was interred for those many terrible years. We visited the mainland prison and his cell where he was subjected to continuously calculated cruelty before being sent to the isolated Iles Du Salut islands from where he attempted to escape. There were no guides even though we paid for a guide and had to piggyback a tour with a Dutch family and their Surinamese guide in order to get more information. I was unnaturally horrified by the prison. I have come to the conclusion that in a past life, or lives, I drowned at sea, hence my hate of boats and ferries and that I once served a long and torturous sentence in a damp, dark cell. Perhaps both took place in my Viking years. In each cell, I witnessed the wretches who had atoned for serious or slight sins, made to sleep at night bolted to a plank of wood and either dominating or being dominated by their cellmate during the day. Other, larger, cells held many more prisoners in a filthy, dark hell where the Sodomites sodomised. Prisoners were organised and jailed according to various classifications and even those who had served their terms fully were subjected to barbarous correction while they awaited freedom and the boat ride home to France. The free were not allowed to leave the prison and had to find a way to pay for the trip home. Human history simply glows with enlightenment. I left a comment in the visitor's book about tolerating the French. It was a joke, I forgot to add the smiley faces.

After that prison visit, I was content to hang out with pestered egg-laying sea turtles and leave the prisons to the French, tourists and ghosts. It was an education to watch a massive Leatherback turtle flounder in the sand, surrounded by glowing red flashlights, smoking Frenchmen and rowdy children. We free camped close to the beach and woke to find that many of the freshly laid eggs had been devoured by stray dogs. A miracle and survival. French Guiana is France, according to the little nation's inhabitants. The vehicles occupying the same single lane roads as our English built, South African assembled Land Rover were either Peugeot, Citroen or Renault, all small and driven rapidly.

As French Guiana is so completely remote and disconnected from the rest of the continent, there are very few Overlanders and even fewer campsites. It was suggested to us that we would be able to camp in the little picnic areas which were infrequently to be found next to the road but with so little experience of the country we were unsure that this would indeed be a safe option and we had not come across any picnic sites in which the Landy would not be visible from the road. Luisa had found a campsite listing on the internet before we had crossed into French Guiana, and we headed for that location only to find that camping is not common in French Guiana and sights referred to as camps are typically base camps with indoor accommodation for those wanting to kayak and canoe the many beautiful and fast-flowing jungle rivers. The camp we found was one of these base camps but the owner;

242

astonished to have a South African family in a Landy show up at his gate, offered a parking space at the end of a driveway where a wooden gazebo provided protection from the regular afternoon thunderstorms. When asked how much the camping would be he shrugged his shoulders and told us not to worry about it. After a few cold beers and a pasta dinner, we went to sleep listening to the flowing river and the raindrops falling on the rooftop tent. Climbing into the tent at the end of the day was to retreat into our own little home, our own private space. Luisa and the kids would usually watch a movie or a TV series on her broken pink laptop while I curled up into my little canvas corner to dream the dreams I love until I fell asleep to dream dreams over which I have no control.

There is a space station in central French Guiana near a neat little town called, Kourou. The space station accounts for the majority of the tiny French Departments income and is a vast complex with multiple launching sites. In season there is a launch two or three times a week, but we had been delayed in Suriname waiting for the French Guiana visas and missed the launch and had to settle for a tour around the site. The tour bus was comfortable, air-conditioned and full of French tourists. The tour guide spoke only in French and we had to be content with giving the kids an improvised tour, inventing interesting facts. This is a French villain's secret lair and, if you are lucky, you might see James Bond parachuting in to save the world. The rockets are actually full of sweets to feed the aliens on the moon. A trip to the tourist information centre and museum set the record straight, seeing 007 would have been a treat though. Tourist tours aren't my cup of tea, and at the start of a tour, I am looking forward to the end. Luisa despises this about me; I have to be tricked and threatened to do anything touristy. These kinds of excursions are excellent education for the kids though, they get to see and experience things which other children can only dream of or will never even know existed. It is the cornerstone of our children's education, the ability to practical experience and learn without the fear of failure or pressure to succeed, with no exams or tests, just the freedom to enjoy learning through experience. Through our travels, they have learned to make the impossible possible and what better lesson could they learn. We have had our fair share of criticism, the most hurtful came from a fellow Overlander who made statements far above his pay grade, but we have to believe in our hearts that what we are doing for our children will prepare them for life and not hinder them.

South of Cayenne we met a man who was referred to us by the kind gentleman, Bernard we had met behind the Land Rover/Ford dealership in Suriname. His name was Gilles and we were invited to stay at his house and were soon to learn that he was actually a famous man in France and in aviation circles. Gilles was the air traffic controller the day that the Concorde crashed and was the last man to speak to the captain, advising him that the tail of the supersonic aircraft was on fire minutes before the very last Concorde to ever fly, crashed into the ground killing everyone on board.

We parked the Landy at the back of Gilles yard and enjoyed a tour of his property and his knowledge of the local flora, followed by a few beers and conversation and even engaged in a bit of gossip.

We had a knocking sound coming from under the Landy to attend to, which we suspected was caused by the worn engine mountings. Through JP, a friend of Gilles, we arranged to use the engine hoist of a Land Rover mechanic in Cayenne. We drove to the little city and easily located the workshop. The internet had suggested that the engine mounting replacement could take six men and an equal number of hours to complete, but Luisa and I now work well together. We parked the Landy outside the workshop and rolled the hoist into position, connected the chains, loosened the relevant bolts and slowly lifted the TD5 engine. Within an hour the new engine mounts were in place and bolted. A test drive revealed the knocking sound was still there and the steering was now stiff, which should have been impossible, but on closer inspection, we found that Luisa had cable tied a water pipe to the steering arm. The friendly mechanic returned from lunch, no doubt relieved to find that his hoist had not been nicked by us dodgy Africans. He lay under the Landy and felt around then had a go at the exhaust with a crowbar. The horrible roads we had been driving lately had slipped the exhaust off its mounting rubber. He slid everything back together and the knocking stopped. We could have saved a few hundred dollars if I had spotted the problem and not relied on the advice of the Surinamese mechanic. The old engine mounts were quite knackered though, better to have changed them when we had parts available than to have the mounting go in the middle of nowhere. We thanked the mechanic and returned to Gilles' property for a French braai and a few glasses of wine. We were relieved to have food presented to us simply because, on our daily budget, we simply could not afford even the most basic foodstuffs in French Guiana. However, wine, fabulous cheese, delicious crunch baguette and dried sausage were relatively cheap, and we made a habit of eating sumptuous picnics. At the braai, there was an eclectic mix of local residents, two of whom were journalists who asked if they could return to interview us for a local television news program which sent regular news to the mainland. We agreed and awaited them the next morning. The jungle sun was cooking by the time they arrived to film us breaking camp while the kids did some typical outdoor home-schooling. My large man breasts were sweating profusely during the filming and we were amused to watch the broadcast a few days later, my blue shirt wet beneath my ample bosom. You might have had a laugh with us if you had watched the broadcast in Guyana or France.

We bid au revoir to Gilles, JP and the journalists and headed back to the N2 road leading to Brazil. The road was well maintained and led through forests and over a few surprisingly unpopulated hills. French Guiana has a terrible history of death and misery and it is only in the last 50 years that the little territory has accommodated residents without killing the huge majority. France had been fighting the English, Dutch and Portuguese for possession of the territory since its discovery by Christopher Columbus and had struggled to populate the island. Originally settlers had been sent, but most died quickly, then convicts were sent and most died horribly and quickly, slaves were sent from Africa and they seemed to fare better than the Europeans but fled into the jungle upon receiving emancipation. If disease and Malaria did not kill you, then the local Amerindians had a good stab at you. Unfortunately, we came across very few Amerindians. European diseases had sought revenge and diminished the population as did war and slavery.

There is a newly constructed bridge connecting French Guiana to Brazil but that bridge, though perfectly serviceable, has not been opened to the public. In Cayenne, it was explained to us that the French had built the bridge and paid for the road which connects Brazilian Oiapoque and Macapa, but the money went missing, and one hundred kilometres of jungle mud remains unpaved. We, therefore, had to drive to Saint Georges on the French side of the Oyapock River and arrange a ferry. The more vehicles there are, the cheaper the ferry is, by cheap I mean $250 US per vehicle, sharing, for a ten-minute ferry ride. We visited the police station to stamp out of French Guiana and asked the fat smoking policeman where we might be able to camp (it seems everyone smokes in French Guiana). He had few ideas, but another policeman suggested that we might be able to camp close to a soccer field on the verge of town. We found the field and a covered area tall enough for the Landy to park with the tent open. The policeman, Francois, came to visit us on a bicycle, followed closely by his two small children and later his Brazilian wife. He was a Frenchman who had been in this little Jungle town for three years and they were preparing to move back to France and civilisation. The next day we drove down to the jetty and sat and waited for other vehicles to arrive. A beautiful, nervous

French girl let Luisa use the internet connection and became very flustered when her boyfriend returned while the kids and I were chatting with her. She displayed all the characteristics of a battered wife and we were tempted to batter her boyfriend and throw him in the river.

No other vehicles arrived to take the ferry and we were not going to pay $500US for a one-way trip. At the end of a long day waiting under the equatorial sun, we decided to drive to the French bridge and cause an international incident. A large compound of police, customs and immigration sat at the top of a winding hill. The friendly cops told us we could take a walk on the bridge, but there was no way we could drive the Landy over into Brazil.

We returned to our impromptu camp to find Francois and his wife waiting to invite us to a braai at his apartment, an invitation we gladly accepted. The apartment was set amongst a row of similar apartments with various stages of overgrowth separating and surrounding them. Noisy kids ran in circles around the Land Rover and a few policeman friends came to visit. Francois suggested that there may be other vehicles needing the ferry the next day and true as Bob, the next morning a bejewelled Brazilian couple came knocking on the tent, asking whether we were waiting for the ferry. We quickly packed up and headed down to the ferry to wait three hours for the ferry to arrive then loaded the Landy in low range down the steep jetty. The river was fast flowing and powerful but smooth. The Brazilian wooden houses beckoned, and we sailed under the beautiful new bridge and disembarked again in low range from the ferry onto the uneven ground with a few feet of air between the wooden planks and the soil. The owner of the ferry only laughed when we suggested that a good man would lower the price significantly. With a bitter taste in our mouths, we were back in our beloved Brazil, looking for salgados, the local snacks which we had learned to love and are only found in Brazil.

38

Jeito Brasileiro

Immigration was a relatively simple affair at the offices of the Policia Federal and the vehicle did not need a temporary import permit as the rules for the temporary importation had been amended in the year before the FIFA World Cup in Brazil which we were going to witness.

Gilles had arranged with a friend, Rafael, that we could camp on his property which had a lovely and popular restaurant overlooking the Oyapock River, the name of the Brazilian town is Oiapoque. Rafael kindly led us along a muddy jungle road to the staff quarters where we set up camp for a few nights. The town was a short, hot walk away and Keelan and I would go to town daily along the muddy roads looking for cool drinks and barbecued chicken. Our camp was surrounded by jungle, and huge colourful parrots would visit us daily, hoping to be fed. The bugs truly rule the Amazon and find a way into every crack and crevice, inanimate or living. Mosquitoes, butterflies, spiders, beetles of every shape and colour and insects which defy description. Each with its own defence mechanisms and favourite snack. Your job is to make sure that you are not the snack. A human body would likely only last a few days before being completely devoured by the jungle and its, spiny, exoskeleton, multi-eyed, razor jawed inhabitants.

Amerindian dugout canoes and a variety of other watercraft slid up, down and across the river, the liquid freeway which connected outlying communities to the town where on weekends jungle people would congregate to replenish their supplies and socialise. This is the Wild West, where many illegal activities take place under the cover of the omnipotent green canopy. Brazilian police dressed in armoured uniforms and armed with high powered machine guns would visit the restaurant where we were camped. Illegal gold mining in the jungle is pretty much the number one criminal activity in this area and it is a problem with tentacles that stretch from the Amazon River in the south to the border between Brazil and Guyana in the north, remember that Brazil almost completely surrounds the three, little north-eastern countries. It is virtually impossible to patrol and control a vast jungle area simply because the terrain is extremely difficult to navigate and the men who ply this illegal trade are nail tough and bush savvy. The authorities can only try to maintain a semblance of control of the motor and waterways and corrupt officials within the law enforcement ranks tip the scales in favour of the criminals. The big men in the area all know each other, and our host Rafael seems to be particularly well connected and respected.

We set off in the vague direction of Macapa on the banks of the Amazon River, as we have no GPS we have to ask for directions which is usually more reliable than our old cantankerous GPS ever was. The road is decent pavement for the first fifty kilometres but thereafter a 100 km stretch of jungle mud road, the road the French paid to pave, lies waiting to suck you in. This is one of the reasons that we bought the mud tyres and we were relieved to have that awesome rubber rolling between us and the mud. We had researched this road on the internet before leaving Colombia, and we were shocked by some of the photos of huge trucks stuck up to their axles in cloying mud, a queue of vehicles and their passengers unable to pass the shipwrecked truck until help arrives or equally stuck in the mud. The best time to drive that route is the dry season, and our timing was perfect for adventure, slap bang in the middle of the wet season.

At first, the unpaved road was not at all intimidating. Amerindians communities hugged the road and we enjoyed the scenery. Slowly but surely though, the road began to degrade until the tyres were flinging mud and I was obliged to engage low range, particularly for the uphill sections. The Land Rover is a fantastic beast and with mud splattering the flanks and windows we bumped and slowly gripped our way through horrible deep holes, some so deep that the wheels over articulated and a rear spring slipped out of its mounting. I had to stop after a wooden bridge crossing, which Luisa hates and jack up the rear of the body before convincing the spring to re-seat using a crowbar. By now, the side windows of the Landy were so filthy that the cab darkened, and we were unable to see the scenery as we pass. This is the only real drawback of the big wheels; the wheel arches and mud flaps are unable to deflect significant or even insignificant amounts of mud and water. The other drawback is that the wider wheels also eat wheel bearings as we were to find out.

Creeping along at a maximum of 20kph, we were making slow progress. We had learnt that slow is the way to go as the holes can be deceptively deep and because the Landy is top-heavy, we were experiencing uncomfortable body roll through the worst sections. A few filthy diggers and graders sat parked outside one Amerindian settlement, waiting to be called into action to retrieve trucks which have no business driving and getting stuck on these roads. The wet season must be a lucrative time of year for the owner of the heavy machinery. The only other vehicles we encountered on the road were either Toyota Hilux's or Fiat Sienna's; the latter has proven to be the greatest off-road vehicle ever made. This road was actually worse than the Linden to Lethem route in Guyana but was a sixth of the distance. Keelan and I were having a great time sledging through mud, but Luisa and Jessica were less than thrilled, Luisa because of the red clay covering every inch of the Landy and Jessica because she was struggling to nap with all the bouncing. Jessica has not changed much over the years in that if the engine is switched on Jessica switches off. In her world cars are beds with steering wheels and a noisy piece of metal upfront which Dad keeps staring at whenever we stop.

I monitored the distance on the speedometer and after 95 km's was looking forward to seeing paved road after every corner. The paved road was hiding from us but after five hours and 130 km's I thought I spotted a dark strip up ahead. We rolled forward and had a few last pits to grind through and then felt that sweet feeling of smooth tar, the vehicle rolling along as if on firm marshmallow clouds at an incredible speed. After a slow long-distance crawl, 100kph feels like 200kph. Since the horrible road had taken so long to traverse, we now needed to search for a safe place to camp overnight. A few small, disorganised towns lay along the road to Macapa and we decided to drive into one of the larger towns to buy provisions and see if there was a gas or police station which would let us park for the night. Finding no suitable gas station, we drove into the police station on the verge of town. The police seemed amused by us but were not prepared to let us camp on the grassy area beside the station. A large policeman told us that they were worried about our safety, not because of criminals but because of cobras. Cobras? Yes, they come out at night and are very dangerous. He then showed us photos on his phone of very large black serpents with their heads shot off. Back home in South Africa, there are plenty of very dangerous snakes, I told him that it would not be a problem, we would sleep up in the rooftop tent where the snakes could not reach us then leave in the morning. No way, sorry. They let us hose down the Land Rover in the wash area, and we left to find somewhere else to sleep. The road was very quiet with hardly any traffic and as we drove over a bridge Luisa spotted an area on the banks of the river below with umbrellas and benches, we pulled over and drove down a muddy road to what seemed to be a little community and a small restaurant. I was in the mood for some fish and the kind ladies in the kitchen agreed to make us fish and chips, rice and salad and agreed to let us camp on a large rock in front of the restaurant.

The fish was tender and fresh from the river and after eating we taught some sweet little kids a few English words and phrases. Our appearance causes a stir quite often, and people are surprised to hear that we are South African because we look German or Scandinavian and in these remote areas blondes and redheads are non-existent and foreign travellers very few.

In the morning, with dark clouds looming on the horizon, I checked the Landy's lubricants and coolant levels and inspected the suspension for any possible problems. The Landy had been pulling to the right and shuddering on right-hand corners since we had let the mechanic work on her in Suriname and I had already driven far enough without rectifying the problem simply because I could not figure out the cause. The owner of the restaurant went for a swim in the bulging river and we were surprised to see him emerge from the water carrying four large fish which looked like Tucunaré or Peacock Bass, the delicious fish we had eaten the night before which he had caught on overnight lines. We had some coffee with the family before re-joining the road to Macapa where we would have to organise a ferry along the Amazon River to Belem at the mouth of the mighty river.

The road was no longer bordered by jungle; instead, savannah replaced the jungle and livestock roamed and fed on the long green grass. The Amapa state which lies between Macapa and Oiapoque is one of the best-preserved areas of the Brazilian Amazon, but there are dangerous levels of Mercury in water sources as this is a common chemical used in the extraction of gold. We were in a very different Brazil from that which we had left back in 2013, far southern and northern Brazil are only the same country on paper, but there are signs that the wealth of the south is slowly making its way up to one of the most secluded parts of South America.

As we were driving into Macapa, negotiating by luck and frequent questioning of pedestrians and gas station attendants, we met up with a convoy of filthy 4x4's. They were a rowdy bunch and signalled for us to follow them. They were at the end of an off-road expedition from Belem to the southern bank of the Amazon River opposite Manaus then across by ferry to Manaus and back along the northern bank to Macapa. This is an extreme off-road adventure and of the twenty vehicles which started the journey, only thirteen made it to Macapa. The men were in high spirits as we drove into the city and down to the banks of a very fast flowing Amazon River where we would introduce ourselves and drink a few beers. After a round of beers and photos the convoy, now including a South African Land Rover, drove to the equatorial monument and took photos of the vehicles along the northern and southern hemisphere divide. The president of the Macapa Jeep Club, Portella, invited us to join the rowdy, muddy men at the clubhouse where we could camp. The clubhouse was not a hut with a braai area as we had suspected but was instead situated at the back of a racecourse and had a swimming pool, electricity, a rondavel with a pool table and hammocks and clean, modern bathrooms. Driving into a city we are always concerned about where we will spend the night as we hardly ever stay in hotels and hostels and we were very happy to join in with some drinking and meat-eating after a refreshing dip in the pool. The men remained in high spirits and invited us to join them for a weekend in the Pantanal, or swamp in English, where Portella has a property. We agreed, but the first order of business was to organise a ferry to Belem. A friendly older man called Batalha, who drove a TDi Land Rover 90 equipped with tractor tyres, made some phone calls and the next day we were handed a business card for a ferry operator he had found for us with the help of Portella. They had even negotiated the rate for us. With that done we were free to party with the men until the ferry left the following Tuesday.

The convoy left Macapa, winding through the city stopping to buy meat, beer, ice and cigarettes along the way then proceeding to a wetland where restaurants hung over the water pumping dance music and serving beer and fried fish to people lounging in the cool water. Portella, in the lead in his Jeep, seemed to be searching for an alternative route to his property, a route which we discovered had been chosen for its excitement value. For twenty kilometres we drove through mud and water so deep that at times it flowed over the bonnet of our raised Land Rover. We had just cleaned the Landy and Luisa was not at all happy with the adventure route but soon accepted reality and began to enjoy the drive. By the time we had reached a decent road the sun had set, and we were surprised when Portella led our group down a muddy bank into a stream which ran parallel to the road where we drove for a few more kilometres until Portella decided to lead us up a bank, out of the water and to an intersection where we parked and drank beer while waiting for the rest of our group to arrive before heading out onto a track which led to his property. That night was another round of beer and Cachaça, grilled meat and chicken served with a sprinkling of lime and a lump of rice. The rustic compound consisted of a few old houses set back from the river and a U shaped, open-plan building with a submerged deck which sat on the water's edge. Hammocks hung under shade to the left and right of the wide central corridor where two long tables groaned under the weight of alcohol and plates of food. A braai area was constructed at the entrance of this building, surrounded by a natural pool where large turtles and fish were fed leftovers by a man who permanently manned the fire and picked at a very large and crusty yellow wound on his upper arm. A rotund man with a bushy moustache called Chico, the man not the moustache, kept our spirits high with constant jokes and laughter. A young man ripped the top of a beer off with his teeth and we struggled to communicate almost exclusively in Portuguese. The kids kept themselves busy fishing, exploring the property and going for boat rides. At night they were put to bed before the festivities reached a fever pitch, and they were free to explore in the mornings while the rest of the camp slept off the night before.

Dehydrated and sunburnt, we returned to Macapa to await the ferry. Portella invited us to stay at the clubhouse once we bid farewell to our expedition friends who left en-masse to return by boat and plane to their lives in Rio de Janeiro and Sao Paulo and other far more civilised places. Our kind host came to fetch us for a Women's Day outing with the Jeep Club at the property of one of its members. A short, sophisticated older man who would have not have looked out of place in Rio. His property had tall swaying palm trees, tennis courts and a massive swimming pool. His Land Rover 110 was equally impressive and very well equipped, considering that he was very, very far away from either a Land Rover dealer or parts supplier. After a few snacks off the braai and a few polite refusals of beer and cachaça, we headed into the jungle where the days fun had been planned. Being Women's Day, the woman would take control of the various 4x4's and drive the jungle route. We were at a disadvantage because the Landy was fully loaded with all our material possessions, but we have faith in her and Luisa's capabilities, so we joined the queue to drive into the jungle. The next few hours consisted of mud, thorns, water and more mud. An old Jeep flooded its engine driving into a water-filled pit dug under a massive felled tree. We recovered him and pulled him up a long slippery slope. A traffic jam was caused by a bogged Mitsubishi which we recovered using South African techniques after the Brazilian method failed a few times. I was covered in mud by the time Luisa drove us out of the jungle route. I was incredibly impressed by her and the Landy's performance. Despite the weight we were carrying, we did not take any escape routes except for one and had recovered vehicles while never getting stuck. We held our name and the Land Rover flag high.

After breakfast with Portella and his family in their home above his bustling auto parts store, we headed down to the ferry which was due to depart at 14h00. We were extremely nervous about the ferry ride not only because we would be on the mighty Amazon for a few days but also because we had heard horror stories about drunken crew and passengers and music that blasts at full volume all day and night. We were escorted by the crew onto the loading area then onto the flatbed ferry which was surrounded by three-story passenger ferries. The passenger ferries were indeed pumping loud music and each level was populated by hammocks. Smaller vehicles were being loaded onto these ferries which were definitely not designed to carry anything, but passengers and small cargo. We watched as people drove their vehicles onto unsecured wooden planks, the only obstacle between them and the deep river metres below, over the railing then down another couple of planks into an area no more than a 1.8m high. Only two other vehicles drove onto the deck of our ferry and after a few hours, a crew member strapped the vehicles to the deck with a thin rope. As the sun began to set the ferry eventually manoeuvred away from the dock and made its way out onto the river. Our captain, who seemed relatively sober, allowed us to open our rooftop tent and agreed to plug us into the ferries electrical system. He played American rock music at a low, pleasant volume and we could not believe our luck to have found this ferry. Of course, it was not luck, but the efforts of Batalha and Portella and their local connections which had secured us safe, comfortable passage.

39

The Mighty Amazon River Experience

We sat on the wooden packing pallets which lined either side of the deck and, with an un-obscured view, marvelled at the massive seagoing cargo ships which shared our route, either anchored or sailing. A towering cumulonimbus cloud rose out of the jungle and the setting sun imbued it with various shades of orange, red, white, yellow and shades of grey. The handful of passengers on the ferry joined us to watch the sunset while Luisa and I retreated to sit on the tailgate of the Landy to sip on a bottle of Bordeaux we had bought in French Guiana specifically for this occasion. We then wrote a message, inserted it into the empty bottle and flung it out into the Amazon River. An Amerindian chief sent me a message the other day. "Hey man, did you lose a bottle? We found it. Thanks for throwing your crap in our river". Ahem.

The ferry trip was to take 24 hours and we spent hours sitting on the deck, photographing the jungle and its inhabitants during the day and watching the stars and imagining what lay beyond the lights on the bank at night. Occasional wood mills processed the destruction taking place behind convenient jungle cover, plumes of smoke rising into the air. Houses on stilts formed pockets of habitation, the inhabitants lounging in hammocks, working on their dug-out boats, washing clothing or fishing while watching various boats slip by. A church beckoned sinners and saints every ten kilometres and children made their way home from school in dugout canoes, driven by small smoky engines which spun propellers at the end of a long prop shaft. We passed a town of approximately 150 buildings, the largest we had seen so far and waved to children whose floating transportation was a converted old yellow American school bus, the type Forrest Gump used to go to school.

It was a dream come to fruition, to lie in the roof tent either at night or in the morning and watch the river slide by. If you lay at a certain angle, the fabric of the tent hid the ferry completely and it seemed almost as if we were navigating the river in a floating Land Rover. With the hum of the engine and the soft rock as a soundtrack, we approached our second night on the ferry. I scoured the horizon for the lights of Belem. As magical as this experience was I was eager to roll back onto terra firma, our natural habitat. I asked the Captain how much longer until we reached Belem and his answer, while not completely unexpected, was nonetheless unwelcome. Another 12 hours. What can you do? Throw your toys and demand to be dropped off in the jungle? No, you accept your fate and wait. I resumed my position on the back of the Landy and thought my thoughts. A small leather-skinned man sitting on a pile of pallets beside the Landy began a loud, wrenching cacophony of snorting, hawking, barking and spitting. I endured this nauseating procedure for ten minutes before turning to the man, intending to tell him to bugger off. Before I could open my mouth, he turned to me and smiled a yellow-toothed grin, his one eye gleaming, the other vacant in the deep socket, a rheumy, dried puss cavity an eye should have occupied. I left him to his nasal ablutions and returned to my thoughts, particularly what lay ahead in Brazil. Being spontaneous has its price and we paid that price in Dollars.

Our budget was draining quickly, the Guyana's had been very expensive, and the loss of 40% of our Rand to the Dollar and the regular uninvited fornications of the taxman had depleted our bank accounts significantly. Within a year most of our assets and cash would be used and we had yet to reach Alaska, our original geographic goal. Perhaps we would be able to find some work in southern Brazil, maybe

Florianopolis, the city we had enjoyed so much in the past, would present some opportunities.

A couple joined me on the deck and interrupted my thoughts. They sat together on the wooden pallets, cuddling, kissing and stroking each other. She was in her sixties, wrinkled and back hunched, flesh hanging onto the bones beneath her stonewashed jeans. He was in his early twenties, a fashionable haircut, Adidas trainers and a blue hoody. Deeply in love, they pandered to each other, her reclining in the bowl of his lap, inseparable in the heat and clinging humidity.

Night fell, and we watched the lights go by, looking for the halo of light on the horizon, which might suggest a large city. We passed huts and holiday homes, navigating around islands and other boats, the captain shining a bright spotlight on the river before us whenever he spotted something irregular. Each time he flipped on the spotlight the deck and choppy brown water would be completely illuminated within the beam, the light would swing from side to side, to its limit and suddenly, immediately retreat, leaving your eyes out of focus, the night blacker than before. Vessels approaching would be illuminated by our captain, as if he not only wanted to alert them to our presence but also to inspect their cargo. Sleep came uneasily that night and we awoke in the morning to men shouting and laughing, the scraping of wood on metal and other sounds we had not heard for almost three days. Sounds which seemed alien after the continuous humming of the engine and Boston's, "More Than A Feeling". We were in Belem, uiteindelik!

40

Terra Firma

A quick shower in the suitably marinal ablutions, pack the tent, unplug from the power, have a chat with the captain and drive down the ubiquitous wooden planks onto solid, glorious, littered soil. The early morning city relatively quiet except for rowdy students heading to school and the noisy buses which transported them and the city's workers.

Belem, literally translated as Bethlehem and is also known as Cidade das Mangueiras or the City of Mango Trees, lies 100 km's upriver from the Atlantic and the gateway to the Amazon. Our first task was to find a wheel alignment workshop once we had found our way out of the city. We stopped to buy some croissants and coffee, but the prices were exorbitant since we had been in Brazil last, the combination of a weakened rand and Brazilian inflation put a cup of coffee out of our reach. Luckily the workshop where we stopped offered us some sweet black coffee. I drove the Landy onto the new yellow hoist, first asking them whether it was able to lift almost four tons. They assured me that the hoist was up to the job. I climbed out of the Landy and joined Luisa to watch the work being done. The short round man pushed the green button and the hoist started squealing and shuddering, the front lifting a foot then the rear then the front again before the hoist squealed to a stop. The technicians then started bouncing the hoist while repeatedly pushing the green button, The Landy rocked to and fro, I told the manager to stop, but he assured me that there was no problem. The hoist eventually rose the Landy five feet and the short man went to work with the alignment. Usually, the vehicle does not need to be raised for wheel alignment, but this workshop did not have a traditional pit. After an hour of work and a crowd gathering to see the Landy and us, the manager hit us with a bill of almost R700. Three times what we usually pay for a similar job. He laughed off our protestations and offered an R50 discount before we left with Luisa glaring. The alignment was 50% effective and the pulling and shuddering reduced enough for us to feel more comfortable driving at a decent speed.

Our destination was Lencois Maranhenses, a flat desert area which floods during the rainy season, filling the depression in the dunes with crystal clear water. The jungle slowly retreated as we left Belem and became green scrub which becomes dry and brown in the dry season. At around 700 km's it is a long drive which we completed before the sunset thanks to an early start from Belem. Being a tourist town, Barreirinhas was full of tourist touts who would shout at us from the side of the road and follow us on motorbikes. We smilingly told them to bugger off except for one amiable pest who directed us to a campsite up on a hill. The camp was actually a hostel run by a pleasant stoned Argentine who let us camp on the lawn and take over the patio. I rotated the Landy's tyres, greased the prop shafts and did all the little repairs which are part and parcel of long-term travel. Our attempts to gain entrance to the dunes with our own vehicle were in vain as the town survives on tourism and everyone we spoke to insisted that the only way to enter the park was with a tour. With the budget depleting we simply could not afford to pay for tours considering we are a family of four. Luisa and I looked at the map and found a track which ran along the edge of the dunes and by driving this route we would not need to backtrack 180 km's to the main road to Jericoacoara, where we would complete our circumnavigation of the continent. Heading towards the track we were told when asking for directions to turn around, that we could not drive that route without a guide. Using a map, we had downloaded from Google Maps we pushed on along dirt roads, often backtracking when we missed a turn. At times it seemed as if we were driving on private farms track, scrub surrounding us and no signs of life. The track led through a few wide streams and it was Keelan's job to walk the streams to determine the depth and the best route. After a few exciting water crossings, we came to a T-junction and a bush pub, the drinkers directing us to turn left and continue along a deep sand route. We could see the dunes to the left and were comforted by the fact that we were running parallel to the park. For about twenty kilometres the track remained deep sand which occasionally crossed hills and past remote houses where people chilled in hammocks and sipped beer. A few large palm trees loomed ahead of us at the top of a hill which marked the beginning of the dunes. I deflated the tyres while Luisa walked ahead to check what lay around the dunes immediately ahead of us. With Keelan standing on the Land Rovers side steps we drove down and manoeuvred around the dunes, rounded one large dune and were faced with a floodplain of disjointed streams and large depressions of water which would have to be traversed individually. The girls suggested that we turn around, Keelan and I insisted that we are in a Land Rover and this is exactly what she was made for. Keelan stripped down to his underpants, earning the superhero nickname, Underpants Man, in preparation for the task of assessing the water crossings. Luisa joined in the fun, and I was jealous of them cooling off in the water while Jessica and I sat in the hot Landy, we don't use our aircon as it reduces power and fuel economy and only gives you ice cold kneecaps and no relief for the passengers in the back seat. Over the next couple of hours, we crossed many water hurdles and white sandy expanses before finding our path blocked by a large dune. Luisa scouted ahead and after a long while returned with the advice that the only way to go was up the side of the dune and along the edge of a little blue lake. We were getting to have the Lenclos experience without expensive guides or being herded around in the back of a Land Cruiser, I could not suffer that indignity. Where Land Cruisers can go we can go further. After having spent the last few months in the Amazon Jungle it was a relief to have a change of scenery, a place where you could look far into the distance and see a horizon. The white sand and blue water of the dunes in stark, beautiful contrast and cool water offering a respite from the windswept and sun-baked sands.

Rounding the lake and dune, we came to another floodplain where sand gave way to mud and tough grasses being chewed by equally tough goats and donkeys. To the right, a kilometre away, we could see fences and scrubland and far in the distance what looked like power lines. A few tracks of earlier vehicles remained in the cloying mud on the verge of streams and pools and we had to make our way forward. Luisa and Keelan scouting the route, careful to choose a path with the least amount of backtracking. The power lines and a few small houses were approaching slowly and with a sense of relief, we drove off the tracks onto an established sandy road. Laughing, we drove along the track congratulating ourselves for making it out of the dunes until we realised that the road too was flooded and our adventure for the day was not yet over. At places, there were two roads running parallel to each other, the one offering an escape route from the other. At times I would drive along the one road to find a dead end and a steep bank which led directly into the flooded road. Underpants Man was working overtime to plot the route and advise where to put the wheels. At one section the road was flooded for almost 200 metres, and Keelan had to walk to the end and back, trying to line up with the wheelbase of the Landy to ensure that we did not fall into a hole. Luisa filmed with a GoPro while I pushed the Landy through the water in Low Range, second gear, trying to maintain the correct speed to create a bow wave as we fought forward. At one point the road looked too flooded and deep to navigate safely, the road itself cut over the years of seasonal flooding and walled in places by steep banks. I walked to a house and asked a little girl to call her Papa. Her Mom eventually came to the window and pointed out another track around her neighbour's house which we followed until it re-joined a drier section of road and a T-junction. We sat debating which route to take to reach a town which we could see on the map, but had no idea how to reach it. As we were discussing our options a young local appeared out of the scrub to our right, we asked him which way to get to the town and he led us through a maze of tracks, which we would have never been able to negotiate on our own until the dirt met cobblestone. Many of the houses we passed were attractive and brightly painted, and we stopped to ask two pretty girls which road to take to get back to the main road. They directed us to a split in the road and a bridge, Luisa then asked me why I always asked the pretty girls for direction. "Were they pretty? I did not notice". I taught Luisa to punch when we first met, and I have regretted that instruction ever since. After a day on the road, my left arm resembles tenderised, bruised steak, especially after a day driving through towns in Brazil, getting lost and often stopping for directions.

Stopping at a gas station or Posto as the Brazilians called them, I took out the compressor and reflated the tyres and headed for Jericoacoara, pronounced jeri – kwa – kwa – ra in Brazil and known as Jeri to its inhabitants. We still had 400 km's to cover and we were all quite tired after the morning's shenanigans. The Landy was running great despite the hard work she had done all morning; however, there was a strange vibration at between 90 and 100kph. We had to slow down and travel at 85kph, which made the road that much more tedious.

41

Circumnavigation Complete!

Arriving in Jeri we had successfully completed a circumnavigation of the continent. A true Guinness record type circumnavigation would technically have been a strict coastal revolution within a certain distance of the coastline. We had never intended to break any records and had left the coast often, but a look at our route on the map confirms that we have followed the contours of the continent and had been to every country except Bolivia. As far as I know, very few families have achieved that journey, and I do not know of any Africans crazy enough to have attempted it.

We had reason to celebrate and the Landy celebrated by losing a hubcap and spraying oil all over the right rear tyre. I found a gas station and got to work replacing the wheel bearing which had expired. I had spare bearings, from the blue brand with the bad name and within an hour had the greasy job done. Luisa went hunting for beer and meat in preparation for the night's festivities. Leaving town, heading for a campsite outside of the main national park but situated next to a blue lagoon, we came across a German TD5 Defender driven by a bearded man and decorated by his attractive girlfriend. As Landy people do, we stopped and blocked the road to have the usual how, where and when discussion. They said they might return to the camp we were headed to, they were just searching for a Venezuelan Overlander who they had met earlier. Saying goodbye, we rolled on and found the camp, set up, had a swim in the blue lagoon and started the fire.

Markus and Katherine joined us when they returned, and after we killed all the beers, they brought some lovely wine to the table, we matched their wine with a bottle of Diplomatico Rum from Venezuela. They then produced a bottle of vodka, and we raised them a bottle of Jägermeister. The kids were happily fed and watching a movie in the tent while we partied downstairs. Markus has a wicked sense of humour and he focused that on Luisa who became happily insulted. They traded insults and the conversation moved into that zone of drunken ridiculous where sober people fear to tread. My memory of that night is vague, but I have flashes. We headed to the lagoon to skinny dip, the booze ran out and I guided a naked Luisa back to the tent then we stood on the pathway for half an hour arguing about which way to go. Luisa was convinced that we must turn left, and I knew that we must continue straight. Anyone who has ever tried to convince a drunken Luisa of anything will know my pain. She then tripped over her own feet and landed with her bum in the sand. Naked and sandy, she reluctantly followed me back to the camp and climbed into the tent without first having a shower. I went and had a wash at least and put on some clothes before going to bed. The morning was bleary, noisy and had a bad taste. Keelan was making a huge fuss over the amount of sand brought into the tent that night and was scolding an apologising Luisa who pleaded with him to please go away. Before I could face the world, I dragged myself and the kids down to the lagoon and a swim, hoping that my body would absorb the clear cool liquid and rehydrate my battered organs. The beach bore evidence of our frivolity. Empty bottles littered the shore, and my boxer shorts lay draped over a sunbed. With Keelan and Jessica's laughter ringing in my ears, I quickly cleaned up and waded slowly into the lagoon. That day and the next the family chilled while I prepared the Landy for the 5000-km drive down to central Brazil to a town called Coquieral. Our Brazilian friends, Daytrippers, had a family farm there and they had invited us to join them for a few days before they left for their Trans Europe trip in their blue Defender TDi. We only had a few days to get down there and having driven that road before, we knew that it would be a long, hot journey. I changed the engine oil and checked the transmission oils, the prop shafts, the wheel bearings, all the fluids and ran a test on the Nanocom to see if there were any faults on the ECU. I was almost finished servicing the right front wheel bearing when a storm broke. I was drenched in seconds but, since all the internals of the wheel were safe from the wet, I continued working, drenched to the bone, while Markus and his camera snapped pics of me. I actually enjoyed working in the rain, refreshing, but my tools needed a good clean dry after the deluge.

Raul, the Venezuelan, Markus had been searching for, had arrived earlier with his beautiful wife and a friend in their huge motorhome with a BMW and KTM motorbikes perched on a platform at the rear of the vehicle. They invited us to an Asado, a braai and as soon as the rain stopped, a fire was started, and Raul's friend began making Caipirinhas. Luisa swore she would not drink for a week after the earlier festivities, but those Caipirinhas can be deceitfully smooth and convincing. Soon the meat was devoured with good sprinklings of coarse salt, and the refreshments flowed. A Spanish long-distance cyclist with a sweet singing voice joined us and Markus took out his camera to record the silliness which continued into the early hours. We Overlanders live an alternative existence generally. There is no weekend or Friday night. Every day is Saturday and a group of Overlanders together is an opportunity to let your hair down, swop stories, make great food and reconnect with the tribe. As much as we were enjoying ourselves we needed to hit the road south, but before leaving we swapped details with Raul and Markus, and Luisa showed Markus the route we had taken through the dunes to the Lencois Maranheses. Markus is a professional cameraman, and after he traversed the route he sent us a fantastic video complete with drone footage.

42

Bad Bearings Good People

The road ahead was almost 3000 km's, and we had about five days to get down there. We had driven this route in 2013 when we headed to Foz Do Iguazu and that trip had taken almost nine days of sleeping in gas stations, waking up early, driving all day. I was not eager to drive exactly the same road again and Luisa plotted a route which would not be much longer but would cover new ground. Leaving Jeri on a Sunday, the road led first towards Fortaleza and then turned south. We passed charming loved and ugly unloved towns and slammed the anchors as we passed a butchery in one of the better towns. Outside, standing on the pavement, was a tubular rotisserie with four rotating levels. This first level was hung with cuts of red meat called Picanha which was dripping fatty deliciousness on the second level of pork Eisbein, which in turn dripped on a level of sausages and more cuts of meat, dripping the combined flavour onto the whole chicken. The server offered us, tasters, while locals came to buy the exquisite meat and chicken to complement the salads, rice and beans they had prepared for Sunday lunch. We settled on an Eisbein and some fresh bread which fed us for lunch and dinner. The dinner was eaten at the back of a gas station where we had set up camp for the night. The new route consisted of a few off-road sections as it was far from the main north-south route which, north of Brasilia, is a dual carriageway full of trucks and days are a nightmare of overtaking eighteen-wheelers in a right-hand drive Landy on left-hand drive roads.

Our overtaking procedure consists of me driving up towards a truck or slow-moving vehicle, smaller vehicles I can overtake without assistance if I can see through their windows, but trucks are simply too obstructive. On approach before I reduce speed, I say CHECK, CHECK and move the Landy towards the centre line. Luisa and Keelan will crane their necks and say either NO or CLEAR. They are not allowed to say GO because it sounds exactly like NO in a noisy Landy and we have had a few near misses when I have heard GO when they say NO. If the road is not clear, then they have to tell me how many and what type of vehicles are approaching and if there is a hill, a dip or a corner. When it is clear to overtake, they will then check my blind spot and say CLEAR! It may sound complicated, but it works for us. I searched entire South America for a blind spot mirror and they simply do not sell them. I have one on my mirror but is of little use unless we are on a multi-lane freeway.

Continuing after our gas station free camp we found that the paved road ended and for the next 200 km's we drove sandy track, and farm roads often getting a bit lost and having to backtrack. After one particularly hot and sandy track, we came upon a little town where we bought cool drinks. While we were sipping on the sweet relief Keelan spotted a Land Cruiser approaching, it had red and blue marking and looked like a police vehicle but turned out to be a group of Costa Ricans who had driven down to Brazil for the World Cup and eventually let on that they were actually making TV shows as they went. After a few photos and email swops, we went our separate ways and returned to the endless sand roads. That night we reached paved roads and a town called Floriano which seemed pleasant and had large gas station on the outskirts where we could camp but I made the decision to keep going, the next town was 100 kilometres away and since the Landy was running perfectly and the roads were not too busy, we should have been able to cover that distance in an hour and a half. The sunset as we left town and we broke the golden rule of overlanding, do not drive at night! We felt safe in Brazil though and did not expect to have any problems. How wrong we were. To ease the boredom Luisa plugged her pink Sony Vaio into the inverter and an audio jack into the sound system then played a few episodes of the American sitcom, Cheers. Listening to an audiobook or, in my case, listening to a movie or television programme helps the long boring miles pass quicker.

Sam was having a vaguely amusing argument with that horribly shrill, 1950's throwback Diane bloody Chambers when a horrible crunching noise assaulted my ears from beneath the Landy. It is the sound I least want to hear while driving. We had been warned that there was no verge when we had asked a gas station attendant in Floriano about the road ahead. I slowed down as quickly as possible without braking too hard and rolled for a few meters looking for a gap in the shrub next to the road, wincing at the loud metallic grinding with every revolution of the tyres. Immediately anger started boiling in my chest, frustration and a horrible sense of hopelessness. I let out a coarse Fuuuucccck! Then I pulled myself together with a mental slap. Giving in to anger and frustration only makes matters very much worse. The first task at hand was to establish what had imploded, exploded, or come loose. The grinding sound was so bad that I initially thought that the gearbox had a serious malfunction. Running the engine, I depressed the clutch and changed through the gears which were as smooth as butter. I had just put in brand new wheel bearings so ruled those out and checked the rear diff for signs of failure. With no oil leaks, I decided to remove the rear prop shaft and roll the Landy forward. If the grinding sound stopped with the prop removed, then we could isolate the noise to the diff. The grinding persisted, what the hell!? When driving I make a note of every side road, gas station, turn off or cluster of buildings just in case we need to find help or find a place to stop. A few hundred metres back I had seen a dirt road leading to a farmer's gate, if I could get the Landy back there I could get us off the road where large trucks blew past us once every five minutes. I threw the prop behind the awning bracket and engaged diff lock which would allow me to drive with power to only two wheels, the Defender being permanent four-wheel drive. I directed the struggling Landy through a three-point turn and slowly drove back down the rural road, dreading the damage I was causing. After what seemed like an eternity of slow grinding progress we came to the dirt road and the Landy hobbled down to a level area. The kids continued to watch Cheers as if nothing had happened while Luisa and I did some more head-scratching. Looking under the vehicle we spotted oil on the rear right tyre. I needed to jack up the rear of the Landy and check the wheel bearings which crunched horribly as I spun the raised tyre. The bloody, poxy, bastard, motherfunkin brand new wheel bearings I had just replaced in Jeri had imploded after only about 1,000 kilometres. We vowed then and there never to buy that brand again, even if the alternative cost double and had to be shipped in from Singapore. I had been very careful to mount the bearings correctly and mate them with the corresponding race, to use the correct grease and to torque the lock nut to spec. I removed my tools and spares from the load area, changed into some work clothes and got busy. By some paranoid miracle, I had kept the old wheel bearings and would at least be able to get to the next town or back to Floriano to source new bearings. Once I removed the drive member the true extent of the damage and destruction became apparent. Shards of the bearing had dug deep grooves into the stub axle and without a stub axle to hold the wheel in place we were going nowhere. Luisa helped by keeping me topped up with cool drinks and biscuits while I spent the next three hours filing and sanding the stub axle so that the new old bearings would be able to slide on. Sitting in the sand, my hands covered in grease and little biting bugs crawling into my pants and up the back of my shirt, the perfect end to a perfect day. I worked slowly and meticulously and at about 02h30am had the rear wheel back on and spinning nicely. I had seen what looked like a small truck stop a few kilometres before the shit hit the fan, the goal now was too slowly drive back there, open the tent and have a sleep before waking, replacing the prop (I was too tired to put the prop shaft back on (and driving back to Floriano to source some Timken or SKF bearings. Slowly and with the diff lock engaged, we drove back onto the road and headed to the little truck stop. Driving at 30kph with the hazard lights flashing it took another eternity to reach our safe haven for the night. Bright lights came into view, checking my mirrors for traffic from the rear I turned off the hazard lights and as I depressed the indicator stalk a loud banging and clanking came from under the Landy, I stopped the Landy quickly, expecting the worst and noticed that the handbrake would not engage. In my agitated state, I had not removed the handbrake drum which the prop shaft holds in place. The drum had dropped off and rolled into the bush either to the left or right of the road. What next! We drove the Landy onto a flat dirt area under a large tree and next to the only truck parked up for the night, opened the tent and put the kids to bed before returning to the road with head torches to search for the handbrake drum. For two hours Luisa and I searched, being careful to avoid snakes and spiders as we pushed through the bush. Exhausted and empty-handed we returned to the Landy for a quick clean and deep sleep. Lying in the tent, unable to sleep, I listened to the occasional car or truck passing, enjoyed the cool morning breeze blowing through the window and thought about what needed to be done and what could I have done differently. I fell asleep as the rising sun turned the air dark blue and the birds began to sing to be awoken at 08h00am by the heat in the tent and a dogs ceaseless barking. Luisa was already up and searching the bushes for that elusive bloody drum. I joined her after a glass of water and dug even deeper in the bush, thorns cutting at my exposed arms and legs. Another two hours of searching until I decided to search the area Luisa had been searching while she returned to the Landy to feed the kid's breakfast and make a cup of tea. I walked over to the side of the road she had been parading all morning and spotted the drum almost immediately lying on top of the grass, shiny side up. Luisa!!! Too relieved to be angry and understanding that she probably did not know what she was looking for looked like, we moved the Landy under the shade of the tree and re-attached the prop shaft before driving the 60 km's back to Floriano at 60kph, listening for another failure, and interpreting every shake and shudder.

In Floriano, we found an internet cafe and began the search for bearings, but the town is so small and remote that none of our Brazilian friends were able to help out except to suggest that we could order the bearings from Sao Paulo. I had also kept the old oil seal which seemed in good order and essentially needed two-wheel bearings and a retaining washer as the existing washer had been destroyed by the failed bearing. Locals directed us to a road with many parts places and we made our way there to search for a bearing with the corresponding part number. At the third auto spares store, we found the Timken bearing! That was the good news, the bad news was that the bearing cost R$140 (Brazilian Reals, which was about R1000). We needed two bearings, and the assistant refused to lower his price. The decision was made to head out to the large trucker's station, outside town and have a good night's rest and continue the search for the bearings at a better price the next morning. At the truckers' station, we set up camp as far from the trucks as possible and enjoyed a couple of cold beers and a bowl of pasta before hitting the sack. Refreshed, we continued our search after breakfast and in the late morning came across a parts shop ran by a man called Clebert. They had the Timken bearing at half the price of his competitor down the road. He did not have a retaining washer but could arrange to have one made for us. We were relieved to have come across this store and that we had not handed over the money the day before. I set about preparing to replace the bearing on the Landy parked on the road outside the store when Clebert asked our lunch plans. I was happy to eat a sandwich and keep on working so Luisa and the kids were invited to

Clebert's home for lunch, an invitation they quickly accepted. With hardly a wave they jumped in the car with a friend of Clebert's and only returned at 5 pm. I dismantled the wheel bearing and gave the stub axle another good sanding and filing before installing the new races while one of Clebert's employees ran off to a workshop to have a retaining washer modified. After a few adjustments and trims, the improvised washer fitted perfectly and I was able to complete the installation being very careful to grease and torque the system correctly. Clebert then invited us to spend the evening with his family and said we could camp outside his townhouse. They invited a few friends over and while the kids played PlayStation and rode bikes with the neighbourhood kids we prepared South African shooters for our new friends. The shooters are called Melktertjies or milk tarts in English and consist of vodka mixed with condensed milk which is then chilled and served with a sprinkling of cinnamon. Sweet and dangerous, a treat I am sure they are still enjoying in Floriano to this day.

The next day we returned to the road after a hearty breakfast. We have learnt to accept the problems we face during our travels as a test from the Gods of the road, as Paul Theroux refers to the powers who govern a traveller's luck and misfortune. Being gracious and level-headed when faced with problems is not only wise but is also fortuitous. Meeting good people who will open their hearts and homes will restore your faith in humanity.

43

Copa Mundial

By that evening we had reached a range of low red mountains which formed part of a national park. The park entrance fee was very dear and as they only offered day camping we were directed to a compound nearby which had camping. The compound did not offer camping but did have dorms which usually accommodated students and volunteers who came to study the local archaeological sites or work in the pottery studio on site. The kind manager allowed us to camp for free and the next day arranged for us to be given a tour of the studio where the kids got to make clay bowls, Keelan, at 14, towering over the man giving instructions. This is a part of the children's education which is the simplest and most enjoyable. A hands-on experience which very few children are fortunate enough to have.

Our destination the next day was another national park which we reached as the sun was setting. The guard allowed us to free camp outside the entrance gate and to use the electricity and bathrooms. We had been told great things about the natural wonders which lay inside the park, but the rude staff insisted that we needed a guide and the guide's fee was more than we were prepared to pay. They were happy to upset us and see us leave, less work that day and more time to play games on a cellphone. That was the last time we ever tried to enter or visit a national park in Brazil.

Despite the mechanical problems we were making good progress and within a few days we had made it down to Belo Horizonte, a city which rises out of the horizon as you approach. Surrounded by mountains, with skyscrapers and greenery surrounding the city is prosperous and beautiful from afar, a welcome contrast to underdeveloped northern Brazil.

The first game of the World Cup was kicking off later that afternoon and we had a few hundred kilometres to cover before we would reach Coquieral and our friends, Isabella and Rafael. The road became a fantastic double lane highway once we left Belo Horizonte and we made very good time, arriving at Isabella's parent's lovely home as Brazil scored their first goal. The family and friends were gathered around wearing their Neymar Jnr football shirts and Isabella's dad thrust an ice-cold Brahma in my hand. Time to party, Brazilian style, which I have to tell you, is second to none.

Isabella's family offered us a cottage on a smallholding they had outside of town and invited us to make ourselves at home. The cottage is set beside a forest and a small fruit orchard filled our table daily. Green parrots woke us with noisy chatter every morning and a lone toucan would regularly float amongst the tallest trees. The long, cool patio faced a coffee plantation and a herd of cattle would visit the watering hole next to the cottage twice a day. A rural paradise, exactly what we needed after the last couple of months of constant travelling and camping. The town welcomed us curiously, little kids would run beside the Landy and we generated many smiles and waves. Isabella and Rafael left soon after a wonderful American overlanding family, Stevie, Tree and Soleil came to visit with a large Mercedes Sprinter and a cache of Tequila and Argentinean wine. The mini Overlander get together was exactly what you would expect when the tribe re-unites. Meat was burnt, tales were told, someone notoriously clumsy managed to set himself on fire and all of the world's problems were solved before the sun rose to chase us to bed.

After our dear friends left, we were alone on the farm and the decision was made to head down to Florianopolis and see if there were any opportunities to work teaching English. I was reluctant to leave, but the budget needed a boost more than I needed to hang out on a farm.

The drive to Florianopolis from the farm takes two days, including a drive through the infamous Sao Paulo city and we were disappointed to find the glorious island covered in fog and wet with rain. Another American Overlander family, Adam, Emily, Colette and new-born Sierra, who we had first met in Peru, invited us to camp in the garden outside the cottage they were renting in a neighbourhood called Campeche. They are a super chilled, highly creative, vegetarian family who has courageously chosen to raise a young family on the road. The first few nights were fun, but some dick decided to rob the family on the third night, which poured cold water over the romance. While a newborn baby and a precious little girl slept in the bedroom with her parents, a walking piece of faecal matter grabbed what he could and made off not only with material goods but also a huge slab of tranquillity. This was the first crime we had experienced on our journey apart from some clothing stolen in Argentina and felt helpless at the loss of this sweet families' possessions, including a hard drive containing all of Adams most recent photos and, most significantly, little Sierras birth pictures. A neighbour had a CCTV camera monitoring the sandy alley next to the house but was reluctant to share the video; the cops left us to do the investigating and hardly made any effort at all. If you know a thief, go punch him in the teeth. Hard.

With no hope of recovering our friend's possessions and our efforts to find employment unsuccessful, we left a few days after the robbery, giving Adam's family some much-needed peace and quiet. Our third visit to the campsite in Lagoa de Conceicao, Florianopolis coincided with the World Cup match Brazil vs Germany. We wanted to head to the pub on the corner to watch the match and enjoy the festivities but decided to try and save some money, make burgers and drink some beers in the camp kitchen and watch the game on the large TV then head down to the pub for the second half. The German football Blitzkrieg surprised Brazil completely, as much as the French were overwhelmed by the military version of that tactic in 1939. The neighbourhood went quiet, no singing and no fireworks, even when Brazil finally scored. A drizzle of rain damped the world outside our kitchen, a wife berated her husband, the night died.

These were my thoughts the next day. Brazil is immense and developing. Brazil has everything. Brazilians are the kindest and most accommodating people we have ever met. But Brazil suffers an identity crisis, insecurity and chronic low self-esteem. Watch Senna, the documentary which depicts the Formula 1 stars rise and demise and the one thing which will strike you hardest, other than his death by insatiable bureaucracy, is the sentiment expressed by his countrymen. That he is the only good thing about Brazil. A nation revered him as a saviour, through sport. Senna was not a typical Brazilian, he was Southern, wealthy and he had an opportunity which he fulfilled.

The World Cup was controversial and protested before the tournament began in Brazil. I understand the Brazilian public's violent opposition to the construction of elaborate stadiums while millions remain disenfranchised. The only consolation I have to offer them is the reality that Futebol is popular and loved, that the stadiums will not remain a burden to taxpayers that eventually the stadiums will pay for themselves. South Africa hosted the World Cup in 2010; our football team is overfunded, over supported and trophy poor. The last major trophy claimed by our national team, Bafana Bafana, was the African Cup of Nations, which was won in 1996. Rugby and Cricket are my nation's most successful sports, but the World Cup stadiums built at great expense in a country sorely lacking education, housing, employment, healthcare and opportunity were built solely for the purpose of football. These white elephants cost millions daily and are not suitable for any sport other than football and the occasional Duran

Duran concert. Perhaps, definitely, race politics and blind politicians squandered an inheritance and an opportunity. Cold comfort.

Brazil's loss to the Germans (and the Dutch) was not only traumatic and desperate but was also wholly undeserved. I speak only of the people of Brazil and not of the sport. We have travelled to many countries and have been amazed by the love and generosity we have experienced in Brazil. The World Cup for them was not only a matter of national pride but also a statement of their place in the First World. Individuals failed, and a nation is polarised, separated, despondent and dismayed. They should not be. Brazil is a nation of love and passion and they will always be champions to me.

We missed the warm comfort of the farm back in Coquieral. I sent a message to Isabella's mom and dad, Christina and Luis, asking if we could take care of the cottage for a couple of months and they, thankfully, welcomed us back. A new plan had been hatched around a fire one night. Luisa had been talking about going home for a few months, and I was determined to keep on travelling until we had reached Alaska, minimum. With the taxman owing us a chunk of change, a family in need of some visiting time and a bunch of errands to be run it was decided that Luisa and Keelan would fly back to South Africa for a month while Jessica and I stayed on the farm and I would work to complete this book.

44

Coffee Country Cottage

Arriving back in Coquieral we were warmly greeted, and we arranged for the kids to attend the local school with the help of some new friends. Jessica would attend the junior school, and Keelan would attend the high school. Both kids walked confidently into their new schools with huge, nervous smiles, schools where they knew not one person and where they could not have looked more foreign if they had descended from the skies in a spacecraft. Back home in South Africa both kids had been shy and lacked the confidence which the world demands of them. A group of little girls huddled around Jessica as she walked into class the first day; she was absolutely glowing with happiness as her instagang gabbled away in Portuguese. None of the teachers spoke even a word of English and Jessica had only a few phrases of Portuguese in her linguistic arsenal, but she would have to learn very quickly. Keelan had a far greater command of Spanish and Portuguese and he is often my translator when I run out of words. His first day of school was going to be completely different from little Jess' experience. Both kids had been very excited that morning and, as they were going to attend the afternoon classes, had plenty of time to change their wardrobes repeatedly. Keelan and Luisa walked into the high school and were led to a classroom where Keelan sat down, took out his own home-schooling books, and gave Luisa a long; you can go now Mom, look. Luisa, the overprotective mama bear, would have been happy to sit there all day and protect her little cub from the horrible world, but this world was warm and inviting, and she had no need for fear. I had also worried that Keelan might send tender glances towards the wrong girl, whose boyfriend would be eager to write his name into the tough guy hall of fame by beating up the foreign kid. Brazilians are not raised that way, and I make a habit of judging people and communities by the behaviour of their children. I anxiously waited with Jessica in the Landy for Keelan to come out of school at 5 pm. The bell rang, and Keelan exited the metal school gates surrounded by a group of kids but strolling along as if he did this every day. 'How did it go boy'?', 'Fine'. A smile on his dial, as my Dad would say. He waited until we made it back to the cottage and I was ready to explode before telling us about his day. He had sat down in a seat at the back of the class and once Luisa had left his new schoolmates had only one distraction to study. The teacher had to work quite hard to get the attention of the class and eventually gave up. Discipline is not a big deal in Brazilian public schools, and the teacher accepted that the kids would not be able to concentrate until they were used to the big mop of blonde which had invaded their world unannounced. The bell ran for a recess and Keelan wandered out into the yard, ready to explore. A new friend, Miguel, took him to the cafeteria where they were fed a free meal of meat, rice, beans and salad, a large group of kids hovering nearby. Returning to the class before the end of recess Keelan sat on a low wall with Miguel. Slowly the entire school began moving towards him, smiling, laughing and joking. He stood up and walked around the corner and the happy mass rounded the building slowly, continuing its curious advance from all sides. Keelan did his best to understand and answer the quickfire Portuguese questions and posed for photos and selfies. There was absolutely no aggression or vindictiveness. Asked today whether he had any bad experiences Keelan says 'no, Brazilians are kind people'.

We settled into a blissful rural routine, I tended the garden, did some maintenance on the Landy and worked on this book. Without full-time employment, you would imagine that we would lie in hammocks all day reading and taking naps, but the reality is quite different. We always found something to do with our time and Luisa had her hands full taking care of the remnants of our immigration business and fighting with the taxman. The tickets were booked from Sao Paulo to Johannesburg and as the day of departure approached we became unsettled. Luisa and I have hardly spent more than a day apart since we began working together and Keelan is my left-handed right-hand man, my soul would be on that plane back to South Africa. A welcome distraction arrived in the form of a tough as nails Toyota Surf and its precious American overland cargo. We had hung out with James and Lauren with Team America in Bariloche and knew that if you want late night bonfires and good times, then these are your people. The next few days were filled with excellent conversation, a picnic and fishing, fires, fireworks and more than a few refreshing drinks. Before we left to drive the long bumpy farm road to the fishing spot I tied three empty beer cans together with a cable tie then attached them to the chassis of James' Toyota. I was going to laugh my ass off when he drove down the road and stopped the truck in a panic, not that James knows how to panic, to check which part of his rig was falling off. No chance of that. We drove all the way to the other farm and back without any excitement. Disappointed I showed James the prank and he just laughed, his old Toyota makes so many noises that he now he just turns the radio up. Problem solved.

James and Lauren hit the road to the Brazilian coast, and Luisa packed for South Africa. If she returned to Brazil and told me that she wanted to return to South Africa and resume 'life', then I would have to accept that the dream was over. I was sure that once the novelty of being home wore off that she would agree, keeping to our nomad lifestyle is our future, for the next few years at least. I cooked all our favourite meals in the days before they departed, buttering them both up with love and food, reminding them why they should love Jessica and me above all else. The day came, and we awoke with the sun for the long drive to Sao

Paulo. Coming from the north we were fortunate that the airport was not too far into the city, a city famous for torturous traffic and crime. We had almost missed our plane to Buenos Aires back in 2012 and could not afford for them to miss this plane, Luisa, they say, will be late for her own funeral and I despise being tardy. We were on time and said our sad goodbyes. Keelan understood that he was being sent to take care of and help his Mom, not that she needs anyone to take care of her, I explained that we are a tribe and he is a young warrior. As a young warrior he needs to take on responsibilities that he was not going for a holiday but needed to pull his weight and do what is asked of him. He agreed and promised to make me proud. I don't know if it is possible to be prouder of my son, but he always finds a way to impress me with his quiet intelligence and courageous humanity. Jessica and I watched quietly as one half of our existence walked away, waving and crying.

Back in the Landy Jessica had the unenviable task of navigating out of the city, using a temperamental Samsung Galaxy which charged when it felt like it and took regular, unscheduled naps. I had memorised the route on the way in and driving slowly we made all the correct turns and were soon back on the BR381 without the assistance of the damned tablet. Tollbooth ladies were shocked when Jessica rolled down the window and thrust out her little hand full of Reals.

Returning to the farm we created a new routine without the input of our noisy matriarch and the permanently hungry teen. 'What do you want for breakfast Jess?', 'pancakes', 'what do you want for lunch Jess?', 'hot dogs', 'dinner?', 'pasta'. Every day the same answers. And during meals, she would constantly chat about her day and dreams and any crazy little thoughts which popped into her head. For years I had been trying to get her to eat more and talk less at the table because she loves to yak when we are all within reach. Now, the more she chatted, the less she would miss Mommy and the terrorist, I would sit and listen every night until her food was cold. The more time we spent together, the more I heard her true voice, her full personality, undistracted by a sibling or a bustling mother. I decided to thank Isabella's family by renovating the cottage which was in dire need of painting. There were two small bedrooms, a living room and a large kitchen with walls burnt black by the traditional Brazilian wood burning stove. In places, the plaster was cracked, and outside entire chunks of plaster was missing. Well-crafted wooden chairs and tables furnished the house and would look as good as new with a good sanding. I had a task to keep my hands and mind busy and have always loved manual labour as meditation, taking satisfaction in the before and after of a job well done.

That month slowly trudged by. Luisa and Keelan skyping regularly and reporting how our home country had or had not changed and realised how they had been changed and in many ways improved by a simple life lived on the road. They would sit on the other side of the Atlantic and chew on South African delicacies while chatting with me. Biltong, droewors, boerewors, Mexican Chili chips, Tex bars, Ouma rusks. Pure torture which they enjoy heartily until I switched off the computer in protest. Within the first week Luisa had already decided that more than anything she wanted to be home, and by the home, she meant with the Land Rover and us, wherever we might be, as long as we were together, that is where home is.

My work on the cottage continued daily. I soon had the lawn growing and built a fire pit on a huge tree adorned ant mound, overlooking the cottage; I had chosen ivory base colour paint and added tints so that each main area had its own look. The outside walls were variations of ash brown and the interior walls were closer to the original ivory. The metal-framed windows and shutters were painted a reddish chocolate brown, and the old yellow cottage began to take on a modern appearance. Standing on a ladder in the kitchen painting the upper reaches one Wednesday afternoon I was putting on the finishing touches when the metal feet of the ladder slid on the carpet I had laid on the tiles to prevent a slip. My legs fell between the rungs twisted the knee on my scarred right leg, my back seized, and pain shot through my body as paint from the cup in my hand splattered all over the kitchen counters, the food and the cutlery. Squirming in pain, I checked my body for blood and found only a few scrapes and then I checked for broken bones and found only instant blue swelling. What a big baby. Hobbling, I cleaned up the paint before it dried and gave up on work for the day and smoked a horrible palheiro, tobacco wrapped in corn husk. Not long after that accident I was limpingly painting the outside walls and was attacked by a swarm of small wasps that lived under the roof. Luis had a look and told me to spray bug spray on the wasps at night, and that would chase them away. I did not want to kill them and instead tried smoking them out, and in thanks, they attacked me again. By now the love was lost and I bought a big can of bug spray when picking Jess up from town, then waited for nightfall to get my revenge. I closed all the doors and windows and left Jessica playing with her dolls on the rug in the cottage. I told her to stay still if any wasps came her way and not to swat them. Dressed head to toe in black I unleashed biological war on those little stinging bastards. A few died, a few buzzed out and were shot down. Job done, that was easy. I opened the door to the cottage to find Jess sitting quietly staring at the ceiling. 'Papa, look at the light'. Thousands of wasps were buzzing around the light in a frenzy. Jessica crawled over to the front door and I put her in the sealed Landy. Thankfully the panicked wasps were only attracted to the light and ignored her completely, hence the advice to spray them at night. I was able to spray and retreat, spray and retreat, spray and retreat until they were all dead, lying in black heaps on the floor after two hours of genocide. That was not the last bug invasion either. Sitting on the loo after dropping Jess off at school, I heard a buzzing noise which I assumed was the fridge. When I stepped into the kitchen though I found an entire swarm of bees had moved in with us. There was no way I was going to kill the bees, so I lit palheiro after palheiro and puffed and blew, puffed and blew until the bees got the message and I got a head rush. I was also fighting a daily war with another breed of wasps who were trying to build a nest in the Landy's rooftop storage and tent. The green parrots who woke us every morning were trying to break through the ceiling cornice and make the cottage their large luxurious nest. Stray dogs, would rummage through our trash and sleep on the patio at night when we locked up. We were under siege. The beauties of spring. Another unwelcome visitor was a lobisomem, the Brazilian werewolf. We had seen one running on the beach near Rio, trying to break into kiosks and now we had one living near the farm. Before Luisa and Keelan left for South Africa, something rushed past Luisa as we were locking up for the night as she went around the corner to turn on the outside light. I saw something dark rushing in the shadows and then we heard a howl which put the fear of God in both of us. A cow moo-ed in distress and we slammed the doors shut. Lying in bed about ten minutes later we heard the howl again, a little further away. We agreed that we had never heard any animal howl like that before. Brazil is full of these bloody creatures. At night sitting on a tree stump watching the fire in the fire pit, I would feel like I was being watched and sometimes found myself running like a little girl, arms flailing to the cottage when my courage ran out. Not really, just kidding, my arms are too manly and muscular to flail.

My friend Marcelo, the Uruguayan and fellow beer addict, sent me a message inviting me to a Land Rover Festival taking place in Sao Lourenco, a small city only 180 km's away from our little farm. Naturally, we were intrigued and enrolled for a weekend of all things Land Rover. With Jessica as my trusty navigator, we set off for Sao Lourenco on a hot and sunny afternoon. We did not know it then, but a severe drought was on its way to Minas Gerais and there was no moisture in the air at all, very bad news for our new coffee-growing friends. Coffee is the dominant crop in the area, and we saw plenty plantations and little rural cities with names like Tres Coracoes, Three Hearts and Tres Pontes, Three Points, which referred to three large hills. We arrived at the festival not long after Marcelo, and as we were registering we shared a beer with two new friends, André and Luis, the four of us became a gang for the weekend and spent the weekend drinking beer, eating meat and wandering around the small exhibition area. The Landy was a very popular attraction in the camping area, and I felt terrible that I had not taken the time to scrub and polish her and present her in full expedition mode but, living on a farm, she would had been covered in dirt by the time we reached the main road, in any event, we were there to meet likeminded people and look at other Landy's, not to be part of the event. Jessica was very happy to make friends with another ten-year-old whose Dad's Landy was parked a few feet away, and I was liberated of childcare duties as Jess, and her new friend spent the whole weekend zooming around on bicycles. I did have a scare when I woke, groggy, one morning to find that Jess was not in the tent and nowhere in sight. I found her playing with some puppies, without a care in the world. There is one aspect of Brazilian culture which I admire particularly and that is the importance of family. Men and women work very long hours then return home to spend the evening with the kids, walking in the park, riding a bike or doing any variety of other family-friendly activities. Many fathers are inseparable from their children and drop any macho pretences to care for, feed and entertain their kids, often late into the evening. To this day, I do not know when Brazilians sleep because they always seem to be busy doing something or going somewhere. A child is treated like everyone's child and in return,c the children are respectful, curious and comfortable in their own skin. This is true in almost every South American country but is especially true in Brazil. I never felt that my kids were unsafe, but they have been well trained to recognise stranger danger.

Most of the Landy's present were Defenders and Series with some of the newer, curvy things driving around. Most impressive on show were a few Series 1's and a TDi Defender 130 on triangular tank like rubber tracks. Defenders are extremely rare in Brazil despite the fact that they were manufactured in Brazil for three years in the 2000s and as a result, they are very expensive. A Defender 130 like ours would be worth around $60,000 US in 2014. I might have been tempted if someone had thrown that kind of money at me, but then I think of the tears I would cry, and I realise that she is worth more to me than a pile of dollars stacked that high. That said if you offer me $70,000 US I will buy some tissues and wipe away the tears. A few of the characters we met at the festival were almost as interesting as the Land Rovers. There was a Swiss-Brazilian aviator and environmentalist, called Gerard Moss, who had set a few world records for aviation, including the first solo flight around the earth in a motor glider. Other new friends included a gentleman who has a glamorous life touring the world with his equally glamorous wife, restores wooden yachts at his citrus farm and a Japanese Brazilian who wore a magical white coat. He could conjure fresh sushi, prestigious wine and delicious dessert from that coat, I made sure to stand near him as often as possible. Though the language barrier remained high, we managed to communicate and understand most conversations. The night before we left I was called up to the stage and presented with a wonderfully decorated ceramic tile, the prize was for Land Rover from furthest away. André is holding on to it for me, there is no place in an overland truck for a ceramic tile unless you are a wealthy European whose truck is large and luxurious enough to need tiled floors. Believe me, they exist.

After what had seemed like a lonely eternity, the time came to fetch Luisa and Keelan from the Sao Paulo airport. Jessica was navigating into the city, and when she suggested that I turn, I doubted her and drove straight into a huge traffic jam. I asked other trapped drivers for

GRAEME BELL

directions and the advice was misunderstood and we ended up driving on a freeway leading to the south of the city. Even though I re-assured Jessica that it was not her fault that I did not take the turnoff she continued apologising while trying to find a route back to the airport. I took an off-ramp, asked advice from a taxi driver and made it to the airport and parked five minutes after Luisa and Keelan had reached the drop and go terminus. It was a typically rowdy reunion, screams of joy and long sweaty hugs. They just wanted to get back to the farm and sleep, but we still had a five-hour drive and plenty to talk about. They also had 170 kgs of luggage which needed to be stuffed into the back of the Landy. Having raided our storage unit back in Plettenberg Bay, Luisa now had clothing we had left behind, two bicycles, all our favourite foodstuffs and a huge box of Land Rover spares which she had bought while visiting her Mom in Durban.

With the family reunited, we were ready for the next phase of our journey, shipping the Land Rover from Argentina. With hugs, thanks and promises to return one day we left Coquieral and our new friends. Of all the places we have stayed this little Brazilian town, which you will struggle to find on a map, seemed like the kind of place we could live happily for the rest of our lives. I was busy writing a letter to my Uncle Alan earlier in the month and I had an epiphany...

"I still dream of being an artist of sorts, of building a home with my hands, of learning to weld sculptures, carve in wood, create structures with form and beauty, make furniture, to work with clay, to have a little home in the woods, next to a lake full of fish where I will create a Nirvana for my family, where I can build a studio and a workshop where I can be creative and productive every day. A little farm, secluded but connected to the world, a place travellers will visit. A place where we can live off the land and live an honest, peaceful existence.

And then I remember. I am an artist; at least I try to be. I have written a book! Writing is an art form, is it not? I am busy rewriting and editing the final draft here on a little farm, in a little cottage with oranges and naartjies waiting to be picked. I have my dream right here right now, but I was so busy dreaming about my dream that I failed to realise. It is not our home and we will have to leave eventually but as I sit here I look up I see a wild olive tree with wood carved seats arranged beneath it, I see coffee plantations, wild cacti and bamboo forests on the verge and another small forest to my right. I smell the fresh earth and the rain which has just fallen; I hear the birds signing, parrots swooping and my family quietly going about their lives in the cottage behind me".

45

Misty Mountains

Not wanting to drive the bloody BR381 for the sixth time we chose a route to a mountainous area and a town called Morrettes where André, my new friend from the Land Rover festival, had recently finished building a house and invited us to stay with him for a week in the jungle. The route wound through the mountains and passed some very poor and remote towns where the rain never seemed to stop, and the youth dressed up in their best clothing to party at the gas stations, it must have been a Friday night when we passed through. Anyone who drives mountain passes often will know the frustration of a destination 100 km's away and a road that takes four hours to drive. Endless switchbacks and blind corners, either hunting for power to climb hills or using engine braking on the downhill's so as not to fry the brakes. We had misjudged the road and length of the route and night descended long before we reached our destination. The mist descended, and visibility was limited to twenty metres, maximum. With the headlights on dim, we inched forward, hour after hour until we dropped into a little town with wooden statues dotted along the road and a tourist office set on the grounds of an old mine. The office was open 24 hours and though they would not let us camp near the office, we could camp in a soggy, stony parking lot across the road and use the bathrooms. The town itself is only a hundred kilometres from Curitiba, one of Brazil's most beautiful and modern cities but reminded me of the little, hard-edged and weather-beaten villages in the Carretera Austral in Chile. Unlike those villages here litter was strewn along the streets and in the many streams running down from the surrounding hills. At the town exit, a processing plant billowing smoke lay waiting for us along with early morning prostitutes waiting for horny workers to end their night shift. Nearer the highway to Curitiba, the towns began to appear wealthier and more residential, less utilitarian and far more inviting than those little-unloved homes of men and women who eke out a living extracting minerals and wages from the bedrock.

Within an hour the Landy was juddering along the cobbled, narrow roads leading down a mountainside through an impeccably maintained botanical garden of jungle and wildflowers, down past lodges and stately holiday homes. We met André as we drove along a long straight road which led into the historical centre where an ancient train still runs a weekly passage to Curitiba. His wood and glass home sat atop a hill at the end of a jungle road. The perfect base for exploring the area on the bikes which Luisa had brought from home. Keelan spent much of his days either on the bike, or falling off and ploughing the dirt with his face. He reminds me of a young me, pushing the limits of two wheels and traction, earning scars like medals of bravery. My precious bike returned every day with a new wound, bent handlebars, scratched paint, flat tyres, ripped handles and pedals full of clumps of mud and grass. Keelan would be similarly wounded, but less expensive to repair. We had never heard of this area and, yet it was one of the most beautiful places we had been in Brazil. A week was not enough to explore and appreciate the diversity of this magical mountainous forest, but we had to head to Panama, and that meant getting down to Argentina and arranging the Land Rover's passage on a boat from Zarate, a port town upstream from Buenos Aires. André had kept our bellies full and our faces smiling; his offer to return will be accepted on the second round in South America if life sees fit to award that to us.

Meeting wonderful people is a blessing on this journey and a family who we had met on our last visit to the Florianopolis campsite, invited us to stay with them in the city of Blumenau. The city has the second largest Oktoberfest in the world and, by some miracle of circumstance; our visit coincided with this very German Brazilian experience. Our hosts Sueli and Flavio, a George Clooney look-alike, had kicked their sons out of the little, designer decorated, apartment above the garage and welcomed us to stay as long as we liked. A very tempting proposition, indeed. Our time with them was spent touring the city, drinking the fine locally produced beer at the Oktoberfest and taking drives into the beautiful mountains nearby to swim in rock pools, marvel at waterfalls and doing some cave exploration, in complete darkness and without a guide. Blumenau City is located in Santa Catarina state, and with its history of German, Danish, Italian and Swiss immigration seems a world away from northern Brazil. Driving through little towns with immaculate gardens and pretty, double story houses, one can't help but think of the most recent wave of German immigrants, particularly towards the end and after World War 2. One little town en-route to the mountains, a slice of Europe with its happy, organised exterior had the highest suicide rate in all of Brazil. Pale men walked German Shepherds and Rottweiler's along the streets and a very Germanic atmosphere prevailed. Well, what I imagine to be a Germanic atmosphere having never been to Germany or even Europe except for a layover in Greece, which doesn't really count as Europe, does it?

Joseph Mengele, the Auschwitz labour camp Angel of Death, lived a day's drive from the farm in Coquieal in the late sixties and seventies until he drowned swimming in the sea near Sao Paulo in 1979 in a town called Bertioga. Candido Godoi, a town of predominantly German and Polish immigrants, has a strange tale to tell. The average rate of twin birth is 1 in 10, much higher than the average. Some speculate that Mengele continued his Sobibor extermination camp experimentation with twins in Candido Godoi, others suggest that the high prevalence of twins predates Mengele's immigration to Southern Brazil and that the phenomenon is caused by genetic isolation and inbreeding. Other famous Nazis known to have lived in the southern Brazilian states are Gustav Wagner and Franz Stangl, colleagues of Mengele from Sobibor.

Keep in mind though that German immigration began long before the rise of the Nazis and it would be unfair and inaccurate to see anything sinister in the culture of a community over a hundred years old. And it is immediately obvious why those immigrants would want to settle here when they had a planet of choices. With an abundance of sun, water and fertile land, the European farmers could double their production and triple their wealth without the threat of a frozen winter turning the soil into rock. And this is the area and community which gave the world Gisele Bundchen the supermodel, Oscar Niemeyer the architect and Ernesto Geisel, the president of Brazil from 1974 to 1979. I think we all owe the community a debt of gratitude for giving us a Gisele.

46

Uruguay, Part Three or Four?

Our route to Argentina led through Uruguay, and it is always illuminating and refreshing to visit a country for a second or third time and revisit a culture you enjoyed. One of our tasks in Uruguay was to draw as many dollars as we could afford in anticipation of a costly shipping process. Uruguay, like Brazil, was that much more expensive for us this time around due to the fall of the rand and our tax woes. However, because we were able to free camp in public parks we were able to afford a few slabs of famous Uruguayan beef which we grilled while watching a traffic jam of cars and motorbikes threading through Parque Rivera outside Melo. Uruguayan cattle are small by African standards, and most have a simple life living in the hills munching on sweet, thick, green grass. Uruguayans eat more meat than any other nation on the planet and the Asado is an almost religious experience. Salted grilled beef with a thick strip of crispy fat is accompanied by beer and wine and maybe a salad for the girls. Tacuarembó, a small city to the west of Melo also offers free camping in established campsites and lakes for swimming and fishing. Locals flock to the lakes every afternoon and weekend to Asado and socialise under large trees. Rural Uruguay is very relaxed and peaceful; siestas are common even in the larger towns and small cities, which can be a nuisance when you need to buy a litre of milk or a loaf of bread. Life rolls along at a gentle pace, people are friendly, inquisitive and relaxed. Unlike the French Overlanders, we met when leaving the camp. They had spent the last two years dividing their time between France and southern South America. She, a thick-lipped, short-haired and a well-rounded lady with a ready smile and a head cocked to the side, tell me more, I know it all. He a stooped back, a grizzled beard, a wiry build and the demeanour of an oil rig welder or perhaps a used BMW salesman. Their truck was massive, imposing and modern with every convenience you don't need. Our Land Rover looked up at the truck defiantly and pissed on her oversized tyres. We took out our travel dicks for measurement and that conversation you learn to dread when meeting many Overlanders. Yes, well when we were in Afjerkistan we found a bearing for our Pinzgauer in a little shack run by a Mongolian chief we had met in Gankakistan in 1983. No, we never buy water, we just tell people we need 50 litres then fill up with 400. Did you do all that with kids? No. And you go home every six months? Yes. Bugger off then, we win. It is something akin to professional jealousy and admittedly unfortunate that some members of the tribe just don't get along with others and it is often the most boastful, flag-waving travellers who are the most irritating. Perhaps that is why we are nomads, we don't really get along with other humans, and we try to avoid each other. I understand psychology, and I am not immune to a bit of arrogance. That psychology is simple. As aspirant world travellers you begin the preparation for the journey nervous and doubtful, researching, hat in hand, asking long-termers for reassurance and advice on everything from water to tyres to insurance to campsites. Then you begin travelling, and the sky doesn't fall on your head, you meet normal non-travelling citizens while travelling and they look at you with awe, treat you like the world-conquering hero you dream to be, and they admire your courage, strength and wealth. You feel great, you believe your own hype and you may even resent meeting people who might make you feel less than your new opinion of yourself. Someone who claims to have travelled further, with superior intelligence, in better style, without a single breakdown on roads which make you tremble and to places you have never heard of are not the people you want to meet when you spend your days soaking up the stares in a shopping centre parking lot, or the questions of taxi drivers while waiting for a light to change or the look on someone's face when you tell them you are from there, you have been there, and you are going there. I imagine it is like Bono meeting Prince, Michael Jackson meeting God or Madonna meeting a mirror, pre-1999.

A massive storm cloud banked across the sky, a tsunami of water vapour rolling forwards, expelling wind and fire, sending us scurrying to the relative warmth and safety of the Landy and ending our tepid conversation, au revoir Frenchie! No, no need to give us your email, blog and website address, we have enough information, thank you. The Landy pointed her nose in the direction of the Argentine border while the family stuffed tampons and hygienic pads into the gaps in the Land Rovers doors, trying to stem the flow of water which pours in if we drive in storms any stronger than a butterfly fart.

The hunt for dollars continued in a wet Paysandú. Luisa withdrawing the maximum 200 dollars at the rare ATM which accepted our African plastic while I drove in circles looking for a suitable handicapped parking or loading zone to guiltily accommodate while the treasure hunt continued. Keelan provided security while Luisa harassed each bank teller and ATM along the main drag. The grand total on hand was $3,000, and our accounts back home groaned with the weight of the new debt we had incurred. At an exchange rate of fifteen pesos to one dollar on the Argentine black market, we were hoping to stretch our African money a bit further. All told though, with the weakness of the Rand and the many bank fees incurred for international withdrawals the profit was negligible. Leaving Paysandú, we entered Argentina via the bridge over the Rio Uruguay which led to a drive-through immigration queue. We did not realise that we were dealing with a toothless, large and grumpy Argentine customs lady until she asked for our insurance documentation. Our passports had been stamped out of Uruguay and into Argentina almost simultaneously and without our knowledge. We did not have insurance for Argentina, and as we had already officially left Uruguay it was too late to head back to Paysandú to buy some. Luisa handed over our 'improvised' insurance document which we had used to enter French Guyana. The official was not happy. Where is the SOAT? Suddenly we could not remember a word of Spanish and our insurance document was written purely in English. With the help of Google translate toothless, large and grumpy was able to determine that we were covered for Argentina. The next hurdle was a toll gate which accepted dollars at the official rate or Argentine pesos. A kind lady in the duty-free shop allowed us to buy a few chocolates with dollars and gave us change in Argentine pesos at the black market, also known as Blue Dollar rate. The rain continued to pelt us as we headed towards Colon searching for a money changer. At the first fuel station, I quietly asked a pretty attendant where I could change dollars; she pointed at an ugly attendant who made us wait until we gave up on patience and demanded prompt illegal service. His rate was less than we expected, but with the sun setting behind the saturated clouds, we reluctantly exchanged $100. The city roads were strewn with leaves and storm debris, and we searched for a supermarket, eager to relive a Venezuelan type shopping experience of paying a tiny amount for rare quality goods with stacks of toy money. Inflation on both sides of the Southern Atlantic raised its leg on that idea, and we were disappointed to find that the goods on offer were still bloody expensive. Then the search for accommodation began as the rain fell even harder. The Rio Uruguay had burst its banks and the campsite was closed, the cheaper hotels we could find were too expensive or filthy or offered no safe parking for the Landy. Outside town we drove along slippery, muddy roads to another campsite we had been told about, but there were no facilities to shelter us from the storm and the little huts on offer had not been cleaned since they were built, and the linen had not been washed since it was spun by that arthritic Vietnamese teenager. We had seen what looked like holiday cottages back along the main road, but no-one emerged to negotiate with us at any of the holiday complexes and we eventually, reluctantly settled on a roadside motel with safe parking for the Landy, a kitchenette, a small bar and splotchy white stains on the bedding. We slept fully clothed.

47

Overlander Heaven

Arriving in Gualeguaychu a few hundred kilometres south of Colon, we debated whether we should stay and research the shipping or head down to Zarate where there are apparently few options for camping. The campsite where we had stayed back in 2013 was flooded and deserted but there was a cluster of pretty double-storey cottages next door and while we sat outside the gates trying to hack into the Wi-Fi the owner, who had driven past us on our way in, drove up and asked if we needed a place to stay. The rooms were small but modern and clean and overlooked the river, green lawn and a braai area. He proposed a daily rate equivalent to $50 a day which we negotiated down to $30 a day at a rate of 15 pesos to the dollar. The cottage had a bunk bed for the kids and a private room for Luisa and me, who predicted a few bottles of excellent Argentine wine and some lovemaking in the not too distant future.

Travelling with and sharing a rooftop tent with kids is detrimental to a healthy sex life. Luisa and I had explored our options and often resorted to slow motion, short-term tantric sex when the kids were sent for a shower or a walk which is never long enough. Discretion is the word, and a rocking rooftop tent is either an obvious sign of a boogie session or a bee invasion. Sometimes we get caught and I have received mid-coitus Facebook messages from the boy child. Bluhding 'You disgust me' bluhding 'we have to SLEEP there' bluhding 'don't talk to me'. Don't ask me what I am doing on Facebook during coitus, I won't tell. A head popping into the tent or a whole body flying up the ladder is not uncommon. If Jessica catches us, she will ask what we were doing under the covers and we will say, uh, wrestling. Yay, she will say, I want to wrestle too. Uncomfortable. If Keelan catches us we can expect an evening of dirty looks and a sense of betrayal. 'Why would you even do that?'. Now that he is fifteen he understands a bit better and, one of the reasons we don't get an extra tent. There are plenty of Latino girls around who wouldn't mind 'wrestling' with him. It is all too sordid, and frankly, you shouldn't have asked. Actually, it is one of the questions that often comes up when we are with other Overlanders, and we have had a few drinks. 'You've got kids, so how do you, you know, do IT?' 'We don't', is the short and sweet and painfully truthful answer. I can imagine all those overlanding couples, the newlyweds or those living in sin, the retirees with a lust for life, bonking their way around the planet. They bonk at Perito Moreno, they bonk under the stars, they bonk in the Grand Canyon and at the Pyramids of Giza, they bonk on the beach and bonk in the mountains and bonk whenever and wherever the fuck they feel like it. We, simply, don't.

Moving on. Luisa and I sat doing the maths on the shipping and flights to Panama. The quotes we were receiving for the shipping were far more than we budgeted for and we were informed that the vehicle had to be empty with the contents shipped separately, the cost of which equalled the shipping of the Landy. The only option for shipping was Roll-on-Roll Off or RORO and we had heard horror stories about theft from vehicles. Then, on top of the shipping costs, we would have to fly to Panama. We had known all of this before we had reached Argentina, but we were counting on the blue dollar rate to render the procedure affordable. It was not working out that way. It would be cheaper, theoretically, to drive up to Cartagena and then take the new ferry service across to Panama. The ferry had been rumoured for a while, and a German businessman had actually bought an old Canadian ferry and run around the Darrien Gap with a few motorbike Overlanders on board. Then the powers that be shut him down. Other, fake, ferry services also existed, they would insist that you pay in full upfront for the service then disappear into cyberspace with your cash. Rumours also abound that the reason that a ferry does not consistently run is that the USA does not want a quick, convenient and cheap service connecting South and Central America. The War on Drugs and a fear of Foot and Mouth disease put paid to another rumour, a road to be built through the Darien Gap by the Brazilians. Regardless, we need to cross that blasted 100 km gap. A few successful crossings of the new ferry and images of overland vehicles embarking and disembarking solved our problem, potentially. It would be much cheaper if we drove up to Cartagena through, Bolivia, Peru and Ecuador and into Colombia, we would be able to visit old friends and travel the only country we had missed on this South American journey, Bolivia. We are Overlanders, and we get that name by travelling overland, not shipping around continents. And we reserve the right to make bad decisions and change our minds whenever we want. This trip is on our dime, after all, mistakes are school fees, and life is a learning experience. Can you hear the wine talking?

With that decision made, I prepared the Landy for the long drive north and inspected every part while Luisa planned the route and worked on the logistics, time frames, expenditure, route, camping, etc. The Dakar rally would also be taking place in Chile, Argentina and Bolivia, a great opportunity for us to witness an event I have always been fascinated by and disappointed by the erratically lousy television coverage. Storms continued to rage intermittently outside our warm little cottage and let up only after a week. We hit the road north and spent the night sleeping at a designated free camping area next to a toll gate before making it to Cordoba and found a nice city with cheap and nasty camping at the municipal park. The Landy's engine area had been making a weird noise, like a sandpapery rubbing noise which came and went. I figured that the noise was either coming from the alternator or the viscous fan pulley bearing. As far as we knew Cordoba was the last major city before the

Bolivian border and the last chance to buy any major parts. After getting directions and advice from some auto parts shops we found a corner in the city which had two bearings suppliers. The one was SKF and they had the bearing at a high cost, next door was an old store run by an old man and his beautiful granddaughter. She looked at the part number and pulled an American bearing of the shelf, assuring us that, though the part number was slightly different the number which needed to correspond did. Both Luisa and I were impressed by her knowledge. Many girls as beautiful as she was would find working in a little, old bearing store beneath them, but she seemed to have her head firmly on her shoulders, a credit to herself and her family. OK, maybe I was a little more impressed than Luisa was. The Landy also needed a new deep cycle battery to run the fridges and LED lights; the old battery had developed a rotten egg smell and no longer held a long-term charge. An old man sold us a Willard battery at a good price and directed us to the municipal camping. Along the way, the Landy developed a wobble and emitted another grinding. A bearing had definitely expired but not the fan bearing, these were the tell-tale signs of a wheel bearing going through the throes of death. It was not one of the bearings I had recently replaced, this was an old bearing set succumbing to the pressure of the wide mud tyres. The camping grounds were litter-strewn, and the only sites with electricity points attracted the most enthusiastic litterers. A large stretch of grass bordered by unused braai areas and therefore free of litter seemed the best place for us to set up for the next couple of days while I changed the wheel bearings, a job I really enjoy. As a kid playing with Lego and Mechano, I always dreamt of working with real metal, mesmerised by the perfection of cogs and gears. Working on the wheel bearings is a job that requires knowledge, patience, special tools and technique and is rewarding in its greasy perfection, the satisfaction of the parts working and fitting together, rolling smoothly. Private Pyle re-assembling his M14.

WE WILL BE FREE

Outside Cordoba, we entered a sleepy little town called Jesus Maria and found the best large camping site we have yet come across in South America. Beneath a sign saying Camping Los Nogales, two women stood and chatted about Tuesday. We asked them if Camping Los Nogales was a nice camp, they said it is OK, we asked if it had a pool, they looked at each other, no, no pool. Tiene una piscina? No. It was a very hot day and the kids were complaining about the heat. Keelan, in particular, had developed a very bad habit since we had come to South America. He took to growing his blonde locks long to attract Selena Gomes look-alikes but then refused to open his window while we were driving because the hair would whip his face. We tried giving him Jessica's alice band and hair clips and beanies, but he would never tie his hair back. And Luisa does not get hot; she can sleep in a rooftop tent in full blazing sunshine under a down duvet and not even break a sweat. I often overheat due to my beer sustained padding, and often I would turn to them while sitting in traffic in the tropical heat to find that neither would have their window open. The first thing we saw as we drove down into the campsite was green manicured lawn, and then we spotted not one but two massive swimming pools, full of cool mineral water pumped out of the ground. It was immediately decided that we would spend a few days at the camp. The bikes were taken down from the roof of the Landy and Keelan, and I set off to explore the town. In Cordoba, we had discovered an ice cream store called Grido, and it seemed there was a Grido on every corner. They served huge triple scoop crunchy cones dipped in nuts and chocolate and little water-based lollies, perfect for killing a thirst. Each ride into Jesus Maria would include a trip to Grido and I suspect that is why Keelan was always ready to ride with me to buy beer, wine and vegetables and excellent cuts of meat for the fire. By the third evening, I had discovered that a rocking of the front left wheel was not caused by a worn wheel bearing but by a swivel bearing, which we needed to buy before we re-joined the road north, any excuse to hang around in the camp a little longer. The kids were doing home-schooling at a picnic table under the trees, and Luisa had Wi-Fi for all the administrative duties which drive her day. I could work on the Landy and sew some new mosquito netting into the windows and doors of our otherwise indestructible rooftop tent. The camp owner, Carlos, took a liking to the family and my Led Zeppelin t-shirt and invited us to visit his home on a farm on the other side of town where a G-string wearing beauty emerged from the pool and hugged us hello. I did not notice the G-string at all, Keelan apparently did though. Carlos and Vicky's lovely home is from a bygone era and is easily a hundred years old. A relaxing afternoon spent chatting in the shade was followed by a walk past fields and vineyards to the front door of a cottage surrounded by trees. A man wearing only a pair of shorts in the afternoon heat opened the door and welcomed us into his home. Carlos, who does not speak English, introduced us to Ricardo who also does not speak English, which is not a problem because, by now, we can understand and clumsily speak Spanish. The problem we have with the Spanish in South America is that every country speaks a different dialect of Spanish and has different words for common things. And the Brazilians speak that sao mao tao pao (pronounced saauw, maauw, taauw, paauw) Portuguese which is from another planet completely. Ricardo walked us down the passage where polished muskets hung on the wall, traditional Argentine pots and clay bowls adorned furniture of hardwood; wax rubbed and undamaged in their antiquity. The passage led to a workshop and two large wooden doors which opened to reveal two stainless steel tanks of at least 1000 litres each. The floor of the winery tiled with cool damp terracotta tiles regulating the temperature inside. Ricardo produced both Malbec red and Torrontes and led us to his cosy, family kitchen and produced a bottle of each wine, cheese, a large homemade salami and crispbread. We sipped and nibbled and savoured the wine, chatting until the sun lay to rest on the windowsill. Leaving with a case of wine under his arm,

after Vicky came to fetch us, Carlos drove us back to the camp and lit a
large fire in the camp entertainment area. Carlos hit the turntables and
got the party started, playing a selection of music to see what got the feet
tapping and the head nodding, refining the selection, his mission? To get
us shaking it on the dance floor. I sat sipping on Fernet Branca and coke,
a northern favourite, my dancing days long behind me, but Carlos is not
a man to quit. The next night we were invited to join them again and
then every night thereafter for a full week, Carlos preparing excellent
meat as only Argentines and Uruguayans can. Cuts like the thin salted
Matambre, the thicker, redder, salted Lomo and chorizo sausage. We
would bring beer and wine, salads and breads and Luisa's, by now,
world-famous potato bake. Every night we told them we were leaving
the next day, they said sure, ok. The actual last night we danced until our
feet hurt. Carlos had patiently read our body language throughout the
week and had us in the palm of his hand, Vicky danced, her slim body
and long black hair moving to a new rhythm with every song. She was
the queen of the dance floor before the kids were born and she still had
all the moves, dressed in a white tennis skirt and a white Puma jumper,
stylish and happy. I do not believe that they thought we would actually
leave until we rolled up outside party central in the Landy all packed up
and ready to go. Stay for one more Asado; have a swim in the pool,
what's the rush? Leaving great people really hurts, you form a
connection with someone, and you have to wonder, will I ever see this
person again, will their lives be happy and healthy?

That afternoon we reached San Miguel de Tucuman, a nasty little city,
where we intended to apply for free Bolivian visas instead of paying $50
per head at the border. The Bolivian 'consulate' was extremely well
hidden and closed on a Monday when we located it after three hours of
driving in circles, on a Monday. With little option for camping, we
pushed on for Salta, enjoying the well-built winding roads and surprised
to find a city with some of the charm of colonial towns like Cuzco and

Arequipa. A neighbourhood set against the side of a hill reminded us of the beautiful house we had rented in South Africa. The camp we settled on was a municipal camp and a gathering point for Overlanders either heading south from Bolivia or heading north as we were. We were guided into the camp by fellow Overlanders and social network friends, Toby and Chloe driving a V8 Ford camper. The camp, Camping Xamena, was a semi-permanent home to the juggling, trinket, bracelet, and knickknack making, dreadlocked Argentine travellers you are likely to spot peddling for coins at any large intersection of many South American cities. They are a breed of traveller unique to Argentina and have a gipsy air, a carefree disposition, and a penchant for marijuana and tents and seemed harmless enough unless provoked. A number of other overland rigs populated the dirt camping area next to what has to be the largest swimming pool I have ever seen, unfortunately, the pool was empty and would take ten days to fill. The camp itself has space for over 500 tents and a large ablution block which, by the grace of a sweet, merciful God, they clean twice a day. A fire was lit in the braai area behind the Landy, and our new friends joined us for a night of laughter. We can be a bit over the top and Luisa can be full of interesting, unshakeable, mildly offensive, or stingingly offensive opinions which need to be taken with a bag of salt and a sense of humour. If the girl can't dance, then she gets bored and starts playing quirky mind games. I am immune. Luckily, she took an immediate liking to Toby's and Chloe's and they escaped unharmed, mostly. The next night we forced more meat and wine down their throats, the following evening pretended to be making vegetables for dinner then cackled wildly and threw more meat on the fire. With our African carnivore reputations beyond reproach and our new friends praying for mercy and the company of people not as fresh from the bush, we kissed and hugged goodbye climbed in the Landy and turned the key. Vroom, vroom, ve ve ve da doon. Engine dead.

With a pink face, pinker than usual, I began a flustered diagnostic process, plugged in the Nanocom diagnostic tool and finding no faults logged, switched the ignition on, lie in the dirt and put my ear to the fuel tank and listened for the familiar whizzing and whining of the fuel pump. Nothing. The fuel pump had been making a whining noise since I had changed the fuel filter during a service in the campsite where we hung out with Team America and their Toyotas in Bariloche at the beginning of 2013. Since then the whining had continued intermittently, even though I changed the fuel filter regularly. I try to fill the tank with the best fuel available whenever possible and had started adding a bit of two-stroke oil to the mix to compensate for the lack of lubricant in the locally available diesel. In Argentina, the buzzing and whining seemed worse than in other countries. Now the poor, hardworking pump had given up the ghost, not too surprising considering the quality of fuel she had to run on in both Africa and South America. The Landy odometer was sitting on around 270 000 km's, and that pump had served for those entire hard kilometres and for twelve years. I was not going to complain. Actually, a grin soon made its way onto my face. Of all the places we could have broken down, here we were, in a cheap campsite with a great little bakery next door and a town full of auto parts stores. This is why we love our Land Rover so dearly, she has a soul and was telling us to get our shit together before we entered the altitudes and remoteness of Bolivia. She is a faithful girl. It took a while to convince Luisa that the fuel pump failing was actually a blessing in disguise. The next morning, after doing some research to determine whether we might be missing some important clues, we changed into our work clothes and set about dropping the tank. The most difficult part of the procedure was to get an arm between the chassis and the body to the top of the fuel tank where four colour coded connections had to be disconnected. Luisa was doing an OK job, but her boobs were in the way because I only own one axle stand and could not remove the wheel. A slim Swiss

Overlander, Michel, put his arm in the gap with room to spare, unclipped one of the connections and then walked away, not succumbing to social pressure to finish the job and lend me his Electrical Engineering degree. It's as if he was teasing us. With the tank out from under the Landy and resting on the picnic table, Luisa and I set about opening the lid of the pump gently with a couple of hammers and screwdrivers. Another Overlander, John, travelling with his lovely girlfriend Betti and a Mercedes truck, helped me test the fuel pump directly from the battery. It whizzed a few times then stopped, we then pumped water through it while connecting it to the battery but found that there was something grinding internally, and the pump eventually gave up completely. The pump itself sat within a larger conical plastic structure and could not simply be replaced with another pump. Luisa and I spent the next few days riding around Salta on our bikes looking for a replacement pump, possibly an external bypass pump and found a suitable, albeit expensive Bosch unit. There were vague instructions on a German website on how to install an external bypass pump with an inline filter, a procedure recommended by my friend Markus who we had met in Jericoacoara. A replacement pump, complete with new plastic substructure, was available in the UK for half the price of the Bosch pump we had found locally. The decision was made to have the UK part couriered over to Chile because customs is a nightmare in Argentina where it is technically illegal to import auto parts. My Mom offered to pay for the part as a 40th birthday present, an offer I could not refuse. With the decision made we now had to just wait for the part to arrive then find a way to either have it brought into Argentina or to courier it to a border town and take a bus to fetch it.

So, what do you do when you have time on your hands, a group of tribesmen to hang out with and an abundant local supply of excellent meat and fine wines? John and Betti gave us a tour of their truck, the camper section of which he had designed with the AutoCAD program and then constructed into a modern, practical and gorgeous home. The kids were amazed by the space and comfort of the home on wheels and looked at me with a bit less admiration. Why do we have to live in a canvas tent Dad, why can't we have a truck with its own bathroom and stainless-steel knobs and stuff, why do we have to get wet when it's raining, and we need the loo and why do we need to leave the 'house' to get something out the fridge. Keep quiet and go play in traffic. John had driven a lot of the route we had travelled, and it was great to have a conversation about places we had been while the rest of the tribe spoke about the regular PanAm route. Our time with them was far too short, but they invited us to join them in Mendoza for Christmas. We were very sad to see them leave. A new overland vehicle would arrive daily, but most would head for the hills over the weekend when the local nightclub pumped music all night and the campground filled with the poorer people of Salta. We became a permanent fixture of the camp as days became weeks. Michel and his feisty wife, Ursi, hung around for a bit longer than expected when their Toyota was broken into in town and their entire precious tech was stolen from the front seat, despite the fact that they had two dogs in the rear of the vehicle. Michel took the robbery personally and took it upon himself to do some detective work and within a few days had found a witness and, eventually, the address of the suspected thief. The cops were less than useless even when presented with solid evidence. The media arrived to interview Michel, and he made appointments with the head of the police and tourism to try and get some action. Still, the police sat on their fat arses. Please remind me never to rob Michel, unless in Salta, then I can take his rig, wife and pooches, no problem.

An endless procession of the tribe coloured our days. A few elderly Swiss couples came and left, an American Overlander couple entered the park but parked very far away from the fun, a Polish couple in a Chevy van with wild children parked next to us for two noisy days. Two

French long-range cyclists befriended us, both were bicycle mechanics, and they helped Keelan service the bikes. A young French couple arrived in a Kia van with some mechanical issues, Luisa said she would help them fix the van then kicked me out of the tent the next morning to go change their wheel bearings and brakes. An Argentine hippie artist couple in a large, homemade camper frequented the camp often, leaving to fix the van and then returning with the same overheating problem. Our job, as resident African carnivores, was to recommend which cuts of meat to buy then show the salivating Europeans how to grill it to perfection, an easy job with such high-quality beef. A fire burnt near our Landy almost every night and we were grateful to have the company of a great bunch of nomads but missed John and Betti, Toby and Chloe and Michel and Ursi, who had all left. They had become good friends, but nomadic neighbours never hang around for very long.

By some miracle of circumstance, we were joined that month by two other South African Overlander couples, the equivalent of two Chinese bumping into each other at an international environment conference. The first Saffas to roll into camp arrived in a yellow Unimog bearing the New Zealand flag. Vic, who had been a professional cyclist and who had left South Africa in the late '80s, told us inappropriate jokes and had a noisy argument with Luisa by the end of the first night. His lady friend, Maria, is a lady from the Cape. Pure class and elegance, nothing like naughty Vic who is going to have us Africans camped on his stately lawn when we eventually sneak into New Zealand. The other South Africans were a lovely retired Afrikaner couple from Oudtshoorn driving a very well kept white Land Cruiser. They had left South Africa with their son and daughter in law in their own Land Cruiser, but had split up and followed separate routes. They only stayed one night in our messy camp before being whisked away to the farm of some very enthusiastic Argentines they had met on the way to Salta. It was good to have some contact with our people, to chat in Afrikaans and disagree about the state of our nation, realising that we came from very different worlds, but from a shared history and similar culture.

With the Christmas holidays approaching rapidly, the pool filling slowly and the locals partying loudly, we became desperate for our pump to arrive so that we too could escape, explore and keep that date with the Panamanian ferry. When eventually the part did arrive in Chile we had it cleared from customs and sent up to Calama, a city very near the Andean border with Argentina. I was set to take a bus to Calama until Toby and Chloe asked American Overlander friends, Emily and Tim, if they were able to smuggle the part over the border. The Chilean division of DHL handed the precious part to a mouth-breathing, retarded, narcoleptic who, with rare determination, found a way to delay the delivery. Emily and Tim kindly changed their plans to be able to retrieve the parcel for us. I hate relying on people or asking for favours, especially when that assistance will cost them time and money and unnecessary inconvenience. I was happy to have taken a bus to San Pedro but as we were booking the bus tickets we received a message saying that Tim had eaten something dodgy and they would be delayed by a day and able to collect the package from the courier in San Pedro de Atacama and a couple of days later pulled into camp and handed us a rectangular green box.

Within a matter of hours Luisa and I had the fuel pump in the tank, the tank re-installed and the bleeding procedure completed. I turned the ignition. Vroom. And this time it just kept on vrooming. A quick test drive around the park confirmed that all was well with the fuel system and we were free to leave. And not a moment too soon. The barbarian horde was preparing to invade the camp with round bellies, loud music, nappies and litter and abomination in the bathrooms. We had been liberated and headed out of town to another camp where the hordes could not afford to enter. It was here that we would celebrate a simple Christmas, my 40th birthday and New Year's. The campsite is called

Alto Valle, or High Valley and had a small clean swimming pool and a tree-shaded campsite. The meat feast continued as we waited for the New Years.

Since we have been travelling celebrated events, birthdays, Christmas, Easter, had become no less important, but less celebrated, less manic. On Christmas morning, the kids were given an MP3 and headphones each and a pile of chocolates. They were happy with the gifts and went for a swim after a delicious camp breakfast, Luisa gave me an IOU and a kiss, and I gave her the same. We had not spent the holidays sitting in traffic, fighting through malls, frantically buying gifts for all our family and friends, then overindulging in a variety of salty or sweet food and a bird I don't consider particularly edible, while worrying about how much we had spent on toys that the kids would probably use a few times before heading back to the PlayStation. Our day was slow, calm and relaxed. We agreed that this had been one of the best Christmas' ever. We also don't have space in the Landy for a mountain of unnecessary stuff. For my birthday I asked for a bag of chocolates like the kids had received and was happy to quietly sit and consider my slow decay. Luisa could not bear me doing what I wanted on my 40th and instead told the camp owners that it was my birthday and they promptly slaughtered a lamb which I spent the day grilling on the Asado inside their entertainment area. That night we ate, drank and chatted with the family before an early night. The best birthday I could have had. And I am not even kidding.

48

Bloody Bolivian Bureaucracy

After a rowdy New Year's Eve in Salta with the camp family's family, when Keelan released his inner pyromaniac and single handily blew up the evening, we packed the Landy and headed uphill towards Bolivia. It never ceases to amaze me how drastically a landscape can change with altitude. For hundreds of kilometres, you may be driving through lush green scenery then round a steep corner and be faced with arid, semi-desert and high winds which suck the moisture out of everything. Quaint colonial villages will give way to dusty dirt and rock houses and streets. From green Jujuy to the dry, high border crossing at Villazon is a less than a day's drive with the nose of the Landy pointed at the heavens, past mountains of seven colours and tourist towns bustling with travellers, many eager to copy the style of the Argentine hippy traveller. Brown clothing, dreadlocks and semi-shaven heads, facial hair, sandals and beads and stoned. Chaos reigned at the Argentina/Bolivia border with busloads of travellers, those bloody orange overland trucks and locals trying to make a few bucks. Getting the passports stamped required a long queue and then cancelling the temporary permit for the Landy required another long queue which worked on a number system. It is very important to remember that when you are dealing with border crossings, you need to be a real bastard, a pushy son of a bitch, with no regard for little old ladies or screaming babies and even less for pregnant women and the handicapped. Why? Because if you are weak you will be trampled underfoot. Luisa is great at this job. I will stand in queue and act dumb and ask silly questions, then get the kids to wait in the queue while I go and tell Luisa the procedure and how to get around the queue. I will then return to the queue and Luisa will then softly elbow to the front saying 'sorry, sorry, I need to ask a question', making eye contact with no-one then sliding our paperwork in front of the official who will sign and stamp, stamp, stamp. Free to go. In Salta we had procured free 30-day visas in Luisa, Keelan and Jessica's South African passports, I chose to use my British passport because I like the colour. My South African passport was almost full and British passport holders do not need a visa for Bolivia. The Bolivian immigration officials had other ideas though; he explained that because I had exited Argentina with the South African passport I could not enter Bolivia with the British passport. We tried to explain our position to any official who would listen, but the only solution suggested was that we ask the Argentine officials to put an exit stamp in the British passport and then the Bolivians would accept that passport. So, basically, the Argentines had to make a concession and compromise their systems and data. Naturally, the Argentines kindly and politely refused, and we returned to the Bolivians with the South African passport. $50 for the visa, please. With no money on hand, no way to do the temporary import for the Landy because it is in my name and unable to enter Bolivia because I had not cleared immigration, Luisa had to cross the large bridge over the little, litter-strewn stream to search for an ATM. Fuming with anger she stomped off into the city, throwing little children and mangy dogs from the bridge, an invasion of sovereign soil. An hour later she returned looking hot and flustered in the dry altitude, a bottle of Coke in one hand. She thrust the money in my hand and climbed in the Landy. I was able to complete the immigration process with the African passport but reached the customs office as they closed for an hour's lunch. You break the news to Luisa, I don't want to frikken do it. The three customs officials had been kind, helpful and patient when we had been randomly walking into closed offices trying to find someone with the authority to change or break the rules. I could not understand though

WE WILL BE FREE

why all three had to sit down and dismember the chicken at the same time. Surely one could man the window, even if he did it slowly. I took my place at the window behind a biker, his girl and a stray sleeping dog and waited impatiently. With lunch digesting the greasy lipped and fingered official slid open the window and sat down to resume the tedium. A little man with a huge moustache tried to get in front of me, but he had messed with the wrong Dutchman, no you can't ask a question, fok off! I pasted a large patient grin on my face and greeted the official respectfully. He asked for my documentation, they tried to make sense of the English and Afrikaans on the green registration form, then called a colleague who knew how to say hello in English to ask me in Spanish what the vehicle registration number is. I pointed it out and helped them through a process, as we have done very many times before. All done, a print out in triplicate, sign here and here and here. Gracias Senor, gracias usted, ciao. Getting back into the Landy, a thick atmosphere of redhead frustration and anger filled the air. I passed the Bolivian temporary import papers to Luisa and asked her to check them while I started up the Landy. 'It says here the Land Rover is Brazilian', 'what?' Dumb Fucks. Um senor, disculpe, but there seems to be a mistake. Que? A thick look on his face, no esta Brasileiro? No, senor. Oh, ok. The entire process had to be repeated, print in triplicate, sign here and here and here. Gracias, ciao, shithead. We had finally defeated the gods in their attempts to keep us off Bolivian soil and drove over the bridge into the last country on our South American checklist.

I almost always experience a sense of relief and excitement when driving into a new country. Bolivia has a reputation for amazing vistas, otherworldly landscapes, roadblocks, corrupt officials and civilian lockdowns. When we had attempted to enter Bolivia in 2013, when the Land Rovers oil cooler failed, we heard stories from many friends of how they had been 'trapped' in towns and cities across the country when locals barricaded the nation's road in protest of this or that. The Land

316

Rover had always suffered from altitude sickness; symptoms included extreme turbo lag and a loss of power. I had done some research and decided to disconnect the MAF, or Mass Air Flow, sensor just before we entered Bolivia. The difference in boost and power was simply amazing; where before I would struggle to maintain 80kph on the flat altiplano above 3000m, I was now able to zoom along effortlessly at 100kph or more. I almost had to rein her in a bit which, luckily, I did just before our first encounter with a Bolivian traffic policeman with a radar speed gun in his hand. There had been no road signs depicting the speed limit and we were surprised when he told us that the speed limit was in fact 90kph. 'And you were driving at 95kph senor'. Ok, good to know, now let us be on our way. He eyed us for a short while, perhaps wondering if these Gringos who pay a spot fine. After the border crossing shenanigans, we were in no mood for a corrupt cop. Perhaps he sensed that we were having a bad day, perhaps his mother doesn't raise poephols, either way, he waved us on with a warning to go slow. Winding along a decent paved road past little villages where tough, tiny villagers live on a diet of dirt, sunshine and a thimble of water a day, we rolled into Tupiza with the viscous fan bearing screaming its tits off. Tupiza is a lovely town, with a road full of pizzerias displaying menus in English and endorsements in every common traveller language pasted on the walls. 'The pizza here was of good quality, enjoyable and fresh ingredients, Ernst und Anna, Germany, May 2011'. It was in that pizzeria that I took the photo which would become the cover of this book. The kids and I sat down and ordered a pizza while Luisa went off to the internet cafe to experience 10 kbps and search for camping. The pizza was good and the ingredients fresh-ish, danke Ernst und Anna. The Dakar had already started in Chile and the unsupported marathon stage was to reach Uyuni and the world-famous salt flats in the next couple of days. I made the decision the fix the squealing bearing before leaving Tupiza, the health of the Land Rover is always very high on our list of priorities. Luisa found a cheap hostel frequented by backpackers and Overlanders, El Refugio. That night we went looking for some street food and found a little restaurant selling fried chicken and chips. 'Four please'. 'No, we don't have chicken'. The tables were full of locals sucking the flesh from bones, and it was still relatively early in the evening. We went to another chicken joint up the road and they simply ignored us. With set prices aimed at the locals, they made no extra income dealing with fussy, demanding (or drunk) tourists who couldn't read the menu and treated the staff like idiots. Realising that we were simply not welcome we returned to the first little restaurant. 'Four please'. The lady looked at Luisa who smiled and asked her to make sure that the pieces were big because her husband, a thumb jabbed towards me standing outside, is very big and fat. A smile crept onto the ladies' face despite her best efforts. 'He is very big and fat' she said. Four small black plastic bags of chicken and chips and a large coke were exchanged for a few notes. We now understood that the people of this town were quick to be friendly if you were sure to treat them with respect, speak Spanish and not walk around like a North Face-clad paleface.

I had a special tool to remove the viscous fan brought over with some spares from the UK when we were fixing the oil cooler in Chile but now found that I needed two special tools, one to hold the fan in place while the other turned the thin 36 nut which held it all together. I had the slim 36 nut spanner but had to improvise the other tool. Working in the unmaintained hostel parking lot I battled under the hot, high altitude sun for two hours. I had bolted together two spanners, a 14mm and a 15mm through the ring section and held the nuts in place while pulling in the other direction with the 36 spanner. I tried every conceivable combination of spanners and g-clamps and vice grips but kept coming back to my two spanners bolted together. The spanner slipped from the nuts when I applied too much pressure and soon I had blood trickling from my knuckles and a bump on my head from hitting the bonnet.

After a tea break I tried again and felt the sweet relief of a stubborn nut loosening. Now with the fan off, I needed to remove the bearing by removing the centre nut which required a 12 Allen key, which I did not have in my very comprehensive toolbox. I remembered having a 12 Allen socket and I remember holding it in my hand back in my garage at home, debating whether I should bring it or leave it. I left it and now had to go buy one. I was directed by the teenager staffing the front desk, watching a rowdy game show, to the central market, a block away, hidden behind high walls. The market was organised by product and service and the first few aisles I entered were devoted to tools and plumbing supplies, bicycles and electrical goods. With Keelan helping we began the hunt which would either be an easy in and out or protracted affair. Typically, the stalls all stocked exactly the same stuff, and not one had a 12 Allen key. One well-dressed little old man had a set of socket type Allen keys but wanted $40 for the set. The searched continued out of the market and into the street, being referred from one ferretaria, hardware store, to the next. Having visited every ferretaria in a ten-block radius we found a well-stocked store near the central plaza. We greeted the store owner cordially and explained what we needed, she disappeared into the back of the store without a word, and we wondered if this might be another chicken and chips, we don't serve tourists, scenario. Five minutes later she emerged holding a fistful of Allen keys, among them an elusive number 12. Bueno. 'How much'? $12, $3 for the tool and an $8 desperate tourist tax, a breakdown of costs that was not volunteered but assumed. Returning to the Landy I found that the Allen key did not fit past the bevelled edge and I had to spend a while filing to tool until it fit with good purchase. The crowbar held the base plate in place while I pulled with all my might on the Allen key which slipped resulting in another bang on the head. I could have lifted the bonnet up out of the way, but it was providing a bit of shade. Another try, the bolt budges and I was able to release the bearing which was well and truly

WE WILL BE FREE

knackered. Luisa and I took a taxi to the other side of town where some greasy guys had a press powerful enough to remove the old bearing from the shaft and insert the new one. We watched them work and were relieved when they returned the bearing and shaft at no cost. Back in the centre of town we bought fruit salad with cream from a kind lady with tiny hands who was amazed at the size of my hands, which frankly, aren't that big. The bearing was popped in the freezer back at the hostel while we went to search for a small camping gas can for my blowtorch. The bearing sits very snugly in its recess in the engine block and heating the block expands the metal into which you slide the bearing which would have contracted from the cold in the freezer. That is the theory anyway. By now I knew every ferreteria in town, and they knew me, but none had the gas can I needed. A drunken man fell in love with Luisa and kissed her hand bravely while I stood two feet over him. Hands off Jose. An afternoon thunderstorm put an end to our search and cooled the day enough that when I returned to work sunburnt and rested I no longer burnt my hands-on the tools which I had stupidly left in the sun. During my siesta I had come up with an idea to heat the front of the engine block with water rather than fire. With the kettle boiled and the bearing freezing cold I inserted plastic bags into the recess and over the pulley below it and poured the hot water slowly over the oily metal. With the kettle empty I slowly tapped the bearing in, struggling to generate force in the tight space and careful not to damage the radiator which I had covered with hardboard. At first the bearing went in skew, but on the second attempt it tapped in perfectly. I sent Luisa off to buy some Loctite; a type of glue used to lock nuts in place and sent her back when she returned with silicone, then sent her back again when she returned with more silicone. Then I had a look in one of the crates in the back of the Landy and found a brand-new tube of Loctite and a furious redhead. With the fan back in place and the fan belt checked for cracks and re-installed, I cranked the engine which purred like a kitten. I was relieved that the fan bearing had been the culprit as I might have replaced it only to find that it was the alternator or some other bearing which had failed.

49

The Dakar!

There are two routes to Uyuni from Tupiza and both take at least six or seven hours. Route 21 is the most direct route but is apparently a very bad dirt road which runs up and over a mountain range and is popular with buses and trucks. With the Dakar Rally now in full swing in Uyuni, that road would be very busy. The other route, Route 14, is almost twice the distance but is paved and leads to Potosi, the highest city in the world at 4090 meters. Normally we would take the rough dirt road, what Land Rovers are made for, but it was decided that the Potosi route would be better; it is not every day that you get to visit the highest city in the world. The Landy purred along the paved road, and I was amazed that she would happily climb hills in fourth where before she would have struggled up in second and third, gasping thin air to feed the turbo and the diesel fire in her heart. Dry, crumbling villages huddled the road and tough little women, wrapped in shawls and long black skirts, wearing English bowler hats above two long ropes of platted black or greying hair, herded goats, and a colourful sheet hung on her back cradling a child or carrying goods. It seems as if rural Bolivian culture is very similar to rural African culture where the women do almost all the work and the men play cards under the trees except here the men were either invisible or playing cards indoors. Christopher Hitchens once said that the key to ending poverty is the empowerment of women, I agree but would add that men need to get off their asses. Once he has built the house he must maintain it and the yard and the fields, he must to carry the wood and make the fire. She should be able to choose how many children she will have and have the opportunity to raise them well. These incredible women worked under extremely harsh conditions but seemed ready with a smile if spoken to respectfully. By the time we reached Potosi we had created a new metaphor for toughness, i.e., 'that Land Rover is as tough as a Bolivian woman'. Chuck Norris is a kitten compared to these ladies. Arriving in Potosi, over impossible roads surrounded by red desert and mines, a stream of trucks and buses labouring in the absence of air, all billowing black smoke, we were reminded of the history of the city, how the mountains had been raped of their silver by the Spanish and of the miners who, to this day, work in conditions so horrendous that they worship the Devil, or Tio, underground because no God can help them down there. Luckily, we did not have time to join the hordes of tourists for a tour into that hell but were surprised to find a pleasant cobblestoned city, trampled by the feet of locals, many tourists and too many evangelical Jehovah Witness' knocking their knuckles raw on Catholic doors.

We had a date with the Dakar and without a GPS found our way down to the road to Uyuni. The city ends abruptly in a vista of green rolling hills and streams and long winding roads. The landscape between Potosi is simply spectacular and we were beginning to understand why so many Overlanders fall in love with Bolivia. We hooted and waved as we drove past caravans of cars parked alongside the road to take photos of the twisted, colourful rocks, the Landy pulling powerfully past slower vehicles on the steeper climbs, still in fourth, putting a large, stupid grin on my face. Why had I not disconnected that sensor years ago? For fear of massive engine failure mostly. Despite our new-found speed and power, the kilometres seemed to be passing very slowly and even slower still when we encountered a powerful, billowing headwind and sandstorm blowing in from the south rocking the Landy. We had been able to buy fuel at a discounted rate simply by asking for a better rate, the rate for tourists being double what the local's pay. A headwind is never good for fuel consumption, especially in a vehicle shaped like a brick and with a quarter of a tank of fuel left we dropped down into Uyuni past a seemingly deserted village clinging to the hillside. A tollgate sits at the entrance to the town and billboards and posters announced the presence of the Dakar Rally. Stopping at a fuel station for a quick rest stop and to fill the petrol jerry can for the Coleman stove, I was shown a sign taped to a post on the forecourt which listed the tourist prices for the various fuels. I, being an Overlander to the bone, then asked for a discount, which was laughed off. I paid a little less than I should have for the 20 litres and gathered my relieved flock for a drive into the city. People might have thought we were part of the rally except for the bicycles strapped on top of the jerry cans. There seemed to be no rally information centre, and we had no idea where we could camp with the best view of the rally participants. A few Dakar buggies roared past us, to huge applause, perhaps searching for a rendezvous point. We had missed most of the action because of the delay working on the Landy in Tupiza, and many of the cars and trucks had already crossed the finish line. Our immediate task was to find a place to camp out of the wind and plan where to watch the action the next day. Driving out of the town and parallel to the salt flats, we found a partially constructed arena with its corrugated roof flapping in the breeze. We circled the arena like a dog before he lay down and found a section of partially completed wall near a Dakar start/finish podium and opened the tent. A group of Bolivians parked their vehicles inside the arena like wagons in a laager amongst the litter and human faeces.

I ventured inside to ask where we could watch the rally the next day, and they pointed down the road and told me that there is a route beyond the next town; everyone would go there in the morning. We were up at 5 am searching for more information and, after driving around the crowded town for an hour and paying for a horrible breakfast and trickling Wi-Fi, found a rally official who told us to head down to the next town. A trail of dust led us to a convoy heading out on a horribly corrugated road running next to a flat unpaved new road, the convoy driving up over earth banks to drive on the flat road until reaching an insurmountable barrier; we would then drive down the banks onto the bumpy dirt road. This on and off-road fiasco continued for thirty kilometres, everyone following the vehicle in front even though he clearly had no idea where he was going. Rally flags blew in the wind as we approached an intersection and were herded off the road by the police, into the flats where a traffic jam of confused Bolivians milled around or headed off into the flat expanse. We too headed off into the flats and parked for a while trying to figure out what the hell was going on, there were vehicles driving in every direction, none who we were tempted to follow. An official rally vehicle drove towards us and we waved him down. 'Where the hell do we go, senor'? He pointed towards the north, 'follow that road and you will find them'. Pushing the Landy through the chaos on the road ahead of us we found ourselves following a track through a market of some sort, then Keelan spotted a trail of dust in the distance, 'that way'! 'Is that them?' We could see some motorbikes but could not tell if they were rally or locals, but headed in that general direction regardless, we did not have any better ideas. By now we were covered in dust and pissed off. This was not the rally experience that I had in mind, not at all. The wheel generated dust storm grew, and we realised that we were rejoining the convoy to God knows where. Another twenty kilometres of chaos and shit roads and again the cops directed the convoy off the road into a field of dust and vehicles heading in every direction. We just kept on following the herd, around and through some poor farmers ploughed field, up over the hill and onto a dirt road where policemen on motorbikes were struggling to keep the road clear. One cop told us to get off the road and pointed at a semi-level piece of land covered in dry thorn brush. We had arrived! A little man walked up to us, stood in my armpit and stayed there for the rest of the day. Somehow, I managed to open the roof tent for the kids and start a braai. Frustration gave way to excitement, especially after Luisa found a truck selling cold beer.

The Landy was the centre of attention until hooters could be heard blaring in the distance, the unofficial signal that the racers were coming. In the distance, the direction from where the racers were coming stood dark mountains, in the sky above dark clouds congregated and helicopters circled. From where we stood we were able to see the dirt track etched into the side of a hill, across a wide, muddy river bed then up along the uneven path to the level section ahead of us then up a steep bank. The first KTM arrived to cheers, flags waving and trucks hooting. Amateur and professional photographers crowded the narrow route including an enthusiastic Luisa, who kept running back to the Landy every five minutes to swop between the two lenses in our camera bag. 'No-one is wiping out' she shouted at me, 'how boring'. Girls. Riders from every nation blasted by on bikes which all seemed, to my untrained eye, to be KTM's. I was inspired, next year baby, we do the Dakar. All we need is a huge pile of money, new bodies and twenty years of racing experience. As the day wore on, the Bolivians drank more and more, and the sun disappeared behind the black clouds. An icy wind began to blow, and the rain began to slash down, turning the red soil into thick clinging clay which clung to our shoes in large heavy clumps and covered the racers. Quad bikes began to arrive as many spectators retreated to the shelter of their vehicles. I truly pitied those brave men and women speeding by, spitting red clay. If I was drenched to the bone and freezing cold just standing there in my wet weather gear, then they must have been going through an icy living hell. Where before the competitors might have waved and nodded at the crowd, now they stared dead ahead, concentrating solely on the slippery track surface, trying not to make a mistake. News spread through the grapevine that the Bolivian rider was approaching motivating the local spectators to crowd the road in a frenzy of cameras and flags. I wandered out towards the top of the long uneven path for a different perspective. A lady in a bowler hat waved a flag and scrambled up the slippery bank in her long black skirt, someone announced that they lost their car keys and everyone within earshot stopped and searched the ground around their feet, some men drank Johnny Walker Red whiskey straight from the bottle and joked with the police. A Land Cruiser ambulance dug alongside the track and changed his position for the tenth time that day. The competitors were now indistinguishable from each other as all wore a layer of red clay and as the sunset became fewer and further between. Once the last Bolivian racer passed on his quad bike, the spectators somehow knowing he was their man, packed up and left, many getting stuck in the cloying clay. I had a chat with a tall man from Santa Cruz de la Sierra, a hot city set in the lowland jungle. He asked if were enjoying the event and I mentioned to him that we were disappointed by the lack of route information, any information actually. He explained that this lack of information was intentional, the rally organisers did not want to encourage spectators, as they earn their money from television coverage, besides, the spectators often caused problems for the racers and the organisers, distracting the racers and even causing accidents. I wonder how much of that is true.

With the last of the competitors completing our section of the course, we made the terrible decision to close the tent and head back to Uyuni for the night. That horrible road had to be driven again, and it was a few hours before we reached Uyuni and drove to the centre of town, looking for a pizza. A young guy came to speak to me when I parked the Landy and we chatted about our journey. He asked if we needed a place to camp, eager not to return to the windy toilet, I said yes, and he said follow me. Three metres from where we were parked lay an entrance to a military base and inside stood a few tents, a few military trucks, a fleet of Dakar organiser vehicles and a row of portaloos. We could camp there with a military guard and, the greatest surprise, the portaloos were spotlessly clean and even had toilet paper.

50

To Titicaca

The next town and the paved road, took four hours of driving in the rain on horrible corrugated and muddy 'road' surrounded by flag-waving SUV's inspired by the rally to be faster and braver and others who bounced along at a snail's pace, trying to preserve their suspension and soothe their hangovers. A train chugged parallel to our path while our windows darkened with mud. The fuel light came on with sixty kilometres of mud road left to drive.

Rolling into a town with a pleasant plaza, looking like those mud-splattered Dakar heroes we found a fuel station and asked the attendant for a good price on diesel. He called the owner who let us fill all our tanks at a mere 10% above local price, gave us a calendar and let us use the hose to wash the mud off the Landy. That night we slept at another gas station, next to a highway with no lane lines, cat's eyes, or illumination, desperately in need of a shower and a hot meal. If you had told us three years ago that we would spend so much time sleeping at gas stations, I don't think we would have believed you. That is not the adventure I had planned for myself, but when you have been driving all day, the sun sets, and you have no clue what to expect of the road ahead, the neon lights of an isolated gas station are very welcoming. Most service stations are open 24 hours and have security and toilets, maybe a shower. At one Argentine YPF station, we found Wi-Fi, hot showers, a barber, a restaurant, a playground, braai areas and spotless bathrooms. That is Overlander nirvana. Here we were not going to be that lucky, but when you have been travelling all day on terrible roads, you simply need a safe place to open the tent and lay your head.

Luisa's research suggested that there was a very nice campsite on the road to La Paz, and we were looking forward to a couple of rest days after the chaos of the Dakar/Uyuni experience. This is one of those times that we wish that we still had a GPS because the maps we had downloaded were not updating as they should, and the tablet would not hold a charge. Only once we drove into El Alto, La Paz did we realise that we had missed the town and turn off to the camp. The traffic was an ignorant, arrogant nightmare and within twenty minutes we abandoned the idea of going to the famous camp in the city and instead set our sights on Lake Titicaca, rumoured to be the world's highest navigable lake but, like most rumours, this was not true. The architecture surrounding us consisted of bizarre, clay brick buildings, most double or triple-storey, many uncompleted and almost all with garish vanity details. Gold gates and window frames, elaborate metalwork and silver tinted windows, the art of opulent poverty. Mud squelched up against the doorsteps of these buildings and packs of stray dogs mated in or slept on or rummaged through the piles of litter and discarded building material which lined the road. This was not postcard La Paz, this was a nightmare to escape, but first, we had to make it through a four-way intersection where only brute force ensured passage. Buses, trucks and taxis pushed in all directions, lanes dissolved as each driver tried to advance his own passage to the detriment of all others. Impatient drivers sat on their hooters as if the sonic insult could motivate metal. I joined in the chorus solely for the ironic joy of redundancy and nudged the Landy forward into tiny gaps which appeared in front of me, the Land Rover's heavy metal bullbar discouraging protest or competition. Slowly we edged forward breathing chalky fumes in the thin air, asserting our rights and smiling dangerously at taxi drivers who dared take on aluminium beast. We could almost see freedom ahead of us and with great relief popped out of constipation like a cork, rejoicing in the novelty of 2nd, 3rd and, occasionally, 4th gear. That insanity takes place every day, all day and it is now a scene I like to remind myself of when I need to be grateful. I could have been born to a woman wearing a bowler hat, my small brown, wet body emerging from under a black skirt to grow slowly in the oxygen-starved heights and mature to buy a yellow Toyota, to spend every day clutching a sheep skinned steering wheel, breathing those fumes.

Lake Titicaca beckoned, and Luisa promised a braai and a beer and a beautiful camp. Rolling up and down green lakeside hills, we arrived at the slipway where wooden ferries loaded vehicles needing to cross the Estrecho de Tequina. I listened to Crowded House while Luisa and Keelan took photos and video of the embarking and disembarking, Jessica sleeping through it all. The geography of the area is confusing with Peru and Bolivia meeting in the middle of an island. Ruta Nacional 2 overlooks the water where few boats sail and pass through Copacabana before terminating at the border with Peru. A police checkpoint blocked the entrance into the historic town and demanded that all drivers leave their vehicles and report to a little white building to have their licenses inspected and noted and to pay a fee for breathing. Young boys hung around the line of vehicles pretending to assist as a disguise for an unsuccessful begging operation. A fat boy jumped onto the Land Rovers step and stuck his head in Luisa's window, 'gimme money, gimme sweets' and barked a wet, rasping cough into Luisa's face. If there is one thing that makes Luisa happy, it is the joyful tenderness of a cough in the face or any nasal projections. When Keelan was a little boy, Luisa had kissed him before heading to the local Spar to buy her favourite scones. As she kissed him he sneezed a huge clump of Ghostbusters slime onto Mommy's mouth and chin, it hung there, swaying, while she trembled in panic and disgust and we all laughed and laughed and laughed. That is her fondest memory.

The slow-moving policeman returned my license and shortchanged me. The lake beckoned, and the colonial town's cobbled street confused.

Travellers packed the streets and the town square; the kids sat in the Landy while Luisa went looking for the promised meat and beer. The ladies carving meat in the market were surprised by our requests for lomo and nyapa. 'Tourists don't buy meat from us', they said, and the ladies selling vegetables and fruit agreed. We had found the one place in town where we could smile and joke with the locals and not be taken for a ride, offered a boat ride, a taxi ride, or a hotel. Other travellers tend to look at us in the Landy either with a smile or a smirk. The smilers enjoy the sight of a kitted Land Rover and a family clearly very far from home, the smirker's do not and perhaps assume that we are rich and privileged and struggle to sit comfortably because of the large silver spoons. If I was a young traveller, I would be a smirker, a hater, jealous and frustrated by my lack of the Land Rover experience.

We had rushed through Bolivia according to Luisa's schedule for reaching the new ferry to Panama. We regretted moving so quickly through an amazing country, perhaps one day we will return. Leaving Bolivia was easier than entering but re-entering Peru was not without its difficulties as we arrived two minutes after a busload of smilers and smirker's who queued in the sun. Keelan joined the end of the queue and kept a place for Luisa. As the sunburn settled they entered the immigration building and called Jessica and me to show our faces to the smiling immigration officer who thoroughly searched our passports for a problem. He refused to let me enter on the British passport and could not find an exit stamp in Jessica's passport for the last visit to Peru in 2013. 'It is in her old passport senor', 'where is her old passport?'; 'I'll be fucked if I know senor'. 'Well, you need to present the exit stamp, or she may not enter'. Breath deep and smile. 'Senor, her passport is valid and look, here she is', 'No, it is impossible'. Is it possible that immigration officers are selected because they are bitter eunuchs? Are tiny penises and equally unimpressive intellect an international pre-requisite for such an important job? I say yes, comrades. However, not all immigration officials are proverbial douche bags, and we sometimes forget to honour and appreciate those who do their jobs without douchery, but with a smile and a stamp and enjoy your day. Luisa had packed the old passports into the communication crate, or comms crate as we call it. The heaviest and least used crate it is packed at the back, behind and under most of our unnecessary crap. We dug out the passport and handed it to the smilingly disappointed official. He stamped little Jess into Peru and only then could I complete the temporary import for the Landy at the Aduana office which closed in ten minutes for a two-hour lunch. A smiling kid in a black uniform sat behind a desk, beside a cupboard covered in stickers of Overlanders, many of which we had met, or heard of or had never met or heard of. The young uniform was struck dumb by the African registration papers and was further perplexed when informed that we had toured Peru before. Looking at all those stickers I assumed he would know how to process our documentation, perhaps he had recently replaced the old customs agent who now sat outside the office at a small table watching the TV on the wall. The young agent had to phone someone to verify whether the Land Rover had left Peru with us in 2013. He made a few unanswered phone calls until he reached someone friendly who wanted to chat for a while, share a few jokes and have a good time. Having apparently established that we had not left Jessica with the Land Rover in Lima, the agent incorrectly completed the relevant forms in triplicate only to repeat the process, slowly, once I pointed out the many mistakes.

51

A New View Of Peru

Our problems did not end once the immigration and customs problems had been solved. Just outside Yunguyo, the first town on the Peruvian side, aviator shaded cops lay in wait. Instructing us to pull over they inspected our paperwork, tapped on the Landy's window and said that one Spanish word every PanAm traveller hates, multa. 'A fine for what?' 'Tinted windows are illegal unless you have a permit'. Force a smile and breathe deeply once again, 'Not in South Africa, there they are perfectly legal and encouraged, there you receive a fine if the windows are not tinted'. A lie, of course. They asked Luisa to follow them to the squad car, even though I was driving, and I joined them. 'Multa, multa, multa'. They showed us a pamphlet which listed the fine for tinted windows. Luisa tapped the tinted windows of the cop car, 'maybe we should give you a fine' she said. 'Dollars, pesos, soles'. 'My apologies senor, but we do not have any money'. We then folded our arms and gave sad, frustrated looks to every car that slowed down to look at the Landy and flash an apologetic look at us. The cops were determined, and we forgot how to speak Spanish. Realising that we were not going to budge the police handed back our documents and told us to bugger off. Welcome back to Peru, Gringo.

We had a long way to go to reach Arequipa, but first, we had to join the road through the mountains at Puno, a city built in monotone along the shores of the lake. I liked Puno, it seemed friendly and welcoming, but we did not stay long after finding directions to Arequipa. The Landy was still running like a superstar and had her work cut out for her for the following six hours of non-stop stop and go road construction and trucks to overtake on blind hairpin corners. Once you have driven in Peru, you learn that to drive safely you must drive predictably. Unfortunately, Peruvian drivers are unable to predict conventional safe driving, so you must drive like them. Overtake on blind corners and rises, speed or drive too slowly, undertake and turn without signalling. At night drive with your brights on, on the wrong side of the road. It is perfect chaos and the best way to drive through the Andes. Though not as wild and otherworldly as Bolivia the scenery continued to amaze us and by nightfall we reached the toll gate above Arequipa, where we had been three times before, once en-route to Chivay, once returning from Chivay, with Bob and Rose, without a thermostat and running out of fuel and once when we were headed for Cuzco. Paying the toll, the fourth time, I accelerated and slowed for the speed bump I remembered hating because it forced me to slow down on an uphill, then pointed the Landy's nose down the slopes of the volcano. I astounded myself by being able to reach Hotel Mercedes without a GPS, which is not that difficult since you only need to take one turn once you enter the city. A minute after opening the tent an insectoid 6x6 MAN KAT truck driving German came over and took his dick out, he wanted to make a comparison, sure that his Asian experience would give him the extra inch. I had been polite until he unzipped his stained stain-resistant khaki cargo pants. It's a game I don't mind playing, just let a man have a leak and a beer first, chances are that if he arrives at the camp long after dark he has probably had a long day. An immaculate Swiss truck stood next to ours, the owner a friendly and funny gentleman who took a liking to us.

The old colonial area of Arequipa has plenty of charm and I found a little restaurant while waiting for the supermarket to open and sell me some eggs and baguette. The restaurant serves excellent fruit smoothies, salchipapas and burger at really good prices. I don't know how I missed it the last three times, well; it is the size of a cardboard box dug into a stone wall. The Land Rover had to be emptied and scrubbed after all the mud and chaos we had driven through, and soon the true extent of senseless baggage we carry was visible to all. The lawn resembled the floor of my childhood room on a Saturday morning when my Mom tipped everything I owned onto the carpet in an attempt to force me to organise and fold. Rugby balls, pellet guns, water pistols, colour-in books and more pens and pencils, paint and paintbrushes than your local CNA. Stained German hovered and sucked on a Camel, and his thoughts, the Swiss and his wife had a chuckle and I tried to throw stuff over the wall while Luisa wasn't looking. Overpacking is a problem for almost all Overlanders, but especially troublesome for those with kids and wives named Luisa. While not wanting to deprive them of anything a normal child and wife are entitled to, you need to consider the impact the weight of hardly used luxuries has on the suspension, tyres, drive train and engine and, by extension, the wallet.

52

Is This The End?

West of Arequipa lies the ocean and the endless expanses of sand which blow up against the Andes. The ocean attracts us like moths to a warm glowing light, the mountains have unparalleled beauty and majesty, but we are not mountain folk. We are feet in the sand, camping on the beach, cold beer and baggy shorts, suntan and sunset people. Peru's coast, however, is not that kind of chilled, hammock and volleyball experience. If you hate palm trees and the colour green, want to surf massive Pacific Ocean waves, then sit on the grey sand next to a fire in jeans and a hoody, surrounded by prehistoric rock structures, being sandblasted by a constant wind then this is your stretch of coast. A well-paved and sand assaulted road runs within view of the sea along almost the entire length of the country and is a much faster, safer and infinitely more boring border to border route than the constantly weaving, climbing and dipping mountain road. In the future, once a new civilisation has grown from the ashes of our current suicidal, consumption-driven insanity, archaeologists will find the remnants of that paved road, chicken bones and tuk-tuks, a VW van with a Subaru motor and six-foot fishtail still strapped to the roof, preserved beneath the dunes.

At the Nazca lines, Keelan and Luisa bought more jewellery carved from bone before we continued towards Lima and that God-awful traffic, asking a Range Rover Classic, with diplomatic plates and a gum-chewing blonde teen in the passenger seat, for directions to Mira Flores. Perhaps one day we will replace the GPS, I don't know if I want to though, we get around ok. We did not hang out in Lima too long, the hostel usually had a vibe and some hardcore Overlanders to drink and braai with, but we were surrounded by a German clique in soft-core campers. We ran screaming for the desert and the road north, leaving on a Sunday when the city traffic is less constipated.

The Landy carried us up along through the coast and back into Ecuador where Luisa had found a cottage in the mountains for us to take a break from the road. It is in this little cottage that I sit today writing these words, putting the finishing touches to a body of work which has taken over a year to write and edit, consuming my thoughts and dominating my days. Luisa has planned our route north to Alaska and the kids have worked to get up to date with their homeschooling.

Looking back over the last two and a half years, I have to ask myself if leaving our safe home and prosperous life was the correct choice. Has the experience been worth our life savings, an uncertain future and the many mountains we will have to climb as a result? Have we helped or hindered our children, and have we compromised their futures by being reckless, spontaneous, impetuous and rebellious? What have we learned and what have we taught?

I awoke the other morning to a tent full of laughter. The kids and Luisa playing together, engaging in wordplay, teasing each other ruthlessly with love and compassion. Well, most of the time, anyway. Keelan and Jessica are on the road to self-determination and a love for lifelong learning. Yes, they do not have the benefit of a structured school education and associated discipline, but we do not see that as a disadvantage. They do not have childhood friends with whom they share every day and dream, but they do have friends from many countries and cultures. The one lesson, the core of their home-based education, is that what we are doing is impossible, we were told we would fail, that the danger was not worth the risk. But, if we can achieve the impossible as a family what will be impossible to them as individuals? With a knowledge of the world, very few people have they will have the keys to success in whatever they choose to do with their lives. Imagine their CV's one day, sitting in front of a suit in an interview. So, you have travelled the world by land and sea can speak five languages, have a distance high school diploma from the United Kingdom and a university degree from Norway. Your interests are sustainable architecture, trafficked rainforest animal rescue, classical guitar recital and Land Rover maintenance. We would like you to be our CEO.

And what of Luisa and I, has our quality of life improved? Are we hairy hippies hoping for a handout, begging our families for money and praying for a miracle? Are we two steps from disaster and a ten-step program? The opposite, except for the hair. I truly believe that we are becoming the best people we can be, confident, hardworking, generous and relaxed. Most of the time. We were born and raised separately as the two halves of one person, what I lack she has and what she needs I provide. Despite our terrible sex life, we have never been closer and work together to achieve our goals. I have her, and she has me, and we believe in each other and love and music. We still have a lot to learn but have decided to keep on travelling, to see the world, learn and grow, teach and love.

Our journey is not yet over.

About the Author

Graeme Bell is a full-time overlander and author. He was born in Johannesburg, South Africa. He is currently travelling the planet with his wife, Luisa and two children, Keelan and Jessica, in a Land Rover Defender 130, affectionately known as Mafuta.

Connect with us

Did you enjoy this book? If so, help others enjoy it too.

Please recommend to friends and leave a review if possible.
Stay up to date with the Bell Family by visiting our website

www.a2aexpedition.com

Alternatively, visit our Facebook page a2a.expedition

Printed in Great Britain
by Amazon